Western Europe Since 1945

D1385674

Western Europe since 1945

A short political history

Derek W. Urwin

Second edition

Longman

LONGMAN GROUP LIMITED
London
Associated companies, branches and representatives throughout the world

© Longman Group Limited (formerly Longmans, Green and Co. Ltd)
1968, 1972

First published 1968
Second edition 1972
Second impression 1977

ISBN 0 582 48811 7

Printed in Hong Kong by
Sheck Wah Tong Printing Press

To Patricia

Contents

Acknowledgements

Space precludes a complete survey of all those who have been my mentors. It must suffice to say that I am deeply indebted to all those students and practitioners of contemporary politics, many of whom are referred to in the bibliography, who have offered in print their thoughts and conclusions on European affairs. I would also like to acknowledge the assistance received from the Department of Politics of the University of Strathclyde. In particular I would like to thank Professor R. Rose, Mr R. M. Punnett and Mr A. L. M. Smith, who read the manuscript at various stages of its development and offered many valuable comments and criticisms. Finally, I am grateful to my wife for providing comments from a 'lay' viewpoint.

In a work of this nature, the main criteria of presentation must be selection and condensation. I have therefore selected for discussion those events which seem to me to be of most value for an understanding of postwar Western European politics as a whole. By so doing and by following each theme through to its conclusion rather than presenting the material in an overall chronological manner, I hope that I have not confused the issue further.

DEREK W. URWIN

Glasgow, April 1967

Introduction

We have learned, whether we like it or not, that we live in one world, from which world we cannot isolate ourselves. We have learned that peace and well-being cannot be purchased at the price of peace or the well-being of any other country.

James F. Byrne (U.S.A. Secretary of State), 1946

On 7 May 1945 Admiral Friedeburg and General Jodl, on behalf of the German Government, accepted the Allies' terms of unconditional surrender in a French schoolhouse near Rheims. At midnight of the following day silence fell over Europe. The Thousand Year Reich had failed in its quest for European— far less world—domination: it had survived for little more than twelve years, or two years less than its much maligned democratic predecessor in Germany, the Weimar Republic. Three months later, the first atomic bombs were dropped on Hiroshima and Nagasaki, and the war against Japan in the Pacific and the Far East finally came to an end.

For six years the continent of Europe had been a battleground between Nazi Germany, Fascist Italy, and their opponents. The Second World War had been all-embracing: the development of military technology had meant that battle was not restricted to limited areas or trench warfare, that the static trench warfare of the First World War was, in fact, completely antiquated and militarily suicidal. Civilian populations had suffered as much as the military forces, not least in the fact that whether a country was a democracy or a dictatorship, the national economy, civil liberties, and social life had all been subordinated to the exigencies of war. In more ways than one the impact of the second world conflict of this century was traumatic—for the individual, for European politics, and for international relations. That there was a new reality was widely accepted in 1945, but its far-reaching consequences were less immediately apparent.

Another chapter of history was closed. Officially the world in

1945 was at peace. With strategic imperatives reduced in urgency or dismissed altogether, the nations of Europe could now turn to the problem of putting their own house in order. Old protagonists renewed with greater vehemency their discussions and arguments as to the type of Europe that would or should rise out of the ashes of war. For, unlike the conceived situation in 1918, it was not simply a matter of picking up the threads of pre-war life. The prime question to be asked, and which was debated more or less incessantly throughout the hostilities by all those concerned with the future, was to what extent there should be change—political, economic, and social. Only a small minority openly desired a straightforward return to the old system. The need for and the unavoidability of change were widely accepted: yet on the other hand not many could grasp that the Europe which by and large had been created by the post-Napoleonic Congress of Vienna in 1815 had expired.

The question of social organisation was not merely to be the concern of Europeans alone. The summer months of 1945 did not herald a new era of peace, but were in reality an interregnum between the six-year struggle against Nazism and Hitler, and the commencement of a new and different type of war. The new Cold War was another struggle for world supremacy, or at the very least world influence, between two incompatible political faiths and value systems, epitomised by the two continental 'super-powers', the United States of America and Soviet Russia, which opposition to Hitler had brought temporarily together. The future of Europe, therefore, was no longer solely in the hands of the European states themselves. This was obvious even in 1945. Europe had been exhausted by six long years of struggle and hardship: the economic viability of the continent after the war was such that it was in no position to determine its own future. Of the former leading European powers, Germany had been destroyed; Italy had been revealed as having a hollow shell; Great Britain was incapable of being the prime mover of a balance of power checkboard; while France was still suffering from the military and moral collapse of 1940. None had the ability or the means to profit from or fill the vacuum which was the direct consequence of the complete and utter disintegration of German hegemony on the continent. Despite the conceptions of the American President, Franklin D. Roosevelt, about the state of affairs in Europe and the political mood of his own people, the meetings of American and Russian troops on the continent— on the Elbe, in Czechoslovakia, and elsewhere—illustrated the future role of these two quasi-European powers in European affairs.

Indeed, it was apparent that Europe would be subjected to a traditional 'spheres of influence' policy of great powers which Stalin, the Russian leader, had already put forward in the war-time Allied conferences as his idea of how the Allies should partici-pate in the political functioning of the postwar world. It was expected, for example, that Eastern Europe would be claimed by the Soviet Union as its sphere of influence, while Western Europe would be that of the three Western Allies. Notwith-standing the fact that the Allies might continue their wartime cooperation in the Security Council of the newly formed United Nations and the Allied Control Councils of occupied Germany and Austria, to all intents and purposes there were two Europes in existence more or less immediately after the cease-fire, one looking toward Russia and one toward the Atlantic. The expected meeting places, the United Nations and the Control Councils, were to be transformed into undeclared battlegrounds.

It is the purpose here to look at the postwar events in Western Europe, or that Europe which looked toward the Atlantic. Without becoming bogged down in the problem of defining what constitutes Western Europe, or even Europe, it will suffice to say that Western Europe is loosely defined here as that part of the continent which remains on the western side of Sir Winston Churchill's 'iron curtain'. The exigencies of space mean that some topics and countries must be examined very summarily or omitted altogether. For this reason, a discussion of the smaller democracies of Scandinavia and the Low Countries is limited to those aspects which have a bearing on the wider themes dis-cussed. Spain and Portugal are more or less omitted completely, for their dictatorial nature has, by and large, placed them even outside the periphery of Western European politics. It is the states of Britain, France, West Germany, and Italy which will receive the lion's share of attention. These countries are important because they are regarded for the purposes of this book as the 'core nations' of Western Europe. Events occurring within these states have important consequences in neighbouring smaller states. They are also in a better position than their smaller neighbours to influence European and perhaps world affairs. Moreover, movements toward European integration are affected primarily by the attitudes of these four states and hence by their internal politics. It might be argued that Italy is out of place here, but as it has been in the forefront of European integration since 1945 and, through possessing the largest Communist Party in Western Europe, has been something of an exposed limb in the Cold War, inclusion is felt to be justified.

To talk of Western Europe as an entity is not to say that there is no inner diversity. Diversity, especially along the lines of the nation state, is still the most pervasive and important feature of Western Europe; it offers a multitude of viewpoints from which the area can be and has been examined. From an overall point of view, however, it could be argued that the basic alignment of European forces, and the most important one for the future of the continent, either defends the retention of the historic nation state system or seeks some unification of European states leading in time to a comprehensive political community which will embrace most, if not all, Western European countries. It is in the latter direction that Western Europe has been moving, albeit hesitatingly. It would also seem to be the most profitable framework to adopt within which one can examine postwar events in Western Europe.

However, an understanding of the forces for and against European integration cannot be fully achieved without some consideration of political events within the various states or of the relationship of European politics to the wider world stage. It is, after all, the individual politics of the respective states which set the tone of, or can hinder and even destroy, movements toward European integration. Furthermore, so much of what has happened in Western Europe since 1945 has been conditioned by world politics, owing to the war and the shrinking of distances, that perforce one cannot isolate Western Europe from the rest of the globe: the ramifications of international relations are so complex that one cannot even begin to consider such a course of action. This is especially true of the relationships of Western Europe *vis-à-vis* the two super-powers. Because America has played such a large role in Europe since 1945, and because much of postwar European politics has been a reaction to the activities and policies of Soviet Russia, the world situation, centred on the polarisation of these two states, has persistently intruded upon European affairs.

Within this world setting, arguments were renewed as to what would be the postwar shape of things in Western Europe. Attitudes and opinions were many and varied, but very generally they can be arranged in one or other of two broad movements which in the immediate postwar years carried on a long and relentless debate on European organisation and arrangements of power. The first broad movement may be termed that of traditionalism, consisting of those who believed, to a greater or less extent, in the validity of tested institutions. For the most part, these people avoided the first postwar political debates, being primarily concerned with their own private social and economic affairs. Nevertheless, their strength was such that their opinions could not be summarily dismissed. Once their own affairs appeared to be again on a sound footing, the pressure and resistance of the 'old guard' to radical social and political change became ever more intense. Opposing this movement were the reformers. During these first peacetime years we may say that they believed in what might loosely be called the ideology and vision of the national Resistance movements, which by and large sought a complete change in the political, social and economic structures of the European states. The ideals formulated by these movements attracted men who had fought against Nazi hegemony over the continent, men inspired by high moral and social ideals, and that minority of prophets who in the pre-1939 wilderness had preached against the stultifying effects of materialism and nationalism on the continent.

Disregarding for the moment the wider implications of international politics, political activity during the first few years of peace in Western Europe was in essence centred on the conflict of these two forces of tradition and reform for the allegiance of the public and for control of the institutions of power. By 1950, when international considerations were intruding even more persistently, the conflict seemed to have been resolved in favour of traditionalism and conservatism. But was it a complete victory? In fact, it was not a simple return to the *status quo*. The effects of the wartime Resistance movements and their ideas could not be erased completely. They continued to play an indirect, but not inconsiderable role in the politics of Western Europe. Because it was a powerful newcomer on the political stage, and because a great deal of political activity in these years revolved around support for or opposition to its proposals for change, the Resistance would seem to be a logical starting point for an account of the politics of postwar Western Europe.

1 The Resistance in the Postwar World

A movement without doctrine, without coherence, without definite outlines, destined to attract much support . . . but not to achieve strong and disciplined action.

Vincent Auriol, 1944[1]

Since the Resistance consisted of potentially revolutionary movements, it is not surprising to find that its leaders were nearly all of a leftist inclination, favouring radical solutions to social and economic problems. The Resistance 'philosophy' embraced, and was willing to embrace, all those who felt that a new spirit should be injected into European reconstruction. Three main currents of left-wing political thought—Communism, Socialism, and 'social' Catholicism—had come together in the Resistance movements along with individuals who advocated a kind of 'Liberal Socialism'. This last was an attempt to create a new type of socialism which would reject the tenets of Marxist determinism. It was basically the social and political philosophy of the shortlived Action Party in Italy. If one had to find a political slogan or motto for the various Resistance movements, it would probably be 'the brotherhood of men'. Brought together during the war by the necessity of fighting a common enemy, men from all these political persuasions desired to forget their differences in an attempt to forge a new and single Resistance party which would direct the destiny of Europe toward a peaceful, harmonious, and socially integrated future.

There were, of course, differences of opinion. Several Resistance fighters, particularly those at the top of the hierarchy, remained suspicious of and hostile to the Communists. Fearing the possibility of a Communist takeover or a desire for influence, they sought to restrict Communists from positions of influence within the movements which would enable them to wield strong

[1] *Le Populaire*, 27 October 1944.

political pressure at the war's end. This attitude, however, was held by only a small minority of Resistance fighters. The vast majority saw no necessity for discriminating between Communists and non-Communists when both shared the same risks and equal responsibility in the fight against German occupation. The Italian Committees of National Liberation, for example, had representatives of all anti-fascist parties.

The vision that the Resistance movements held, then, was in many ways broad and generous. Their programmes for postwar reconstruction were all-embracing. Institutions alone were not sufficient: a new morality and a new belief in the dignity and ability of humanity was to pervade the whole of society. This moral tone is present, for instance, throughout the famous blueprint for the future prepared in 1944 by the French National Resistance Council.

Two main currents of thought combined to present this overall vision and programme. The first was the prewar idea of the Popular Front, previously expounded by such men as Léon Blum, the veteran French Socialist, and Aneurin Bevan. This looked for an alliance between Communists and Socialists, together with any other political movement desiring the same goals. These two parties had collaborated closely in Italy since the early 1930s and had for a short while in 1936 been the governing coalition in France. For many, however, this was too much of a class movement. The dilution of class was provided by the second current of thought, liberal Catholicism. Christian Democracy pursued the goal of class reconciliation. It sought to bring two alienated groups, the working classes and the practising Catholics, into the mainstream of political development, from which, at least outside Britain and Scandinavia, they had long been excluded. Like the other left-wing movements, Christian Democracy considered social and economic rights to be as important as the political rights recognised in Western Europe after 1789, but it argued that these rights should apply to the whole community and that one class should not gain at the expense of others. In other words, Christian Democracy was trying to be a comprehensive amalgam of political forces firmly based around the centre of the political spectrum.

On the continent of Europe the Resistance movements provided one of the few serious attempts to bridge the gap between
the industrial and rural masses, and between state and society.
In countries such as France and Italy the working classes had
usually been consigned to a social and political ghetto (partly of
their own choosing) far removed from the centre of gravity of
national political life. But in Italy, for example, there were in
1945 around 250,000 fighters in the northern partisan groups,
and it was virtually the first time in Italian history that the
peasants had been associated with other social groups in a political
activity. Elsewhere, for example in Belgium, the workers may
have been incorporated into the political system through the
electoral successes of Socialist parties. But without a clear
majority, yet too strong to be ignored by more conservative
forces, Socialists had found it necessary to abandon some of their
principles in order to prevent political rivals whom they
disliked from joining right-wing extremists inspired by Nazi or
Fascist ideology, which they feared even more. Only, perhaps,
in Scandinavia and Britain had the working classes been accepted,
to a greater or less extent, as an integral part of the political
system.

Together, all these forces would work for a new society which,
it was hoped, if based on a less dogmatic socialism, would create
benefits for all and end hardship, privation and insecurity. But
it was argued that if a new society was to be born of a new
political ideology, then those ideologies which were old and
discredited (at least in the eyes of the reformers) must not be
allowed to regain control or influence in the postwar world. It
was believed that a great alliance of all left-wing progressive
movements would possess sufficient strength and popular support
to be able to defeat in elections the older and more conservative
parties. Thus there was born the idea of a single Resistance
party, comprising all those groups which had worked for the
Liberation.

But in its optimism the ideology of the Resistance did not stop
at national boundaries. The new spirit of reconciliation which it
advocated was concerned not only with the creation of a new
society, but also with the need to prevent another war that might

engulf the continent. The causes of past wars in Europe were attributed in part to too much emphasis on nationalism and national pride. Attention, therefore, was paid not only to the pressing needs of national reconstruction after the ravages of war, but also to the need to transcend old national boundaries, now regarded as discredited and artificial, in order to create a revitalised international community which would consist of as much of Europe as possible. Announcements to this effect were made long before the end of the war in Europe. During 1944 several French Resistance groups in France and North Africa emphasised the need for some supranational structure in Europe, based on federal lines, to replace the old system of nation states. The Italian Resistance movement also emphasised the need for a new federal structure in Europe; and some even went so far as to claim that national reconstruction must take second place in relation to the need to establish a new federal Europe. In July 1944 leaders of Resistance movements in several European countries, including Denmark, France, Holland, Italy and Norway, added their signatures to a declaration stating that a completely new federal governmental structure built along democratic lines was required in Europe. Of course, not all Resistance participants and movements—including those whose political views were to the left of the political spectrum—argued for a federal union in Europe. In Holland, for example, a return to the prewar national political system seemed to be favoured by most people. Even sentiment for a unified Dutch Resistance political party had weakened considerably by 1945, and some protagonists had already appeared to argue that leaders of an underground Resistance organised along quasimilitary lines would not necessarily be the people best qualified to operate a peacetime political system.

Nevertheless, the Resistance movements, taken as a whole, still possessed a comprehensive vision of the postwar situation in Europe. Many of their leaders would be content with nothing short of total reconstruction. The historic nation state had proved utterly incapable of preventing wars, therefore some new organisation was required. This was to be supranational in form. The prewar political leaders and political and social systems had, in the eyes of the Resistance, been found wanting. Intranational change was required, and the wholesale victories of the Nazi juggernaut on the continent gave Resistance reformers an opportunity to rebuild from entirely new foundations. The impetus, moreover, did not come only from Resistance movements. Much official American opinion was at least sympathetic to European union. Britain also was seen as a sympathetic supporter. There was little reason for these pan-Europeans to foretell the results of the 1945 British General Election. It was hoped, therefore, that Winston Churchill would continue after the war to pursue a policy along the lines of his dramatic offer to France in June 1940 that 'there shall no longer be two nations, but one Franco-British Union'.[1]

Confident that they had the support, tacit or expressed, of the Allies (even Communists were following orders from Moscow of close cooperation with non-Communists) and that, because of their leadership in the fight for liberation, they would gain the support of their own electorates, men of the Resistance groups looked toward the postwar world with increasing optimism. We must now, therefore, examine the role of the Resistance in Europe after May 1945.

The First Postwar Elections

For all the countries which had been affected by the war, one of the most pressing needs was to hold a general election as soon as possible. These elections gave further encouragement to those in the Resistance organisations who were seeking to achieve a new type of society based on social and economic rather than liberal and political imperatives. The tone was set by the British election of 1945. A massive Conservative majority in Parliament disappeared overnight in a landslide victory for the Labour Party. For the first time in its history, the Labour Party was able to form a one-party government with an assured majority, possessing as it did 393 seats in the House of Commons as opposed to only 213 held by the Conservatives. This was the most surprising election result of the immediate postwar years. Churchill, as war

[1] W. S. Churchill, *The Second World War: Their Finest Hour*, Vol. II, London, 1949, pp. 183–4; 219–20.

leader and Conservative leader, commanded a massive popularity in the country. Moreover, the wartime National Government, which many Europeans identified solely with Churchill, had issued its own plans for social reconstruction in the Beveridge Plan of 1942, which has been called Britain's 'Resistance Charter'.[1] The Beveridge Plan was, in fact, a primary source of the programmes and charters later announced by continental Resistance movements.

Notwithstanding any peculiarly national reasons which may have contributed toward the Labour victory in Britain, the same swing to the left was apparent in most other European democracies. In France the elections of 1946 were dominated by three mass parties of the left which in June obtained 75 per cent of the total vote, and 72 per cent in November: these parties were the Communists (26 per cent in June and 28 per cent in November), the Socialists (21 per cent and 18 per cent), and the Christian Democrats (28 per cent and 26 per cent). A similar tripartite pattern was visible in Italy. There, however, in June 1946, in the first free elections since 1921, the Christian Democrats outstripped their two major rivals, gaining 35 per cent of the votes as compared to 21 per cent for the Socialists and 19 per cent for the Communists. In Belgium and Holland also, these three parties or their counterparts tended to dominate the first postwar elections. Here, Christian Democrat or Christian Socialist parties, which had increased in strength and prestige during the Occupation, had attempted to expand from being more or less pure Catholic or sectarian parties to include all Christians who wished to see a non-Socialist programme of reform adopted and executed. Catholic parties were rewarded with 43 per cent of the votes in Belgium and 31 per cent in Holland, and the Socialists maintained their challenge with 32 per cent and 28 per cent of the votes in Belgium and Holland respectively. In both countries the Communists gained around 10 per cent of the poll, thus emerging as a serious party. In liberated Scandinavia a similar pattern appeared. The major parties of Denmark changed relatively little in their overall strength, although again there were gains for the left-wing parties, while in Norway the Labour Party in 1945 won its first

[1] D. Thomson, *England in the Twentieth Century*, London, 1964, p. 178.

absolute majority in the *Storting* (the Norwegian parliament).[1]

When the smoke had cleared, it seemed that the spirit of the Resistance movements had won a great victory. It was obvious that left-wing parties with their demands for radical social reform were the true representatives of the electorates. The people had rejected any return to the prewar system. Old-fashioned political liberalism had been found wanting, and accordingly had been cast out. Together with the strong social challenge of the Communist and Socialist parties, the new or revived Catholic movements had been the main beneficiaries of the elections. Later elections and developments, however, revealed that Christian Democracy had been lured into a false position. It had been supported by large numbers of liberals and conservatives who, unable to vote in their traditional manner, had rejected the alternatives of Socialism and Communism as being completely unacceptable. Liberal and conservative parties were the chief losers in these first elections: liberalism because of its prewar failures and conservatism because of its support of or silence over the virulent policies of Nazism and Fascism. It was obvious that there was an almost universal demand for social reform along the lines proposed by Resistance propaganda, prompted by the emotional fears of insecurity caused by the war and by the memories of mass unemployment during the 1920s and 1930s. On the surface, therefore, the way seemed clear for the Resistance groups to realise at least some of their aims. Yet these first post-war elections, while seeming to vindicate the optimism of Resistance reformers, proved that they had been defeated in at least one of their aims. At the same time these elections carried the seeds of destruction for other of their plans and hopes for the future.

The Resistance Party

It will be remembered that one of the proposals circulated during the last years of the war was that suggesting a total reorganisation of the old party structure of the European democracies. The key-

[1] Postwar election results for Western European states can be found in D. W. Urwin (ed.), *Elections in Western Nations, 1945–1968* (Occasional Paper, Nos. 4/5, Survey Research Centre, University of Strathclyde, 1969).

stone of this reorganisation was to be the creation of a new and comprehensive Resistance party incorporating all progressive elements in society.

It was soon clear that this proposal had very little chance of succeeding. Several parties had managed to maintain some form of organisation in functioning order during hostilities. Others, especially the Communists, had actually been successful in strengthening and extending their organisation. This was particularly true of French and Italian Communism. The membership of the Italian Communist Party, only around 10,000 in 1944, had leapt to over one million by 1946. In France about half the active participants in the Resistance belonged to the Communist Party. Their activities allowed them to seize a powerful foothold among the French peasantry. Building on their meagre prewar strength in rural France, they gradually achieved an impressive organisational structure maintained by a network of Committees of Peasant Defence and Action. In addition, the war and middle-class support for the Vichy Government gave the Communists an outstanding opportunity of winning control of the French trade union movement—an opportunity which they took. Middle-class support for Vichy suggested that the working classes and their 'true' representatives, the Communists, should be the new rulers of France:

This fact produced the sentiment that was most favourable to the spreading of Communism, the belief that the bourgeoisie was condemned by history and was impotent to reassume the leadership of a country that it had lamentably abandoned, and that the working-class, excluded from power but nonetheless faithful, was alone capable of giving France a future.[1]

The full extent of Communist expansion was obscured by wartime exigencies; it became apparent only after 1945.

In addition, governments and party leaders in exile in London and elsewhere had kept the thought of the old party structure alive. They were extremely loath to be merged with other political forces. In the Netherlands, for example, most leaders

[1] M. Einaudi, J. M. Domenach, and A. Garosci, *Communism in Western Europe*, Ithaca, 1951, p. 137.

welcomed the decision of the monarch to hold consultations with Dutch Resistance heads on the subject of the formation of a new cabinet, but nevertheless regarded the creation of a Resistance party as being completely out of the question. Here the revival of the old party system was accepted almost as a matter of form. In minor countries, such as the Netherlands, however, the old parties had not been guilty of so many faults as their counterparts in the larger countries. Hence they did not have to face so much criticism. The basic problems involved parties in France, Italy, and Germany.

It was the return of the former party leaders, either from exile, semi-retirement or concentration camps, that more or less finally ended the hopes of the Resistance organisations in this respect. Men of an older generation, they were well versed in the arts required of political leaders. Resistance leaders often proved to be incapable of opposing them successfully on this different type of battlefield. In this context Resistance fighters were essentially innocents abroad. They survived the broils of peacetime political in-fighting only if they possessed previous experience or had 'compromised' themselves by joining a 'normal' political party. Only outstanding personalities, such as General de Gaulle, could be exceptions to this seemingly inexorable law. For some, particularly Catholics, adaptation was virtually impossible because of their quite different reasons for participating in the Resistance: religion, not nationalism, had been the *raison d'être* of their opposition to Nazism.

The Communists, too, contributed to the difficulties of the Resistance unifiers. During the war, when minds were occupied by the day-to-day necessities of guerrilla fighting, it did appear that Communism had changed. Local Communist leaders were often young men who, because of the dictates of war, usually acted on their own initiative according to their judgment of the local situation. To their partisan companions it may well have appeared that their prime concern was with the national welfare rather than with Moscow's wishes. After 1945, however, Moscow sought to regain its total influence over Western European Communism and to force it into the rigid code of Communist aims. This return to Russian suzerainty was emphasised by the return of older Communist leaders such as Maurice Thorez

9

and Palmiro Togliatti from their years of exile in Russia or elsewhere. The Communist parties were determined not to renounce their independence to any comprehensive Resistance party unless it was certain that they themselves would control it. Since events consistently proved that this could not be the case, the Communists returned to the policy of building up their own monolithic party structure—a state within the state. Consequently an open and irreconcilable breach in Resistance homogeneity appeared between Communists and non-Communists.

Even during the war there had been obvious signs that the proposed Resistance party would never get off the ground. National Resistance movements were on the whole little more than coalitions of groups claiming allegiance to one political party who were unwilling to forfeit their own individuality. In many areas resistance activity was carried on through and directed by only one or two political parties. In some rural areas of central France, for example, resistance was the Communist Party; its success in establishing an efficient wartime organisation enabled it in subsequent elections to become the dominant political force in these regions. In northern Italy the partisan armies were organised along party lines and owed their allegiance primarily to their party. The best-organised were the Garibaldi brigades, under Communist control (in France the Communist bands were known as the *Franc-Tireurs et Partisans*). These were closely followed by the *Rosselli* and *Giustizia e Libertà* brigades which supported the Action Party; while the Christian Democrats had a loose force of about 65,000 men.[1] Given these circumstances during the war, it is difficult to see how any effective reconciliation could have been achieved in the more relaxed atmosphere of peace when pressures to conform or unite were much less severe. This was especially true of countries where social divisions and cleavages ran deep. Old prejudices would not disappear overnight. In France the Socialist traditionalists determined to stay true to their doctrine. In particular they remained extremely hostile to Catholicism. In fact the party came to be the focal point of anti-

[1] The Rosselli brigades were named in honour of Carlo Rosselli, an exponent of liberal socialism, who was killed in 1937 in Paris by French right-wing extremists, reputedly on the orders of Mussolini's political police.

clericalism, arguing that only class parties should be allowed to exist and preferring to associate with secular politicians, no matter how conservative, rather than with progressive Catholic leaders.

Only two parties were to a great extent directly created under the auspices of Resistance thinking and experience—the French Christian Democrats (MRP or *Mouvement Républicain Populaire*) and the Italian Action Party. The MRP, however, claimed an electoral base in the Catholic religion. Strictly speaking, its ideology was not obtained directly from Resistance experience or aspirations, but could trace a direct descent from earlier Catholic political movements and groups. The Action Party, on the other hand, was the Resistance party *par excellence*. It owed its origin to no other clear source. Under a forceful leader, Ferruccio Parri, it set out to expound the demands of the Resistance in a political and ideological framework which may be described as 'liberal socialism'. In other words, it saw itself as the integrating link between all left-wing parties. It hoped to provide the leadership and common meeting ground of the ideological Socialist left (the Communists and Socialists) and the non-Marxist left (including the small Republican Party and the reforming wing of the Christian Democrats). Some comments on the Action Party, therefore, would help to illustrate the problems facing a possible Resistance party.

The portents were at first auspicious. The pressure for change—*vento del nord* (wind from the north)—of the Resistance forced the resignation of the government of liberated Italy which had been appointed by the King. The two great forces of Catholicism and Socialism—Communism (the two parties having pursued a common course for a number of years) were too evenly matched. The Socialist leader, Pietro Nenni, was unacceptable to the Catholics, while Alcide de Gasperi, the Christian Democrat leader, was unacceptable to the extreme left. Hence Parri was left as the only alternative. He was nominated and commissioned to form a government. Parri, however, did not survive for long. The direct cause of his fall was a realignment of political parties, due to the growing self-confidence of the right and the policy of de Gasperi to keep the official policy of his Christian Democrats as close to the centre of the political spectrum as possible. The dangerous economic and social condition of Italy was bordering upon a revolutionary situation. The middle classes hesitated to travel along unknown territory and accused the Resistance of turning into a Communist conspiracy. Fearing Parri's proposals for extending the purge of Fascism and its com-. mitted supporters to state and private industry, his plans to break up monopolies, and his intense republicanism, they returned to their old traditional values where they felt safe. However, Parri's own lack of political experience, typical of most Resistance leaders, and the fact that the Action Party was essentially a party of leaders agreed on principle but without any significant mass following, also contributed to his failure. The bridge proved to be impossible without the central pillar of political support. Even then, it would still remain doubtful whether the Action Party could have pursued its intended course. Speculation ended in November 1945, when first the Liberals and then the Christian Democrats withdrew their support of the government; on 24 November Parri was forced to resign.

This was the death-knell of the Action Party, and could be taken as the final indication that the ideals of the Resistance movements could not be directly implemented, not just in Italy, but in the whole of liberated Europe. A similar situation occurred in France. Sectional political parties were increasing in strength. Only General de Gaulle had the authority and prestige to form a political movement cutting across traditional cleavages and sectional loyalties. This he was unwilling to do. It would have to be done 'spontaneously' by the people. The mountain would have to go to Mahomet, for Mahomet was reluctant to go to the mountain. The situation in France has been summed up admirably by a leading scholar of the Fourth Republic:

The Resistance party was never formed. The Communists were bent on hampering any organisation they did not control. Some Resisters from the old parties, especially Socialists, were unwilling to lose their former political identity. Christian Democrats who could hope at last to found a major party would not renounce this opportunity for an uncertain fusion with rather reluctant anti-clerical partners. Above all, General de Gaulle, who in 1943 had revived the discredited old parties by bringing them into the National Resistance Council to strengthen his hand in Washington and London, was in 1944–45 still unwilling to forfeit his position as a national hero by stooping to lead a political party.[1]

A different pattern of politics, symbolised by the election results of 1945 and 1946, was to determine the course of events in Western Europe during the crucial first postwar years. If any of the ideals of the various Resistance organisations were to be achieved, they would be engineered by political forces or combinations of such forces motivated primarily from a different base. Furthermore, these forces would be in a much stronger position than Resistance groups as such to claim the credit for social and economic reform.

The Purges

Not only were the Resistance movements defeated in the field of practical politics; they also failed to achieve the most practical policy of their drive for a new morality in Europe. They had set out to purify the European atmosphere of the virulent hate of the previous years. The most obvious and most symbolic way of achieving this goal was to institute and carry through an effective purge of Fascists and collaborators from public life. This proved to be an impossible task. Too much political passion had been generated during the years of occupation. In 1945 and 1946 this emotion was still too strong for any rational system to be devised for punishing the guilty and awarding damages to the victims. The illiberal tone was instituted at the outset by Resistance partisans themselves. In nearly all the liberated countries summary justice was meted out by the more extreme elements of the Resistance before the Allied authorities and the returning exiled governments were able to establish effective control. Even 'moralistic' elements within the Resistance movements could not completely escape this criticism.

In northern Italy several thousand Fascists were executed by the partisans who occupied the larger towns during the German retreat. Mussolini himself was captured and killed after an extremely brief and highly irregular trial. Unfortunately,

[1] P. M. Williams, *Crisis and Compromise*, London, 1964, p. 19.

revenge was not simply directed against the more virulent Fascists. The guise of patriotism and outraged morality provided an excellent excuse for dealing once and for all with old enemies for personal satisfaction or gain. Criminal elements, who had been quite prominent in the partisan movements, and Communists were especially guilty of such crimes. The Communists took the opportunity of eliminating both potential adversaries and ex-Communists who had resigned from the party. Whether or not these unfortunates had later joined the Resistance or the collaborating groups was of no account; what mattered was that they were a possible source of embarrassment. The total number of summary executions of Fascists and collaborators, including even those merely suspected of such political sympathies and associations, was not very high. At any rate, nowhere did it approach the scale of mass murder practised by the Nazis. Nevertheless, no excuses should be offered; it meant that the Resistance had stained its character even before it embarked on its ambitious moral programme.

Once domestic or Allied military governments had been established in France, Italy, Germany, the Low Countries and Scandinavia, a regularized purge was instituted under normal judicial procedure. The burden of supervising this vast cleansing operation fell, on the whole, on the public administrators and the judiciary, who conscientiously attempted to achieve the intended aims. A series of penalties was devised, ranging from discharge from public office through prison sentences to charges bearing the death penalty. This ambitious 'denazification' programme, however, foundered in a welter of recriminations, accusations and counter-accusations.

Nowhere was this more apparent than in Germany, where the purge and denazification procedures were directed by the Allied occupation authorities. Germany was the most monumental problem, for instead of a minority of the population being concerned, nearly every adult had been connected in some way with the Nazi regime. For many possession of a Nazi Party membership card had been the only guarantee of continued employment. The occupation authorities drafted lengthy questionnaires which the Germans had to complete. Even so, it proved to be impossible to determine with any great exactitude who was responsible for a particular crime. Given the complex, intertwining and often chaotic nature of the German State and the Nazi Party structure and machinery, nearly everyone could find a reasonably valid excuse for claiming that the responsibility for a particular action had not belonged to him, but to someone else.

The mood of Germany with regard to the purge changed comparatively rapidly from wariness to open hostility. Germans could not see any sense or application of justice in the whole affair. Moreover, they preferred to draw a veil over the unsavoury past rather than have it continually paraded in full public view. Given the complex nature of the problem, it had proved easier for the Allies to try the minnows first: their cases could be dealt with simply and quickly. Greater offenders often had the ability and the means to throw many red herrings across the path of the inquisitors or to disappear into the obscurity of a totally disorganised German society. This policy meant that the Allies, instead of doing justice, were committing an injustice. For as they became aware of the magnitude of their appointed task and of their inability to deal with it satisfactorily, they gradually accepted the need to wind up the denazification procedures as quickly as possible. The result was that delayed cases were never taken up, that more amnesties were granted to categories still at liberty and to some individuals already sentenced, and that punishments became less severe. After the Allies had resigned this duty in favour of constituted German authorities, the trend became even more marked. It meant that the minor offenders who had been sentenced first received relatively harsh penalties. It was thus not calculated to endear the purge to the ordinary German.

At the heart of Allied policy in Germany, endorsed by the Resistance movements, was the desire to illustrate to the Germans and to the world the magnitude of the wrongs committed in the name of Nazism. The symbol of this punitive lesson was to be the Nuremberg trials of major war criminals held between November 1945 and September 1946. Much time and thought had gone into the preparations for the trials. There was a board of nine judges presided over by a British Lord Justice, while a member of the American Supreme Court acted as chief prosecutor.

The charges against the defendants were 'crimes against humanity' and conducting an aggressive war. They were supplemented by a mass of detail which had been carefully sifted. The penalty was death. Most of the leading Nazis were on trial, except Hitler and Goebbels, who had committed suicide in Berlin as Russian troops were taking over the city; Heinrich Himmler, leader of the ss, who had committed suicide shortly after his capture by British troops; and Martin Bormann, the party secretary, and Heinrich Mueller, the Gestapo chief, both of whom had disappeared. Of the twenty-two Nazis who stood trial, only three were acquitted. These acquittals were perhaps the only results which came as a surprise to Germany. Of the remainder, seven were given prison terms and twelve were sentenced to death. All the sentences were carried out except that on Hermann Goering, who succeeded in committing suicide in his cell. Elsewhere, the same fate awaited other prominent Nazi collaborators. Vidkun Quisling, whose name gave a new word to the English language, was sentenced to death and executed in Norway. In France, the two outstanding leaders of the Vichy Republic, Pierre Laval and Marshall Pétain, were also condemned to death, although in the case of Pétain the sentence was later commuted by General de Gaulle to life imprisonment.

In Germany the Nuremberg trials were received with apathy and cynicism. They merely confirmed the evidence of the other denazification procedures that justice was not being done. The Allies had failed completely to communicate their high moral purpose to the Germans. To the latter the sentences delivered at Nuremberg, coupled with the fact that Russian and French judges were participating along with those from America and Britain, were merely further indications that the whole denazification policy was an act of revenge carried out by the victorious nations on the defeated: it was seen by some as being no different in its intentions from the Treaty of Versailles.

The same effect was noticeable in the liberated countries. The trials of Laval and Pétain in France were the scene of much virulent invective, thus poisoning the atmosphere even further. The general public lost all interest in the proceedings. The dangerous economic situation forced individuals to pay more attention to their own pressing immediate needs. The trials and the purges had inevitably been conducted in a political, not a moral atmosphere. The anxiety of Resistance reformers to lead a great moral crusade appeared, as far as the average onlooker was concerned, to degenerate into acts of personal revenge upon political opponents; whereas the Germans saw denazification as the revenge of some nations on another, in the liberated countries the purge of collaborators was seen as the revenge of some political groups who had taken the opportunity to destroy their opponents.

Even while bearing in mind the many obstacles facing the prosecutors of the purges and the virtual impossibility of implementing any other workable course of action, it seems reasonable to claim that the post-war purges marked a second important failure of Resistance thinking. The ordinary European had not seen justice carried out. Instead, he believed that a great injustice had been done. Many innocents had suffered at the hands of powerful political adversaries, while those who were least implicated with Hitler's drive for European domination had been punished far more severely than more serious offenders. This was partly a consequence of the postwar situation, where unified political direction and social cohesion were lacking. However, another important reason lay in the nature of the action itself. The greatest problem the prosecutors had to face was that of constructing a series of punishments compatible with the crimes committed. And it was here that the whole operation failed from the beginning. No one could point to the man definitely responsible for a particular crime; no one could determine to which grade of collaboration a crime should be ascribed. Above all, the gigantic, almost 'superhuman' scale of Nazi persecution made it seem impossible that any 'human' efforts at retribution could repair or equal the damage already committed. Public resentment at Resistance extremism in trying to force the issue to a definite conclusion may well have caused great harm to the overall Resistance programme.

The Federal Union of Europe

In two of their basic proposals Resistance movements had failed. It follows, almost automatically, that their third important proposal also could not succeed. This was the plan to create a great new Federal Union of Europe. It had been believed that such a radical step could have been taken when the Resistance movements became the legitimate peacetime governments of their respective countries. The return to traditional political and parliamentary life coupled with the failure of Resistance leaders to succeed in this alien environment meant that unless a majority of the parties in a country were agreed, not only upon the goal, but also upon the details of that goal and the methods necessary to achieve it, then the only outcome would be deadlock and the shelving or abandonment of the project.

The Communists, for example, were totally opposed to European union unless it was under their control. Old issues which had previously kept non-Communists apart, as for example the historic hostility between Socialists and Catholics, returned to drive further divisions between the various segments of the Resistance movements. Moreover, the newly constituted governments of Western Europe found and believed that bread-and-butter problems were becoming increasingly important and urgent. Solutions to these problems were what the electorates were expecting and demanding; and unless they were found, the economies of Western Europe might sink without trace. Perforce, economic reconstruction took priority over the ambitious plans for European union.

These plans now had to be sponsored by private associations such as the French Council for a United Europe. These groups could count parliamentarians and even government ministers among their distinguished members, but their policies could not be said to be the unequivocal policy of their government. Like the German Army, the Resistance movements had waged total war, but on what they considered to be outmoded political organisations. Like the German Army, they had attempted to fight on more than one front against a number of strong and well-entrenched adversaries. And like the German Army, they had found the task beyond them. To the more ardent supporters of the Resistance ideals in these first post-war years, it seemed that the vision of a great new society, born of high moral hope, had died of despair and political pettiness.

The French Worker-Priests

At this point it would be advisable to consider briefly another postwar development which, although not related directly to the Resistance, was undoubtedly inspired by it. This was the social activities of reformist Catholics which led to the bold experiment of the worker-priests in France. Despite the equivocal position of Pope Pius XI *vis-à-vis* the right-wing authoritarian movements during the 1930s, the Catholic Church emerged from the war with its reputation enhanced. Vatican opposition to Nazism had gradually hardened during the war. Catholics had often played a leading role in Resistance activities. Partly as a consequence of this, Catholicism became more involved in politics after 1945 through the rise of Christian Democrat parties to positions of strength. Their Catholicism was often of a left-wing variety and sought solutions to social problems which were often of a quasi-socialist nature, although their inspiration was derived from the two basic encyclicals of the Church, *Rerum Novarum* and *Quadragesimo Anno*. At the heart of their beliefs was the determination to wage a crusade for Catholic values in order to reduce or destroy class conflict.

This implied that the crusade would have to be among the working classes which in France, Italy, and to a lesser extent, Belgium and the Netherlands had for long been 'de-Christianised'. Only in France was a radical measure introduced in an attempt to reconvert the workers. Beginning in 1946, the worker-priest experiment was designed to show the working classes, who, except in Alsace, were on the whole apathetic and even hostile to the Church's values and beliefs, that the Church was not divorced from their way of life and even understood their problems. This was to be achieved by the clergy sharing the tasks and life of the workers. By 1951 there were some ninety worker-priests employed in the factories of France's large industrial centres, and the idea had been given the blessing of the French episcopate. By that time the programme was beginning to show some signs of success. The priests had had to work incognito in ordinary labourer's clothes until accepted as equals by their workmates. Gradually they had been able to win the workers' confidence and reveal their true identity. To the sponsors of the scheme it appeared that the formidable first barrier had been overcome and that the priests could now start their proper evangelical mission.

However, the remaining barriers were never tackled. Riots, sponsored by the Communists, broke out in Paris, and during the mopping-up operations a few worker-priests found their way into the police net. Subsequent questioning brought to the surface the horrifying fact that some had traversed the length of the political spectrum, that they had become, if not outright Marxists, at least sympathetic to Marxist ideas. To the traditionalists within the Church, this could appear as a threat which could undermine its whole structure. Although the French higher clergy still endorsed the experiment, they were overruled by the Vatican. Severe restrictions were placed on the remaining worker-priests, while the Pope refused to allow any more to enter the field. The debate over the value of the priests, which was long and bitter, was finally closed when the new Pope, John XXIII, declared in 1959 that factory work and the mission of the clergy were incompatible.

Once again a revolutionary idea associated with the Resistance experience had come to nought. But at least here the experiment was actually tried. Credit must go to the French episcopate for endorsing and supporting the plan, especially as the French Church had in politics consistently come down on the side of monarchy and reaction, which since the French Revolution had been the losing side. But it stood virtually alone among official Catholicism in its worker-priest policy. Political Catholicism had become disinterested in and even hostile to the idea and the experiment. The radical element within Christian Democracy had failed to maintain its ascendancy over the movement. By 1950 the Christian Democrat parties everywhere were led by more conservative leaders: where the same leaders were still in control, they had had second thoughts and were now more conservatively inclined. Moreover, the worker-priests represented a political relationship between Catholicism and the working classes which was not controlled by the Catholic political party. It was therefore a potentially independent power centre and as such an object of envy and jealousy.

The worker-priest experiment was one of the most important attempts, inspired by the Resistance spirit of the brotherhood of man, to establish a new social homogeneity. It was not entirely immune from criticism. Many of the priests had not received adequate preparation for their task, and most operated in complete isolation, unable to fall back upon the Church for advice. This alone placed them in an extremely vulnerable position, where indoctrination was not just possible but probable. Thus it became a gallant failure. But at least it showed the Church, in no uncertain terms, one of the most profitable ways, if not the only way, by which the Church could regain the confidence and allegiance of the working classes. The idea did not die. Only a few years after the Vatican had seemingly closed the matter, the French clergy were once again considering sending missionary priests out into the industrial world. In some ways this is a remarkable testimony to the vitality of the fundamental ideas of human concord which the Resistance experience did so much to resurrect.

The Resistance: An Assessment

After the above brief account of the aims of Resistance reformers and their activities after 1945, we can attempt an assessment of its achievements. At first glance it would seem that the Resistance vision had failed to exert a positive impact on Europe; nowhere was it able to assert a moral authority over practical politics. Its supporters argued that they had been ruthlessly tricked and suppressed by unscrupulous political manipulators and by short-sighted officialdom which could only see as far as its immediate self-interest. Its opponents argued that its conception of human society was essentially unrealistic and entirely incapable of being achieved by political means in existing circumstances. As in most things the truth probably lies somewhere between these two claims.

In the field of practical politics the Resistance programme seems to have proved somewhat unprofitable. But it had only one complete failure—its inability to create a comprehensive Resistance party covering all or most of the radical progressive elements in society. Even today there appears to be little chance of such a party being established on a permanent basis, even among the non-Communist left. Since 1945 there has been only one definitely major arrival on the party scene in Europe, the West German Christian Democratic Union. And even this party developed from the already well-rooted Centre Catholic party of the German Empire and Weimar Republic. All other 'Resistance' parties disappeared or were unable to overcome barriers restricting them to narrow confines. In their moral aim of purging Europe of Fascism the Resistance movements had only a limited success. Indeed their success here may have backfired. Many eminent jurists were doubtful about the value of trying the Nazi leaders for war crimes and about the juridical authenticity of the trials themselves. Quite apart from the technical problems involved, it was argued that the trials at Nuremberg and elsewhere set a dangerous precedent for the future: any victor in a war could claim it was justified on the grounds of precedent in placing the leaders of the defeated nation on trial.

In their attempt to create a European federal union the Resistance movements also failed, yet not entirely. It at least helped to pave the way for the establishment of several European institutions such as the Council of Europe which, based at Strasbourg, began to function in 1949. It also indirectly helped to inspire both the loose union of Scandinavian states which are 'directed' by the Nordic Council and the more intense experiment of economic union of Belgium, the Netherlands and Luxembourg known as Benelux. Above all it can claim some credit for the establishment of the European Economic Community (the Common Market) which came into being in 1957. Admittedly it would be foolish to suggest that these supranational attempts at cooperation and integration arose directly and solely from the Resistance experience. The latter, however, cannot be excluded altogether. For its importance in this respect is that it took an issue which before 1939 had been relegated to the fringe of politics, being espoused by private groups and associations with little or no parliamentary support, and made it an issue which after 1945 was nearly always taken seriously by Western European governments and parliamentarians, whether they supported or opposed it. This radical change of fortune of European federalism was achieved primarily by the dissemination of the idea of union to the various component parts of the Resistance movements which, though changed in their political colouring, survived in the postwar world. After 1945 nearly every political party in Western Europe, with the possible exceptions of the British, Swiss and Swedish parties and the West German Social Democrats, possessed a substantial and influential parliamentary minority which favoured and advocated some form of political and economic union for Europe. The Communists, of course, had their own conception of European union. The recognition that some form of cooperation was indispensable, and not just advisable, was given expression in the Statute of the Council of Europe in 1949: Article I states that 'the aim of the Council of Europe is to achieve a greater unity between its Members for the purpose of safeguarding and realising the ideals and principles which are their common heritage and facilitating their economic and social progress'. The Resistance movements, therefore, had not tried in vain to make Europeans realise that they had a common heritage and a common future.

It was, however, in the legislative provisions passed by postwar parliaments that we see the greatest influence of the Resistance. The French Resistance Charter of 1944, for example, in calling for a 'more just social order' had demanded in its programme for the future a rational reorganisation of the national economy which would benefit the general interest and not just favoured individuals. It also asked for numerous socio-economic guarantees for the workers, a comprehensive system of social security, the nationalisation of many private monopolies, and the right of the workers to share in economic policy-making within industries and firms. French legislation between 1945 and 1950 shows how much the demands of the national Resistance influenced legislative production. Nationalisation was carried out on a fairly large scale; an improved social security system was instituted; trade union rights were fully restored. Above all, alone among the states of Western Europe, France established a national economic planning agency under Jean Monnet (known as the Monnet Plan). Only in the request for the participation of the workers in the economic direction of industries did the French Resistance thinkers fail to see their desires realised. The workers in West Germany, however, did achieve a partial success in this direction.

Comparable legislation, heavily influenced by the native Resistance movements, was realised in other liberated countries. In Britain the Labour Government of 1945 set out to implement as much as possible of its own radical programme and of the social recommendations of the 1942 Beveridge Report which had proposed a comprehensive system of social security covering all aspects of family life. Such reforms were possible because of the control of the various parliaments by left-wing parties which had been the mainstay of the Resistance movements and which had long held similar ideas on social organisation.

Where new constitutions had to be adopted the ideas of the Resistance also made their mark. The West German constitution of 1949 was deeply influenced by the Christian and moral ideas of its drafters who were on the whole confirmed anti-Nazis. In France, although a result of compromises, the new constitution showed much of the thinking of the Socialist Party: the French Resistance Charter had been very largely socialist in its inspiration. In Italy some provisions of the constitution were derived from Communist proposals, while much of what the Action Party, the epitome of Resistance 'ideology', had advocated during and after the war—republicanism, regional autonomy, antitrust laws, nationalisation of some public utilities, progressive taxation, land reform and economic development, especially in the south—were incorporated as principles in the new constitution. Moreover, Resistance adherents had the satisfaction of seeing incorporated into the newly drafted constitutions clauses which provided for the abrogation of national sovereignty in favour of supranational authorities. The preamble of the French Constitution of 1946 stated that 'on condition of reciprocity, France shall accept the limitations of sovereignty necessary to the organisation and defence of peace'. Article II of the Italian Constitution of 1947 declared that 'Italy consents, on condition of parity with other states, to limitations of sovereignty necessary to an order for assuring peace and justice among nations; it promotes and favours international organisation toward that end'. The West

German Constitution of 1949 has similar provisions. Perhaps it is no coincidence that these three states were signatories of the Treaty of Rome in 1957 which marked the beginning of the European Economic Community, the most advanced experiment of abrogation of national sovereignty. However, these states did not possess a monopoly of the willingness to recognise that working international and European associations provided the most satisfactory means of advancing world, European, and national interests. In 1953 a new constitution was ratified in Denmark: it included the provision that 'the powers invested in state authorities, may, to such an extent as shall be provided by statute, be delegated to international authorities that have been established by mutual agreement with other states for the promotion of international rules of law and international cooperation'.

In view of all this, it is hard to say that the Resistance movements failed completely in the years of reconstruction. Although it proved impossible to combine the ideologies of Marxian and non-Marxian Socialism, and those of Communism, democratic Socialism, and Christian Socialism in a single integrated political framework, its limited achievements did indicate the increasing economic and political power of the working classes whose interests had hitherto been neglected or 'quarantined' in many instances. The ideological movements which had benefited from their Resistance participation by and large retained their strength during the early peacetime years. By their political presence they illustrated the changed mood of public opinion and the changing structures of politics. The general opinion of Western Europe was that the *status quo* of prewar days, which had remained relatively unchanged in its basic emphases since the early nineteenth century, could not be regained, and that it would be undesirable to try to turn the clock back. This was to be further stressed by the hardening of the Cold War. But already during the closing years of the world conflict and the immediate postwar years there was a demand for social change. The rejection of the old liberal democracy with its emphasis upon political rights, created by the French Revolution of 1789 and its consequences, and the acceptance of the need for a social democracy with its emphasis upon social and economic rights was forged by the experience of war and resistance. By their efforts during these years Resistance participants played an important role in conditioning the ordinary individual to accept and understand the new social way of thinking.

2 Problems of Reconstruction

The truth of the matter is that Europe's requirements for the next three or four years of foreign food and other essential products—principally from America—are so much greater than her present ability to pay that she must have substantial additional help or face economic, social, and political deterioration of a very grave character.

General Marshall, 1947

The primary task awaiting Western Europe and its leaders after 1945 was that of picking up the scattered threads of European life and bringing them together in some comprehensible and viable whole. It was no academic problem, but a matter of life or death. Failure to solve the urgent economic and political problems of reconstruction could mean the end of any vitality.

The Catalogue of Damage and Disaster

In 1918 when the First World War ended, only the battlefields of Belgium and northern France lay in ruins: elsewhere war damage was comparatively negligible. In 1945 the situation was entirely different. Military and technological development had made war seem universal. Very few areas in Europe had remained immune from the conflict and its consequences. The outlook everywhere was bleak. The development of air warfare had laid even the British Isles open to destruction. The devastation of northern France between 1914 and 1918 may have been more intense, but what the Second World War lacked in quality it made up for in quantity. In every direction whole regions had been virtually defoliated. Industrial production on the continent had slumped; in 1945 and 1946 it stood at only one-third of the 1938 figure. Agriculture had also suffered: agricultural production was down to half the prewar level. Cities had been severely damaged. Millions of acres of valuable farming land had been rendered useless, not only from being battlefields but also through

27

the demands of war. Land was exhausted through overcropping, while the compensation of fertilisation was lacking because commercial fertilisers were unobtainable. Furthermore, the death rate of animals had been extremely high. In the factories and mines machinery had been crippled because it had been overworked and because it had not been maintained satisfactorily: in addition replacements were generally unavailable.

Economic reconstruction after the war started off at a great disadvantage for additional reasons. The war had disrupted and destroyed communication networks. Aiming for a speedy end to the conflict, the Allies had concentrated on the destruction of communication lines. Hence bridges, railways, marshalling yards and shipping facilities had been targets of high priority to Allied bombers. Again, rather than allow such valuable acquisitions to fall into the hands of the advancing enemy, the German military had attempted to destroy them wherever possible.

In Britain, damage was largely restricted to the larger cities and ports; the country had on the whole suffered relatively little damage from the war. Nevertheless, machinery was exhausted and outdated. Even without the war the problem of economic renovation would still have had to be tackled. The war only precipitated and highlighted the process. France, which had never really recovered completely from the drain of manpower and resources inflicted twenty-five years earlier, was once again placed in a critical situation. Several cities were badly damaged: some ports—Toulon, Brest, Le Havre—were practically in ruins. Nearly one-fifth of France's houses had been destroyed. Moreover, two-thirds of its railway stock had been destroyed or rendered useless, while about one-half of the country's livestock had been killed. Summing up the extent of damage the French War Damage Commission estimated the bill as costing France 45 per cent of its total wealth. In Italy the extent of the destruction reflected the various stages of the Allied advance northward through the peninsula and the intensity of German resistance. Damage was greatest in the areas between Naples and Rome, and between Florence and Bologna. Apart from the clash of determined opposing forces, these areas had been the site of static fronts enforced by adverse winter conditions. Although the large industrial conurbations of Milan and Turin, and several ports, had been hit by bombing raids, the industrial complex of northern Italy emerged in 1945 relatively unscathed; the poverty-stricken south had suffered more heavily. It was calculated that overall one-third of Italy's assets had been destroyed.

The picture in northern Europe was perhaps rather brighter. Neither Denmark (Germany's 'model satrap') nor Norway had been the scene of much fighting, despite the fact that the German armies were still in occupation at the end of the war. Norway's resistance, however, had perhaps cost the country dear. The German forces had adopted a 'scorched earth' policy in the northern provinces and much land had been devastated. Meanwhile one-half of Norway's shipping (and three-quarters of its whaling fleet) had been destroyed. The country's main source of international trade had therefore been seriously restricted. Even Sweden did not escape these problems. Admittedly its neutral policy had permitted it to escape the ravages of war, but since the government had placed the country on a permanent war footing during the hostilities, the same problems of reconstruction could not be avoided.

Belgium, too, had fared rather better than its neighbours. The slight extent of the damage was due partly to the rapidity of the Allied advance through the country and its consequent speedy liberation. Only the sea-port of Antwerp, inevitably a military target, and the Ardennes, the scene of the German Army's last desperate counterattack in the west, had suffered serious damage. The basic problems of reconstruction took only a few months in Belgium. The road was made easier by its colonial possession, the Congo territory. During the war the Congo became one of the main suppliers to the Allies of raw materials and minerals, especially uranium. The exiled Belgian Government in London was thus able to accumulate a great amount of credit with which to arrange for food, clothing, shelter and new machinery once it was able to return to Brussels. With all its good fortune, Belgium still had to introduce the same stringent measures of control as other Western European democracies. The Netherlands, however, had not been so fortunate. Dutch opposition to Nazi domination had been marked from the beginning. As the Allied advance approached its borders, both German troops and Dutch patriots played the deadly game of breaching the dykes and flooding the land. At the end of the war the Germans still controlled the country. Since much valuable reclaimed land was under water, the native population was near starvation point and urgent supplies had to be delivered by the Allies by parachute. A government survey estimated that one-fifth of Dutch housing had been destroyed and that the total loss was more than three times the nation's annual income.

There remained Germany itself. On the surface the country appeared to have been obliterated by the Allies' determined advance and the Germans' stubborn resistance. The American Strategic Bombing Survey stated that two-fifths of the buildings in the fifty largest German cities had been destroyed. Very little survived of Frankfurt, while Berlin, three-quarters of which lay in ruins, was commonly described as 'a heap of rubble'. The surface appearance, however, was very illusory. Much of Germany had been spared, in particular its industry and agriculture. The so-called 'German miracle', the fantastic recovery of its economy after 1949 in the face of what earlier had seemed to be impossible odds, was facilitated greatly by the fact that many of its important assets had been preserved. The Allied bombing raids on Germany had been much more successful in scoring hits on private dwellings and public buildings than on industrial plants.

Nevertheless, the damage in Germany, as elsewhere, appeared to be extensive. The German economic miracle was not even a dream in 1945. In 1946 industrial production in Germany was still only one-third of the 1936 figure. In France output at the beginning of 1945 had not reached 50 per cent of the 1938 volume of industrial production. This overall gloomy outlook gave some justification to the pessimistic assertions of those experts who argued that European recovery would take the best part of twenty to twenty-five years. In the event only ten years were necessary for the process of reconstruction to be virtually completed.

These examinations and analyses of the various economic systems were based only on an assessment of material damage. No forecasts for the time-span necessary for future development could take into account the effect of the great losses in human lives and expertise. France had been bled of its young manhood in the First World War; and again the country had suffered greatly. This time the onus fell upon the whole civilian population. Over two million French men and women had been transported to Germany, there to be placed in prisoner-of-war or concentration camps, or to be used as forced labour. Many had died from exhaustion and starvation or had been executed. Of those who returned many more were physical or mental cripples, unable to participate fully in social and economic activities. Civilian losses among the other belligerent and occupied nations had also been high. Military losses were not as great as they had been between 1914 and 1918; only Germany had lost more fighting men in the Second World War than in the First. Nearly two million German soldiers had been killed, while a further two million were reported missing. In addition another one and a half million were prisoners-of-war. Many of those who had been captured on the Eastern Front by Russian troops were destined never to return home.

It was this drain of human material as much as the destruction of actual property which gave rise to the pessimism about any speedy economic recovery. The conflict had been more total than the First World War. Civilians as well as the military had been involved. Nations had given virtually everything they possessed, in spirit as well as in goods. Consequently a feeling of exhaustion was universal. The question had to be asked whether Europeans were psychologically and physically capable of the task of economic reconstruction. This general fatigue and the psychological aftermath of defeat and collaboration must be set as counterbalances to the unbounded optimism of the Resistance vision.

A further important factor was the complete disruption of international trade and payments. The war had changed radically Europe's pattern of markets and commerce. In many ways a vacuum had been created which was filled by the United States. By 1945 American exports had soared to nearly three times the 1938 total. It was the beginning of the 'dollar gap'. America was

now in a position to supply Europe with more than its requirements. On the other hand, American imports were extremely
low and did not balance the exports. Europe, moreover, did not
possess the necessary cash or credit to purchase the available
American products. Economic dislocation had spread beyond
the mere land area of the old continent. The bulk of the latter's
'invisible means' of earning foreign currency, particularly dollars,
had also disappeared. Merchant shipping had been decimated,
while foreign insurance schemes and investments had been called
upon to finance the war.

It was the extent of economic damage and the need to rebuild
the national economies that contributed, as much as any other
factor, to the failure of Resistance schemes for integration. In
many instances economic disruption meant unemployment and
privation to the individual. Many had lost most or all of their
personal belongings. The average individual was more acutely
aware of his own economic wants than of the high moral aims
of Resistance idealists. The emphasis was very soon placed upon
bread-and-butter issues, to the extent that a vast withdrawal
from political activity, and even from association with politics,
occurred.

The Proposed Solutions

The task of reconstruction was so vast that inevitably the initial
progress made was slow and produced almost negligible results.
The new governments had to concentrate their attention on
the demands and needs of the population. This meant supplying
them with essential services. And so the preliminary economic
efforts had to be centred around rebuilding communication
systems to facilitate transport, and around restoring power
supplies. Although this was the general pattern everywhere, the
methods employed to achieve these ends varied considerably.
Once again the debate took place whether one should pursue
a fairly strict *laissez-faire* policy or adopt stringent and permanent
government controls to check rises in prices and wages, hence
preventing inflation. Generally speaking, four main policies were
advocated: that reconstruction should occur within comprehen-

sive national economic plans under rigid government control; that basic industries—'the commanding heights'—should be nationalised; that land-holding systems should be reformed in favour of the small farmer and peasant; and that social security systems should be introduced or greatly extended.

The first solution, complete national government control, was not popular in Western Europe, for it reminded nations of Nazi totalitarianism and of the current Russian formula in Eastern Europe. Only France introduced a national economic plan. However, there was no question of coercion: the government had to be content with direction gained through influence and persuasion, while the actual political situation in postwar France merely emphasised the impossibility of rigid governmental overlordship. However, the principle of planning was widely accepted. It took second place to *laissez-faire* doctrines perhaps only in West Germany: on the other hand, the widespread publicity given to the 'free market' state of the West German economy has generally concealed the considerable extent of government planning and supervision that does exist in the country. The importance of planning in Europe increased when American foreign aid, which proved essential for reconstruction to proceed at a satisfactory rate, was donated only on the conditions that the recipient European nations would present both a plan for the use of foreign aid and some organs for utilising it along these lines. In addition to the Organisation for European Economic Cooperation, which was the main organ of the overall plan known as the European Recovery Programme, national planning organisations were developed: France had its General Planning Council; Belgium a Central Council of the Economy; and Italy a Committee of Reconstruction. These institutions were given the fundamental function of supervising the attempts to overhaul and modernise industrial plants, to reach a self-sufficient level of production, to expand export production, and to find a new trade system made necessary in the late 1940s by the disappearance of traditional markets in Germany and Eastern Europe.

The state apparatus became a prime factor in the various national economies. Nearly everywhere some measure of nationalisation had been accepted as necessary. It was most

33

widely used in Britain and France. The motives behind the nationalisation schemes depended on the particular circumstances. In some instances it came about because of the need to rescue failing but vital industries by injections of government aid: where investment was lacking, governments were usually the sole possible source of additional funds. This was the case with several Italian industries. But other reasons also existed. In Britain for example, the Labour Party implemented nationalisation schemes partly because of its tradition and partly because of the need to reduce the role of private industrialists in the country's basic industries. These reasons also applied in France. But there, for example, the government was virtually forced to nationalise the mines in order to persuade the miners to return to work, while other industries—for example, the Renault car firm—had to be appropriated because their previous owners had collaborated closely with the German occupation authorities.

The pressure for nationalisation diminished after the first flush of enthusiasm in 1945 and 1946. Sentiment for it was retained only among a few Socialist parties, as for instance in Britain where it was virtually an article of faith to the Labour Party's left wing. Generally, it was preferred to use nationalisation only to a very limited extent and only in economic areas where private industry clearly could not function satisfactorily. In Norway the Labour Government preferred a system of privately controlled industries operating within government-designed economic plans. The Socialist members of the Belgian Coalition Government opted for a policy of economic reforms which could be utilised by private initiative. Having a tradition of close collaboration between state and industry, Italy, after currency reform was dismissed in 1946, preferred the old system to one of outright nationalisation. In West Germany the prospects for nationalisation were very poor. When Germans themselves were given the opportunity of administering their own country, they rejected government control as being too reminiscent of the Nazi era and the desperate situation under rationing between 1945 and 1948. They pursued a course of allowing 'unbridled' market forces a fairly loose rein, encouraging investment by means of liberal tax concessions.

An assessment of postwar nationalisation policies is extremely difficult. It is still a very political subject and the dust has not had time to settle. However, it can be asserted with a great deal of certainty that this kind of large-scale government intervention in the control of the economy did permit a more speedy programme of redevelopment and investment. Overall private control could not have achieved the same effect in so short a period of time. It was equally clear that state ownership created nearly as many problems as those it was intended to resolve. It was certainly not the panacea some of its ardent supporters believed it would be.

On the two remaining general policies there was much more agreement. Agricultural production was well below the minimum acceptable level. The means adopted to improve agriculture varied a great deal. Production grants, guaranteed prices, and heavy taxation on land that could be productive made it profitable for landowners to cultivate their property wherever possible. With a limited amount of success France introduced schemes to rationalise its 'patchwork' system of peasant holdings. Italy, possessing the biggest agricultural headache, attempted to redistribute the agricultural land of the inefficient large estates in favour of the small peasant by compulsory purchase and improvement grants. Finally, social security systems were improved with very little argument. In general the Western European nations concentrated upon social legislation and improved social insurance within a framework designed to prevent the recurrence of mass unemployment and the consequent hardship and social unrest.

The Threat of Inflation

Two of the major problems which had to be faced were the needs to restrict the circulation of currency required for reconstruction programmes and to control or destroy the black markets which, due to the shortage of goods, had sprung up everywhere. The level of currency in circulation had increased greatly during the war, but usually strict governmental control prevented it from causing enormous rises in prices. The climate after the war was much less conducive to rigorous controls and

D

prices had begun to rise steadily. This tendency was reinforced by manufacturers who wanted high prices in order to finance their investment programmes in replacing or modernising capital equipment and by the considerable dearth of necessary consumer goods. The need for reinvestment and the imbalance of demand and supply pushed prices in some instances to astronomical levels. The vicious circle was complete when workers demanded large wage increases to maintain their standards of living. This inflationary spiral appeared everywhere. It was perhaps less noticeable in Belgium, which had been in a more favourable position in 1945, and in Britain, because of an austere rationing system. Nevertheless, inflation and the inability to force exports up to its import level partly caused Britain to devalue the pound in 1949. The most significant point about post-war inflation was that it prevented that long-term investment which was the primary basis of the policy of hoisting industrial production up to and beyond its prewar level.

A precondition of any action against inflation and its twin adversity, the black market, was the existence of strong government and strong government measures. On the continent this was forthcoming only in Scandinavia and the Low Countries. Here governments in exile had returned to ease the transition to peacetime conditions. The postwar governments had been quickly constituted in these countries, and they were able to tackle the problem of economic reconstruction without being trammelled by political debates over their legitimacy and the type of political system the countries should possess. Inflation was not destroyed, but it was prevented from reaching astronomical limits. Elsewhere the picture was not so bright. Germany, Italy, and France found it impossible to curb the mushrooming of inflation and the inevitable black market. In all three countries (allowing, of course, for the Allied military government in Germany) the old regimes—Nazism in Germany, Fascism in Italy, and the Third Republic and the Vichy regime in France—had been destroyed or discredited. Hence arguments over legitimacy and constitutions, over what the rules of the political game should be, tended to occupy much attention, allowing for little common ground from which a concerted attack could be made on the economic problems.

Here, government regulations proved to be almost completely ineffective. Nearly all purchasing was done through the black market, and the value of money as a circulating medium steadily decreased. In Germany money was replaced by cigarettes as currency: it was said that one packet could possess the value of an average monthly wage. The threat of total ruin through astronomical inflation, such as that which disrupted Germany in 1923, was once again very real. In France the exchange rate of the franc multiplied nearly six times between 1944 and 1948. In the same period the rate of the Italian lira multiplied five times, and between 1938 and 1948 prices in Italy increased fiftyfold: the financial plight of Italy was further aggravated by the economic tactics employed by the government.

Some degree of price stability may have been achieved, at least temporarily, by 1948, but the other side of the coin was even darker. No control had been possible, and prices had borne no relation to wage levels. The great fall in the purchasing power of the Italian lira has already been mentioned; the fall in purchasing power of the French franc had been nearly as great; the German mark was almost valueless. The consequences were an almost total drain on individual savings, the reduction to poverty of those living on fixed incomes, and the disappearance of the small investor.

Reconstruction and Foreign Aid

By the end of the decade the struggle against economic deprivations was slowly being won. A severe financial squeeze in Italy meant that production was beginning to climb past the prewar level; in France the large investments of the immediate postwar years were beginning to have an effect and prices were pegged while the national income slowly rose. At least the much maligned Fourth Republic had attempted to resolve problems which the Third Republic had ignored. In short, the rate of economic productivity was amazing, and confounded the many pessimistic experts. Industry was back at its prewar level by 1948: agriculture took only two years more, despite the extremely rigorous winter of 1947 and the widespread droughts of 1949.

It did not mean, however, that Western Europe had regained its former eminent world position. The programmes had been ones of economic reconstruction, not expansion. The main target had simply been the attainment of the prewar situation: they did not basically imply an expansion from the 1938 base. The rest of the world had not been standing still. Production and incomes in Western Europe still tended to lag, relatively speaking, behind those of other countries, especially the United States.

Nevertheless, one must not detract from the rate of reconstruction. Considering the difficulties which had to be overcome, it was little short of miraculous. Internally, the lack of effective communications systems hindered progress. A good railway network did not reappear until 1947, while a further three years were required for shipping to regain its feet. The basis of industry, coal production, was generally insufficient. Overall, there was a shortage of miners and up-to-date equipment, while in France, for example, strikes by the rather left-wing miners presented a further barrier to progress. There was a general shortage of labour, particularly of a skilled labour force: the war had taken a great toll in deaths, while its exigencies prevented adequate numbers of recruits from receiving proper instruction and apprenticeships. Moreover, the old class hostility had not disappeared. Workers and management remained suspicious of each other. This was particularly true in France and Italy with their large Communist parties. Despite the massive intervention of government in the economy, investment was still below the levels required.

The new social democracy was in some ways a further hindrance. Social security benefits were inflationary in their effect, but most governments were hesitant to curb them solely for anti-inflationary reasons. The general policy of seeking a more equitable wages structure produced the same effect. Again, the postwar governments were generally committed to a policy of full employment which was usually not justified by the economic situation. Where governments instructed firms not to dismiss workers, inefficiency appeared. Prices remained high to cover costs, while productivity and investment were in danger of stagnating. It placed nations in a position where purely monetary methods of controlling inflation and regenerating the economy could not be used. Furthermore, it prevented any reasonable balance of payments from being achieved.

The foreign trade outlook was the final barrier hindering progress. Imported goods, especially raw materials, had virtually ceased in 1945. Little could be done later by Western Europe to change the situation. Governments, through their own policies and through factors outside their control, were unable to bridge the dollar gap. They had not the means of setting their house in order, yet did not possess the financial resources necessary to purchase raw materials and the required capital machinery from abroad. Furthermore, trade dislocation had been almost complete. Old markets had disappeared, even within Europe. The fall of Germany and its relatively tardy recovery seriously inhibited the redevelopment of European trade.

Notwithstanding the praiseworthy efforts of the European governments in the economic field, it became increasingly obvious that Europe had been literally bankrupted by the war. It simply did not have the resources necessary for improvement and stabilisation. In time Europe might have recovered without outside help, but the process would have been extremely slow and painful. Injections of foreign aid, especially from the United States, were the means which provided improvement and stability within a reasonable period of time.

American aid had taken various forms. During the war there had been the Lease-Lend programme initiated in 1941 by President Roosevelt, which provided material for the war against Germany. Europe may have expected this assistance to continue, but once Germany had capitulated its original justification had gone, and Lease-Lend was therefore summarily ended. However, American aid in the form of food and necessary supplies had had to be provided on the continent to combat the emergency situation prevalent immediately after liberation. But by 1946 only Germany, still under military occupation, was a beneficiary of this aid. The rest of Europe was expected to stand on its own feet.

A measure of assistance was provided by an organ of the newly constituted United Nations, the United Nations Relief and

Rehabilitation Administration (UNRRA) and by American grants to specific nations. Anticipating the creation of the United Nations, UNRRA was formed in 1943 to combat the expected shortages of food, shelter, and clothing. It was this organisation which took the lead in distributing supplies after liberation and in resettling and tracing displaced persons. Overall, it handled over twenty-five million tons of supplies, most of which came from the United States. However, it was mainly concerned with Eastern and Central Europe. Most of the western nations, excluding Italy, rejected the full UNRRA programme and ran their own relief programmes.

Movements toward international aid had also been taking place in the fields of finance. At a conference held in 1944 at Bretton Woods in America, several nations agreed to set up an International Bank for Reconstruction and Development and an International Monetary Fund. The Bank was designed to lend money to war-ruined countries for reconstruction purposes, and to under-developed countries for their development, while the IMF's main purpose was to stabilise foreign exchange, and thereby international trade, by issuing loans to nations showing an imbalance of payments, on the stipulation that devaluation should not take place without prior IMF approval. Again, the United States was by far the largest donor.

These new international organisations did play a valuable role in the tortuous process of adaptation to peacetime conditions, but in the long run none proved sufficient, singly or collectively, to cope with Western Europe's chronic inability to set its house in order. Given this situation, it may well have been that a massive injection of American aid would have been forthcoming. But by 1947 the United States was becoming acutely aware of the worsening world situation. The year 1947 marks the opening of the Cold War, and Western Europe was an obvious target for Communist expansion. In this tense international atmosphere it became necessary for America to recognise Europe's economic shortcomings and to supply even more financial aid to the continent. The recognition came officially in a speech at Harvard University in June 1947 by George Marshall, the American Secretary of State, in which he emphasised the gravity of the situation and proposed the American policy of foreign aid that became popularly known as Marshall Aid.

The introduction and implementation of the Marshall Plan was the catalyst which eventually enabled Western Europe to put its economic house in order, and helped to pave the way for the successful boom periods of the 1950s. By 1950 Western Europe had largely overcome the obstacle of damage. It had achieved a higher gross national product than that of 1938, and a much larger proportion of this product was being reinvested for further development: by 1952 production was more than 200 per cent above prewar efforts. The same general success story was true of all Western European nations, whether they had opted for a maximum or minimum amount of government planning. The breakthrough had been achieved, and by 1955 European trade had doubled.

The Revival of Parliamentary Democracy

The principal task in the field of politics was to re-establish or reconstruct an effective governmental and political structure. In each country this had to be adapted to meet the altered condition of European parliamentarianism and the prevailing mood of public opinion. For the three major continental powers, the problem was more serious. Instead of returning to or slightly altering the immediate prewar system, they had to construct a completely new governmental and political structure.

In political life the end of hostilities saw a general reversion to parliamentary democracy throughout Western Europe. Only in the Iberian peninsula, where right-wing dictatorships remained in force, and in Sweden and Switzerland, which had maintained a somewhat precarious neutrality during the war, was this not the case. It was even true of Britain. It had not been overthrown by Germany, but the imperatives of war had entailed rather severe restrictions on its normal political and constitutional life. The parliament elected in 1935, which should have been dissolved in 1940 at the latest, was extended by yearly Acts. The parties did not fight by-elections as parties. And parliament had had far less influence upon the government than in normal circumstances.

In the liberated countries, apart from France, which had witnessed the utter collapse of the Third Republic and the compromising performance of the Vichy regime, the governments which had fled into exile during the invasion returned to their old offices and authority. Since these governments had been representative of a long democratic tradition and had not compromised themselves by association with right-wing authoritarianism, it was not surprising that very little dislocation was involved in the transition from occupation to freedom in the Low Countries and Scandinavia. The only clash of opinion which occurred was between the formerly exiled politicians and the dynamism of internal Resistance leaders. However, since a difference in fundamentals was not basically involved, compromise and adjustment were possible. In this process the experience of the older politicians was usually decisive. The influence of the Resistance reformers was marked, however, in the steady leftward movement of public opinion and political forces which reflected an acceptance of changed social and economic circumstances requiring different political solutions.

In this re-establishment of parliamentary democracy only one major problem appeared—the return of the Belgian monarchy (though not of the exiled Belgian Government). King Leopold had not left his country during the war, and had subsequently been suspected of sympathising and collaborating with the occupying German forces. This gave extra ammunition to the previous bitter accusations that the King, as commander-in-chief of the Belgian forces, had surrendered in May 1940, before defeat was clearly obvious and that this surrender had greatly facilitated the German sweep westward which had ended at Dunkirk. The debate over the future of the monarchy resolved itself along the already firmly established cleavage of language and race, already buttressed by regional and religious differences. It was the French-speaking Walloons who demanded that Leopold abdicate, while the King was supported by the Flemings. The dilemma proved almost insoluble. For a long time the government refused to allow Leopold to resume his role. When he did return, there was a very real threat that the royal issue would precipitate a civil war. The only way out of the impasse was for Leopold to abdicate. This he eventually did in 1950, relinquishing his throne in favour of his son, Baudouin.

There remained the problems of France and Italy and the question-mark hanging over Germany. In the two defeated Axis powers parliamentary democracy had been destroyed, over twenty years earlier in Italy and twelve years earlier in Germany. In both countries democracy had even then operated under grave disabilities, being utterly opposed by large and influential groups and forces within society which were indifferent toward its success or even actively worked for its downfall. A successful establishment of democracy in these two countries after 1945 could certainly not be taken for granted. The same point could be made about France, though the parliamentary democracy of the Third Republic had from 1870 to 1940 lasted longer than any other of France's numerous attempts at constitution-making since 1789. However, even the Third Republic had been subjected to great stresses which had threatened its survival, from Boulangerism to the Fascist movements of the 1930s. In that France had always possessed a substantial and discontented rightist movement which tended to reject parliamentarianism for authoritarian solutions, and in that it was extremely doubtful whether these right-wing elements had been destroyed or converted, it could not be said with any certainty that parliamentary democracy would flourish on French soil.

Of all the French political forces in 1945 only the Radicals, who had benefited enormously from it, favoured the return to the Third Republic. De Gaulle, the Resistance activists and the three great parties of the left all preferred a new and different constitutional system. Their claims were reinforced by the result of a popular referendum on the subject held in October 1945. Over eighteen million voters rejected a revival of the Third Republic, while only 700,000 were in favour.

A Constitutional Assembly, elected at the same time, therefore had full authority to go ahead and find a new constitutional formula. The longer it debated, however, the more obvious it became that only something closely resembling the Third Republic could reconcile the wide gap between the different ideas on constitutionalism entertained by Frenchmen. The right

43

argued that state authority must not be subservient to public opinion, while the left, following Jacobin tradition, argued for popular control of government through an all-powerful parliament. The gulf between the two had been very wide in the late 1930s: in 1945 it was clear that it had not diminished, and the absence of an unquestionable majority for either side only made the situation deteriorate further. The dominant opinion, in fact, was at first opposed to a parliamentary structure, but it became the only acceptable alternative. The strong reaction against Vichy's stern antiparliamentarianism, and the success of Communist propaganda in emphasising the virtues of republicanism and the dangers to it inherent in the person of de Gaulle were two of the major factors causing this reversal of opinion.

The Constituent Assembly was dominated by left-wing members who represented the Jacobin theory of constitutionalism; together, the Communists and Socialists possessed a slight overall majority. Tracing a direct descent from the revolutionaries of 1793, they forced through a draft constitution which would allow parliament, or more properly a popularly elected National Assembly, to be the only source of authority in the political system. This proposal was anathema to the more conservative authoritarian tradition. The draft was opposed by de Gaulle, who favoured an authoritarian solution, and by the MRP, which preferred something akin to what they understood the British system of cabinet government to be. The opponents of the Communist-Socialist draft were successful in presenting their case to the electorate, who in a referendum on the proposed constitution in May 1946 refused ratification by a small majority, 10½ million votes to 9½ million.

France, therefore, had to start again. A new Constituent Assembly had to be elected and a new constitutional formula found. The new Assembly reflected the mood of the referendum in that the MRP returned with a slightly larger representation, while the Communist–Socialist alliance had lost its majority. A compromise as a result of bargaining seemed to be the only feasible policy. It is not surprising, therefore, that the draft constitution prepared by this second Assembly was less radical than the first draft, but still far from being acceptable to conservatives. In a referendum it was passed by a small majority, and hence became the constitutional basis of the new Fourth Republic. However, those who voted for it (nine million) were only a minority of the electorate. Eight million voted against, while a further eight million abstained. The genesis of the Fourth Republic, therefore, was not approved by a majority of the population.

In accordance with the acceptance of the Jacobin tradition, the lower house, the old Chamber of Deputies, was renamed the National Assembly. The more conservative upper house was considerably weakened, and this was symbolised by renaming it the Council of the Republic instead of the Senate. Old traditions die hard, however, and the Councillors, many of whom had sat in the prewar Senate, claimed both the old title and the considerable powers of the former chamber, thus creating a further area of disagreement. But the crux of the success or fall of the new constitution would revolve around the question of government stability; this involved the powers of the prime minister. In an attempt to guarantee stability, the drafters had formulated a new procedure for electing the head of the government. The premier was still nominated by the President, but before the nomination was approved by parliament and a government constructed, the proposed candidate had to present and defend a policy programme before the National Assembly. If Assembly approval was withheld, France would still be without a government until a presidential nominee could persuade the National Assembly to endorse both himself and his programme. This new technique was never successful. In fact it produced a diametrically opposite result. It harked back to the Third Republic, but, if anything, it made the operation of government more hazardous in the Fourth Republic than in its predecessor. Prime ministers failed to sustain themselves more frequently than in the Third Republic, while deadlocks in the search for a successor were commonplace. Again, it was an illustration of business as usual. The more conservative and moderate forces took over the system and worked for their own advantage. By now it was something of a physical law that the chief beneficiaries of any revolution in

France were the moderate, centrist elements, but never the revolutionaries themselves.[1] The population at large were still alienated from the system; it tended to be cynical about the whole procedure whereby governments were the result of extensive and complicated negotiations among several political parties, and not the direct outcome of election results. Moreover, this popular alienation had the corollary that the political parties became divorced from the electorate. Above all, the French extreme right never really endorsed the Fourth Republic; it represented a force of permanent disaffection.

In Italy the existing constitution was rejected even more decisively by the dominant political forces than in France. This constitution had been established in the mid-nineteenth century and, with its provisions for a monarchy with rather unlimited powers and a large measure of control over the government, was anachronistic and completely unacceptable to the parties of the left. Mussolini had merely suspended this constitution (as Hitler did with the Weimar Constitution). Resurrected in 1943 it had been the basis of official Italian governments until the election of a post-war Constituent Assembly.

This Assembly was elected in June 1946 at the same time as a popular referendum which voted for the replacement of the monarchy by a republic. After nine months it produced a lengthy document which included several new proposals for securing and guaranteeing various individual rights. Although valuable and worth enforcing, it proved impossible to reconcile these radical moves with the traditional and the actual operation of the Italian political system. Very few radical changes were made in the structure of government. Apart from providing for the establishment of a ceremonial presidential head of state in place of the monarchy, the draft suggested only an electoral basis for the upper chamber. Several provisions, however, did bear the imprint of Communist planning. The Communists had worked hard in the Assembly to produce a design which would be amenable to a Communist government when it came to power, 'so much so that it was said that the Constitution would have required no modification to permit the functioning of a Com-

[1] D. Thomson, *Democracy in France*, London, 1964, p. 132.

munist popular democracy'.[1] However, the Communists were never given the opportunity. The ability of de Gasperi, supported by the middle classes, and the relative speed of reconstruction barred the way to power for the Communists. Moreover, in its functioning after January 1948, the new constitution was little different from its nineteenth-century predecessor. Many of its novel suggestions were never implemented. Government and politics, as in France, became divorced from the public, who considered politicians and administrators as being motivated only by self-interest and greed.

The events leading up to the West German Parliamentary Council which met in Bonn in 1948 to discuss a new constitution are described in more detail in a later chapter. The West Germans had the additional handicap of Allied supervision and possible veto of their discussions and proposals. In the event this counted for very little. The constitutional draft reproduced much that had existed in the Weimar Constitution. The most important changes were, first, the greatly increased powers of the upper house, based on the federal principle, which gave added emphasis to the relatively decentralised nature of the political system. Second, the abolition of virtually all the *political* powers held by the president in the Weimar Republic meant that he was left as a *ceremonial* head of state only. Most of these powers were given to the federal chancellor, the head of the government. Third, several clauses reflected a distrust of the whims of public opinion and 'mass democracy'. These techniques, particularly the clause stating that a chancellor can be overthrown by parliament only when an alternative candidate has already been chosen by the opposition (the so-called 'constructive vote of no-confidence'), were designed to strengthen and stabilise government. The constitution has had a marked success, confounding its critics, although again it did not work out in some instances in the way the drafters had intended.

Postwar Parliamentary Democracy

By 1949, then, the three major powers of continental Europe

[1] G. Mammarella, *Italy After Fascism*, Montreal, 1964, p. 157.

had adopted parliamentary constitutions, thus joining most of their smaller neighbours in the democratic camp. Whether these constitutions could be maintained and this particular type of democracy guaranteed were questions which could be answered only after a process of trial and error. The important point about the restoration of parliamentary democracy in Western Europe was the universal return to old and tried political systems and methods. Even in France, Italy, and Germany, where the old democratic systems had been attacked not only by authoritarians of both left and right, but also by numbers of influential democrats, the new constitutions faithfully reflected the salient characteristics of their ancestors. Radical innovations were often shelved or assimilated and converted by tradition.

This illustrated that each country has its own interpretation of such a term as parliamentary democracy, that accepted practices are more important than foreign ideas, and that attempts to graft one's own institutions and the ideas behind them on to the body politic of a foreign nation, as the Allies contemplated with Germany and Japan and as the colonial powers did with their colonies, can be a futile and often dangerous venture. The British authorities in Germany, for example, essayed to fashion local government institutions in their occupation zone in the mould of British local government. This was alien to German ideas on the subject; in nearly every instance, the German local authorities reverted to traditional and accepted German patterns of local government once independence had been secured.

But after the interim period of authoritarian domination, parliamentary democracy in Western Europe had changed somewhat. There was, as has been pointed out, a more general acceptance of governments playing a more extensive role in society and the economy. This implied stricter limits upon 'pure' parliamentarianism. Henceforth, parliaments would be clearly relegated to a secondary position. The decline of parliamentary influence brought with it accusations of government bureaucratisation and the problems of curbing governments and holding them responsible.

This was accompanied by a greater emphasis upon party organisation. The first successes of the 'regimented' parties forced others to think along the same lines; it was particularly true in later years of the reactions of non-Communist parties in areas where the Communists were very powerful. Where regimentation had previously meant that the parties were confined within narrow ideological limits, there was now a greater concern for a mass party which would have a large national following irrespective of various sectarian claims such as class and religion. The best example of this change is the great expansion of the West German Christian Democratic Union from a relatively narrow Catholic base to a dominating national position with support from most social groups.

This trend inevitably led to the belief that the number of national parties would decrease. West Germany emerged with two parties clearly far superior to all others. France and Italy seemed to be dominated by only three parties. Elsewhere, as in Norway and Sweden, where multi-partyism still existed, the imperatives of politics—that one party (in these two cases the Socialists) was capable of acquiring an absolute parliamentary majority—meant that the several parties were often obliged to enter one or the other of only two coalitions. Despite the disintegration of the tripartite system in France and Italy, this generalisation remains substantially correct, for parties were quite often offered the simple choice of supporting or opposing the political system, thereby creating a pseudo-variety of a two-party structure. It was hoped originally that this trend, which seemed to be strengthened by constitutional and electoral techniques, would help to eliminate the deep ideological cleavages between the parties.

The other side of the coin was that with increased regimentation the parties often tended to become ridden and fossilised with bureaucracy. Decisions were made within the party with which the individual felt he had little relation: the world of politics and decision-making was removed even further from his own world. Party manipulations and manœuvres in certain countries, notably France and Italy, gave extra weight to the feeling that people were alienated from politics and political decision-making. When these attitudes were added to the belief that too great an involvement with political ideology could be disastrous, as the

Second World War and its aftermath had shown, the general result was a relatively massive withdrawal from association with active politics and a widespread apathy and scepticism about the sincerity of party argument and activity. This process of 'depoliticisation' did not, obviously, apply equally to all countries; it was much less marked in Britain, the smaller continental democracies, and in France during the early years of the Fourth Republic. Nevertheless, it would perhaps be valid to say that it was a characteristic of Western European politics in the 1950s. The retreat from political activity also implied a retreat from political ideas. Ideology was now suspect. People no longer accepted what could be called 'pragmatic ideologies', let alone a *Weltanschauung*, a comprehensive philosophy of life. In some ways this withdrawal was a consequence of the parties compromising their firm ideological bases in the search for a vast new number of supporters. But it meant in the long run a decline in party membership. The problem of finding new voters was replaced by that of retaining existing members: parties which relied only on membership dues for their finance were placed in an extremely difficult position. Virtually the only real ideological cleavage remaining was that between Communism and Western democracy. This cleavage, intensified by the Cold War, more or less dominated European political thinking for almost a decade. Only when people had learned to accept the threat of thermonuclear warfare did a revival of concern for more 'domestic' ideologies occur.

Although parliamentary democracy had been re-established without a struggle, the disinterest with which it was regarded was a perpetual source of worry. The apathetic masses were opposed by those—Communists on the left, authoritarians on the right—who had not accepted the parliamentary regimes and remained ideologically militant. The twin problems of public apathy and constitutional legitimacy were the most serious problems which some postwar governments had to tackle. For the new regimes in France and Italy—and to a lesser extent in West Germany (where it was the suspicions rather than the actuality that counted)—these were problems around which every government had to centre its whole activity.

3 The Breakdown of Wartime Arrangements

We really believed in our hearts that this was the dawn of the new day. The Russians had proved that they could be reasonable and far-seeing and there wasn't any doubt in the minds of the President or any of us that we could live with them and get along with them peacefully for as far into the future as any of us could imagine.

Harry Hopkins[1]

The United States emerged from the war as undisputedly the strongest military force. The Democratic administration under Franklin D. Roosevelt and Harry Truman and a substantial number of the country's political leaders had abandoned the traditional policy of isolation. 'Americanism' would have to run the risk of contact with foreign bodies, for there was a general acceptance that America had world responsibilities which could not and should not be evaded. The difference in American policy between 1918 and 1945 was that in the latter case Presidents Roosevelt and Truman generally had the support of Congress and other influential leaders; in 1918 President Woodrow Wilson had been almost isolated in this respect. It is not surprising, therefore, that the United States should have displayed a great interest and played an active role in world affairs.

American Foreign Policy: Theory and Reality

The foreign policy beliefs of American leaders during the war about the future pattern of world relationships did not receive any sustenance from postwar reality. It was assumed that after the cessation of hostilities the active role of the United States would have certain limits: its specific aim would be to restore the world to normality and sanity. Military action and the build-up of defensive military alliances were not part of American

[1] R. E. Sherwood, *Roosevelt and Hopkins: An Intimate History*, New York, 1948, p. 870.

conceptions about the world to be and the American role in it. President Roosevelt did not interpret the belief that Americans should accept a more active world role as meaning involvement in any place at any time. His plans for and his conception of the postwar world were therefore framed in general terms and on the basis of a limited world role for the United States. In this way he hoped to avoid the pitfalls into which undue optimism about the willingness of Americans to play a dominant world role had led President Wilson in 1919. America's major allies in Europe were thus also assigned a role in the postwar world. The arrangement which Roosevelt and his advisers envisaged was that Britain would resume its role as the policeman of the Mediterranean and the Middle East, that France would be the dominant continental power in Western Europe, while Russia would have a hegemony of influence over Eastern Europe. The four powers would be united in Europe in their guard over Germany, while in the world at large they would take the lead in international policy within the newly established United Nations. Roosevelt may have been pragmatic in his understanding of American public opinion and its moods, but his assessment of the globe was sadly naive. Lulled by a false sense of the innate goodness of humanity, the Americans regarded themselves as participating in a story which had come to an end: good had triumphed over evil and everyone would live happily ever after.

American policy-makers were apparently unable to conceive of the Soviet Union, the acknowledged new dominant power in Europe, replacing Nazi Germany as a grave threat to the European and global balance of power. . . . President Roosevelt and the American Government did not aim at re-establishing a balance of power in Europe to safeguard the United States; they expected this security to stem from mutual Russo-American goodwill, unsupported by any power considerations. . . . The expectation of a post-war 'era of good feeling' between the Soviet Union and the United States was characteristic of the unsuspecting, and utopian nature of American war-time thinking, which held that war was an interruption of the normal state of harmony among nations, that military force was an instrument for punishing the aggressor or war-criminals, that those who co-operated with this country in its ideological crusade were equally moral and selfless, and that once the war was finished, the natural harmony would be restored and the struggle for power ended.[1]

This fundamental naivety was to cause the American Government to undergo a painful period of reappraisal and readjustment in the very near future.

Roosevelt's policy, moreover, was based on two assumptions which proved to be erroneous. Both had serious consequences on the direction of postwar international affairs. The first assumption was that the Allies would continue their policy of cooperation into the postwar world. The first indication that this would not be so came in disagreement over the occupation of Germany. Very swiftly that defeated country came to resemble four distinct nations with four distinct policies. Germany, however, was merely a microcosm of the new world-scale alignment of powers. The second assumption was caused by an overestimation of the strength of the Western European powers and an underestimation of the toll taken by the war on their resources. Britain found that all efforts had to be directed toward stabilising the national economy; no resources could be diverted for acting as a foreign policeman. When Britain asked for American help to subdue Communist guerrillas in Greece early in 1947, the implication was that Britain could not fulfil the role assigned to it in American thinking. This fact had perhaps been obvious for some time. Simultaneously, the United States had to recognise that France had never been in a position to assume the leadership of Western Europe. Threatened internally by a strong Communist Party which was steadily moving toward an aggressive hostility to the Fourth Republic, endangered by a threat of latent right-wing authoritarianism under the possible leadership of General de Gaulle, riddled by irrelevant and historical, but deep and irreconcilable social cleavages, France could hardly maintain adequate supply lines for the colonial wars in which it was already involved. On the other hand, Roosevelt's spheres of influence policy, which had accommodated the demands of Stalin at Yalta for the application of this traditional form of Russian foreign policy, had given Russia a free moral hand in

[1] J. W. Spanier, *American Foreign Policy since World War II*, London, 1962, pp. 14–15.

Eastern Europe, in addition to *de facto* Russian military occupation. The hegemony of influence offered at Yalta soon became a hegemony of power.

American conceptions had therefore become illusions. Britain and France were too weak to play a distinctively positive role. With Germany prostrated, a power vacuum had opened between the United States and Soviet Russia. If America did not wish to become isolated and confined on the new continent, steps had to be taken to prevent Russia occupying the vacancy in Western Europe. By 1947 it was clear that these representatives of totally opposed ways of life were to force other nations into two conflicting camps as they jockeyed for dominance over each other, while at the same time strengthening the cohesion of their own alliances.

The Role of the United Nations

The United Nations Organisation was to be the outstanding symbol of the approaching moral peace. But the disruption of the wartime alliance meant that the international body was never given a chance of functioning in the way America had conceived. It would not have been unjustifiable to assume that the new organisation would be completely ineffective and deadlocked by the world cleavage. It retained some importance, however, for apart from the shortlived Allied Control Council in Germany, it was the only body in which American and Russian representatives could meet, even if the two were almost invariably opposed. More significant is the fact that once its teething troubles were over, the United Nations proved to have some values, unforeseen by its founders, which were created by the changed world situation and balance of power.

The foundation of the United Nations by the major allies at Dumbarton Oaks, Washington, in 1944 had a precedent in the establishment of the old League of Nations by the war victors in 1919. Because of the existence of a previous international organisation, the drafters modelled their new creation fairly closely on its predecessor, taking into account its good and bad points. It was obvious that the United Nations could succeed only if it became a world organisation. One great drawback of the old League of Nations had been that it was essentially an institutionalisation of the old European balance of power and concert of nations game, being little more than a solely European organisation. Accordingly the final Charter of the United Nations was approved by fifty nations meeting in San Francisco in 1945. The organisation had two general functional bodies. First, based on the old League structure, was a General Assembly where each nation was allowed one representative and one vote. Above this was a Security Council where permanent membership was given to five powers: the United States, Russia, Britain, France, and China. The remaining six seats were filled by election by the other members of the General Assembly; these temporary members served for two years. In addition, several specialised agencies and committees were established to provide coordination and assistance in various social, economic, and cultural fields. Finally, the United Nations was given the task of supervising the colonies of the defeated Axis powers and of preparing them for independence. The new international body steadily proved itself to be truly international as new Asian and African members added to its world character.

One fundamental difference between the League of Nations and the United Nations was the constitutional recognition in the latter that the major powers should possess special privileges. Some form of recognition along these lines had been demanded by Stalin at Yalta as a necessary precondition for Russian participation. Stalin's views, however, were not divergent from the general opinions of the other leaders, especially Churchill. Accordingly, the Security Council, with the permanent representation of the major nations, was intended to be the centre of the new organisation. Here the great powers would thrash out their differences without being distracted by too many other states. Some such central arena was necessary for the prosecution of postwar aims. If not, then a complete breakdown of wartime preconceptions was inevitable. The major powers strengthened the Security Council and their own positions within it in three ways to meet the Yalta agreements. First, the Security Council rather than the General Assembly was given primary responsibility for maintaining world peace. Second, the major powers were guaranteed permanent representation on the Council. Finally, and probably most important, each of the permanently represented nations was under Article Twenty-seven of the charter given the power of veto on Council decisions. The big five therefore had to agree on an issue, otherwise no action could be taken. This was perhaps no more than a formal recognition of the fact that the major powers would, veto or not, place their own national interests first rather than go along with a policy to which they were opposed, although the agreement had been that the veto would be used only against a proposed course of action designed to enforce peace in a 'trouble-spot', and not against any Council discussions aimed at finding a peaceful solution to a problem.

Again, the functioning of the United Nations did not take the direction planned for it. The changes occurred within the Security Council. It had already been debatable whether China should have been given a permanent seat on the Council. In the event, China proved to be the sick man of the Council: the corrupt government of Chiang Kai-Shek was fully engaged in a losing battle with the Communists under Mao Tse-Tung for control of the mainland. The issue was resolved by 1949 when the Communists ousted the Nationalist armies from all positions on the Chinese mainland, but Chiang Kai-Shek, although confined to Formosa, still held the Council seat. The other four major powers gravitated within the Security Council to the basic alliances forged by the cleavages of the Cold War. Russia pursued an increasingly ethnocentric course; the Soviet veto in the Council was used by the Russian delegate as a matter of course on almost every issue that arose. The other three nations tended to band together, as if the unanimity of their three voices was a symbol of the alliance.

The inability of the Security Council to fulfil its previously assigned role forced more limelight and responsibility to focus on the General Assembly. Here resolutions were relatively easier to adopt. There were no veto powers allowed, and unanimous decisions were not necessary; all that was required was a two-thirds majority. The General Assembly could often act when the

Security Council was prevented from doing so, usually by the Russian veto. As the number of member states increased, this role of the United Nations correspondingly grew in importance. The Afro-Asian states and the neutrals demanded attention and found they received it because of the extreme polarisation of the two power blocs. The influence and prestige of the Secretary-General of the United Nations, despite the vendetta upon the first occupant by the Soviet Union, illustrated that this body still had some authority, and was in a far better position to arbitrate in disputes than the old League of Nations.

But the United Nations found itself powerless to intervene or arbitrate effectively in matters intimately affecting the security of America or Russia, as events in Cuba in 1962 or in Hungary in 1956 illustrated. The European continent also fell into this category. The global polarisation took its most crystallised form in Europe. Wars for ideological supremacy could be fought in Korea, Vietnam and elsewhere, because here there are areas of 'no man's land' or areas claimed by both sides: the situation is essentially fluid. In Europe the dividing line was clearly demarcated: the continent had been carefully separated into two opposing camps. Any transgressions could not be concealed, and the consequences of a nuclear war were obvious. Moreover states like France and Italy might have hoped to play the great arbitrator between the two sides, but economic and political pressures forced them to make a choice: only the traditional neutral states, Sweden and Switzerland, or those in precarious positions, Finland, Austria, and perhaps Yugoslavia, could avoid this fate. Europe therefore was not a major concern of the United Nations, except where one state was clearly isolated from its colleagues in its alliance. The 'keep off' signs were unmistakable. Its most important actions lay elsewhere—in Israel in 1948, in Korea in 1950, in Suez in 1956, in the Congo in 1960, and in the Indian subcontinent in 1965. Decisions on Europe, it seemed, could only be reached with the mutual consent of the United States, the Soviet Union, and perhaps the continent itself. Since the two sides could not agree even to disagree within the Security Council, it was not surprising that the United Nations could neither provide the connecting link in Europe, nor prevent the two sides drawing further apart and ignoring the suggestions of what was, after all, their own creation.

The Peace Treaties: Necessary or Irrelevant?

The third area where wartime plans for the future failed to materialise was in the Allies' relations with the defeated Axis powers. Quite apart from the almost insoluble problem of the fate of Germany, the victors had had to formulate policy with regard to the minor defeated belligerents: Italy, Hungary, Rumania, Bulgaria, and Finland. At Potsdam, it was decided that this responsibility would be delegated to the foreign ministers of the three major powers. For this purpose a formal Council of Foreign Ministers was constituted, which first met in September 1945. Later meetings were held in Paris and New York with the participation of the French foreign minister.

The details of the peace treaties to be signed with the minor Axis powers were the sole responsibility of these four representatives, but consultations were held with other interested nations to take regard of their opinions. Three common features emerged from these treaties: the traditional victors' policy of altering territorial boundaries was followed, reparations were demanded, and these countries' military independence was restricted by limitations placed upon the size of their armed forces. On the whole, however, the demands were not too exacting. The policy of radically rewriting the map of Europe was not pursued: in contrast to the past, territorial emendations were relatively minor. Apart from the problems connected with Italy, the most important points were that the peace treaties had conceded Russian claims made at Yalta for *de jure* recognition of territory acquired by Russia during the war. Thus Russia received *de jure* recognition of its *de facto* occupation and annexation of Bessarabia (formerly belonging to Rumania) and of Karelia and the sea-port of Petsamo (formerly belonging to Finland). The greatest changes in the map of Europe, the wholesale westward movement of Poland's frontiers and the disappearance of the Baltic states of Estonia, Latvia, and Lithuania, were *de facto* changes and not part of the peace treaties. The new Polish boundaries are still temporary in theory, awaiting ratification or further adjustment by a peace treaty made by the Allies with the whole of Germany. It was only in the late 1960s that West Germany seriously began to consider the possibility and advisability of publicly acknowledging the permanence of Poland's western boundary.

The main problems were with Italy, about its boundaries and the future of its colonies. While France claimed some territorial compensation from Italy, and the Austrian population of the South Tyrol were placated by the guarantee of a statute of autonomy within the Italian State, the real threat lay on Italy's eastern frontier. Here it was confronted by the Communist regime in Yugoslavia. Marshal Tito of Yugoslavia and his Russian supporters were adamant in demanding territorial compensation from Italy. The areas in dispute, long a bone of contention between the Slavs and the Italians, were the city of Trieste and the province of Venezia Giulia. Italian opinion was equally firm that these demands should be resisted. The Western Allies conceded the legitimacy of the Yugoslav claim to Venezia Giulia, whose population was mainly Slav. Trieste, with a large Italian majority, was a different matter. Ethnic considerations allowed most of the province to go to Yugoslavia, but the impossibility of finding an adequate solution for Trieste was illustrated by the first formula adopted: that Trieste should become a free city on the lines of prewar Danzig. The success of such a formula could never have been seriously entertained, especially as the city would be a buffer between two antithetical ideologies. It is not surprising, therefore, that both Italy and Yugoslavia refused to accept and ignored the provisions of the treaty. A compromise was not evolved until 1954, by which time Tito had broken with Stalin and had embarked upon his policy of national Communism within a neutral state. The new solution was that the city itself should go to Italy, while Yugoslavia should assimilate the hinterland. The loss of territory has never been entirely accepted by Italy, as questions on the subject in the Chamber of Deputies in 1970 illustrated. However, it is perhaps significant that the question of territorial revision was not raised during the visit to Italy of President Tito in 1971.

The Allies also failed to agree upon the future of the Italian colonies. The innate anticolonialism of the United States frowned upon them becoming colonies of another power, while no one was anxious to see Russia acquire a foothold in Africa. The problem was handed by the four Allies to the United Nations, where it had to face the same difficulties and obstacles. By 1949 the United Nations decided on a policy of independence, apart from Eritrea which was attached to Ethiopia. Libya was granted independence immediately, while Italy was given the task of supervising Somaliland's progress toward independence on the stipulation that this was to be as soon as possible. This operation was not to the liking of America's leading European partners: for Britain and France it had been one solution to be avoided. Independence at some date was more or less inevitable, but by occurring when it did, it helped create a precedent for the nationalist movements in Asia and Africa which troubled the colonial powers of Europe in the 1950s.

All this lay in the future. The immediate point to be made about the peace treaties is that by the time they were ready to be signed they were largely irrelevant, negated by the changed international climate. Italian political leaders may have entertained ideas of being a neutralist state, acting as a link between East and West. But pressure from America was being brought to bear on the Italian Government to enter the Western power bloc: international considerations and domestic dangers made this step almost inevitable. The gesture of a treaty by the West to Hungary, Bulgaria, and Rumania was meaningless. These countries had been 'liberated' by Russia in the closing months of the war and were now integral components of the Russian defensive system behind the iron curtain. Only Finland was allowed by Russia to retain a precarious neutrality, poised between the two power blocs. Being the only European country whose main border neighboured Russia itself that was not part of the Soviet system, it was obvious that Finland would be susceptible to Russian pressure and extremely chary of pursuing any policy that might annoy its powerful neighbour. The West tended to recognise that Finland was more or less within the Russian sphere of influence. The Soviet Union itself would no doubt be pleased to utilise Finland as a profitable shopwindow to illustrate the 'true liberality' of Russian policy.

There remained the peace treaties with Germany and Austria. Unlike the other Axis powers, these two states underwent a full military occupation by the major Allies. Thus any peace treaty with Germany and Austria was attendant upon the concurrence by the Allies on a common policy. The changes in Allied policy, the failure to achieve a common agreement in Germany, and Austria's ten-year wait for independent status are to be discussed in detail in a later chapter.

Berlin: Symbol of Postwar Actuality

The iron curtain ran through the middle of Germany. The division of Germany was therefore the most dramatic aspect of the failure of wartime conceptions and of postwar reality in Europe. And within Germany the most dramatic event that pointed to the failure of any continuity in cooperation was the Russian blockade of Berlin and the subsequent Allied airlift. Berlin became a symbol of the Western decision to confront Russian aggressiveness with an equally determined resistance. The blockade of Berlin by the Soviet Union, which started in June 1948, was partly a reaction to the Western Allies' decision to create an independent West German state, partly a reflection of the desire to eliminate the West from the most exposed outpost of its alliance, partly a determination to end the anomaly of having a Western 'fortress' in the heart of Russian-controlled territory. The Russian decision was also motivated by a fear of Germany. This was not a fear that Germany in the future could once again bring Russia down in single combat: the consequences of the Second World War were that Germany could never match the military capacity of the Soviet Union. It was rather a fear of what a united healthy Germany could contribute to an alliance focused around the United States. Such an alliance would commit America even more strongly in Europe and would moreover give the United States an advanced field position virtually overlooking the main road to the heart of Russia. A test of strength was therefore necessary: Berlin was the selected battlefield. The purpose was to see whether the American resolution was sufficiently determined to maintain a military force in Europe even at the risk of becoming involved in another war. If the American nerve failed, then the way was open for Russia to attempt to bring Germany within its own orbit and so increase the opportunities for Russia to expand even further in Europe.

All road and rail communications between the Western-controlled sectors of Berlin and West Germany were closed. At the same time pressure was brought to bear upon the German city government in Berlin to concede to the Russian demands. In return the Soviet authorities promised to restore electric power and other essential services that had previously been supplied by Russian or Russian-controlled authorities. The answer of the West was given rapidly. The United States promised to support the city administration by the inauguration of a massive airlift of essential goods and materials. The airlift was supported unequivocally by the other Allies, but only America had the capacity to guarantee the necessary supply of planes and provisions required to maintain West Berlin as a functioning entity. Throughout the remaining months of 1948 and the early days of 1949 the airlift continued to build up in intensity. Though its cost was tremendous it was successful in that foodstuffs, raw material, and fuel in more than sufficient quantities were being received by the West Berliners.

It seemed that the United States was determined to maintain the airlift for as long as proved necessary. The policy of the economic blockade clearly could not by itself bring about the Western evacuation of the city. Russia admitted defeat in two ways. First, a separate Communist-controlled city council was established in the Russian sector which claimed that it was the only legitimate German government in the city, and not the democratically elected one which only recently had moved its offices and agencies to the Western sectors of the city because of Russian-inspired obstructionism. Second, the blockade was called off in May 1949 as abruptly as it had been started. Thereafter Berlin lived under an uneasy peace, punctuated at frequent intervals by the alarums and excursions of either a possible military takeover by Russia or the Western abandonment of the city, although it is doubtful whether the latter was ever seriously mooted as a course of action.

Nevertheless, the Berlin blockade, the first real test of strength between East and West in Europe, set three important precedents which have been maintained in all subsequent arguments and clashes over the city's future. The Soviet Union has not used or seriously threatened to use military force to win control of the whole city; on the other hand, the stand of the Western Allies seemed to imply that only a military invasion would compel them to leave Berlin. It was also clear that the Western Allies were not altogether willing to use military force themselves to assert their rights as occupying powers in Berlin. It may be gratifying to realise that the use of military force on the question of Berlin seems to be frowned upon by the rules of the game. But there is no room for complacency; what it means is that the Soviet Union has had to turn to other methods to gain its ends. While the West has been reluctant to take any positive action, as the refusal to play any role during the workers' uprising in East Berlin in 1953 illustrates, the dangers that the West has to face from a gradual erosion of its position are as portentous as the threats of a military takeover. This was stressed by the after-events of the most emphatic action taken in Berlin by the Russians since 1949—the building of the notorious Berlin wall in August 1961. The United States rushed in a token show of extra troops, not to defend the city but to restore confidence. President Kennedy emphasised America's determination to defend the *status quo*, but it was a different *status quo* from that which existed before the erection of the wall. Then movement of Germans between the two halves of the city had been relatively unrestricted; now the two were distinct entities with hardly any contact with one another. It is further action of this type rather than the open use of force which presents the greatest danger to the West's position in Berlin. These events in Berlin are also in some ways a microcosm of the larger game played throughout the continent: as the overt threats employed in the opening years of the Cold War were either thwarted by Western action or failed in themselves to achieve the desired result, the struggle changed to one of attrition, where victories were the outcome of erosive tactics, perhaps slight in themselves, but overall significant for what the two blocs saw as the effectiveness of their security.

4 New Governments and Their Problems

To secure for the workers by hand or by brain the full fruits of their industry, and the most equitable distribution thereof that may be possible, upon the basis of the common ownership of the means of production, distribution, and exchange, and the best obtainable system of popular administration and control of each industry and service.

British Labour Party Constitution

Never before ... such flagrant civil war within a government.

Gordon Wright[1]

It will be profitable to examine in slightly more detail the internal politics and operation of government in the major nations of Western Europe during the first crucial postwar years. Although the economic problem was universal, different political situations and complexions implied that different political events would occur and different solutions be sought. Germany was still in a special category: the progress of Germany from virtual annihilation to a new political sovereignty and confidence merits separate treatment in a later chapter. In Britain we must attempt some assessment of the performance of the first majority Labour Government: where France and Italy are concerned we must appraise the experiment of tripartism.

The British Labour Government

The result of the 1945 general election gave the British Labour Party a convincing victory. For the first time it achieved an absolute majority of seats, and hence was in a position to put its programme into practice without fear of complete obstruction by necessary coalition partners. To observers this Labour victory was perhaps the most surprising European election result,

[1] *The Reshaping of French Democracy*, London, 1950, p. 222.

perhaps the only surprising result. Elsewhere the groundwork had obviously been made by the strong left-wing participation in the Resistance and the obstacles facing an immediate conservative comeback. In Britain, Churchill was at the height of his popularity and it had been confidently expected that he would lead the Conservatives to a sweeping victory. But again, the necessary preconditions for a left-wing victory had been prepared in Britain. The whole nature of wartime planning and government control of the reconstruction of the national economy and social way of life was a factor which greatly helped the Labour Party, quite apart from people's memories of prewar days, of the Conservative association with appeasement and Munich, of the 1926 general strike, and of the long depression of the 1930s.

In 1940 the problem facing Britain was that of sheer survival. Of the three belligerent nations left in Western Europe, the pressure was on Britain as it was not on Germany and Italy. A maximum effort was required to mobilise the community in such a way as to obtain the maximum effect from a limited amount of resources. This policy was based on the assumption that for an indeterminate period the British Isles would be in the position of a besieged city. A vast rationalisation of the economy and of manpower was achieved, based on the beliefs that everyone should contribute something and that from the overall product everybody should receive a fair share. The speed and efficiency with which this reorganisation was carried out meant that the operation of a large-scale black market stood very little chance of succeeding, or even of beginning to function at all. British wartime domestic policy rivalled that of the Communists during the reorganisation of Russia in its determination to standardise economic opportunities throughout the whole community. In place of a traditional acceptance of a hierarchical society, emphasis was placed upon an egalitarian economy.

In fact, many of the ideas of a welfare state and a planned economy held by the Labour Party were introduced during the war. Overall, the man in the street was affected by two general trends. First, he obtained his greatest ever share of the national product; and second, his standard of living reached a new peak. It was obvious that these trends, reflecting more governmental social services and regulation of the economy, were irreversible. A party which wanted, or was even suspected of wanting, to set the clock back would be committing political suicide. In this sense, the Labour Party was more acceptable to the public than the Conservatives.

The postwar needs and the general policies which the postwar government, of whatever party, had to follow were clearly delineated by circumstances. The first and obvious political point was that the social services must be extended to embrace a whole new field of social security. The financial outlay for this scheme could only come from a continuing policy of heavy taxation. But the experience of war and unemployment had somewhat conditioned the electorate to accept this stringency. Then there were the obvious economic imperatives. Britain would have to pursue a policy of large investment in order to maintain and modernise the scope and methods of production; and the export drive had to be greatly increased in order to achieve an effective balance of payments. This last point meant that a high proportion of British production would have to be diverted from domestic to foreign markets. These economic policies were essential, for postwar Britain would be completely dependent upon imports to satisfy the needs of its population: domestic resources and overseas investments had been largely consumed by the war effort and its rising costs. The flow of imports had to be balanced by a correspondingly large flow of exports. Thus a considerable percentage of British goods, especially luxury items, had to be channelled to the export market. In turn this meant increased efficiency and output in the factories; and consequently higher taxation and prices to meet the necessity of industrial modernisation. While this might mean full employment it would have some obverse effects. The austerity necessary for the success of these measures would not guarantee increased consumption, while heavy taxation might tend to deter substantial investment.

Nevertheless, these imperatives were accepted by both major parties. For many Conservatives acceptance came only reluctantly as the sole means of reassuring Britain's status as a world power and the country's economic stability. For the Labour Party, on the other hand, the means that had to be adopted to meet these necessities were in complete accord with traditional party policy. It may well be that this fundamental difference between the parties was realised in some part by the electorate. In any case, a substantial number of voters accepted the Labour Party as being capable of managing affairs in the light of the changed situation. The Labour Party, of course, had much more than a manifesto with which to confront the electorate. It had possessed virtually a monopoly of the management of domestic affairs during the war: Ernest Bevin, for example, one of the party's outstanding leaders, had created a minor revolution in his handling of the Ministry of Labour. Conservative ministers in the National Government had been more directly concerned with the prosecution of the war itself, continuing the long tradition of the party's great interest in foreign affairs: the Foreign Office and service ministries were, on the whole, led by Conservative politicians. This distinction between the two parties was apparent at all levels. Conservative Members of Parliament were more inclined to enlist in the armed services, while Labour Members because of their age and interests, remained in the House of Commons and helped both to supervise the domestic war effort and to consolidate the party's plans for the future. Nowhere was this dichotomy more apparent than at the top. While Churchill toured the world as a leading director of the Allied war effort and concerned himself primarily with military plans, the Labour leader, Clement Attlee, remained in Britain as Deputy Prime Minister and governed in domestic affairs virtually as Prime Minister. The differences were still noticeable during the election campaign: the Conservatives offered only Churchill's leadership against Labour's presentation of a fairly comprehensive programme of socio-economic proposals.

Labour's Performance

These reasons partly explain why the Labour Party found itself in power in 1945. They also help to illustrate the basic continuity between the wartime National Government and the policies of the Labour Government. The programme of the Labour Party was drawn from two basic inspirations. First, policies were drawn from the basic tenets of Socialism which the party had incorporated into its 1918 constitution; and second, the party relied heavily upon the economic arguments of John Maynard Keynes. Keynesian economics had a great influence upon Labour plans for the future welfare state—particularly in their ideas on slum clearance and housing construction, on a large extension in educational facilities for teachers and students, and on the vast expansion of what was to be known as the National Health Service.

The parties may have argued about details in these spheres, but underneath there was a fundamental agreement on what was necessary. It was on the introduction of Socialist-inspired legislation that the Conservative Party found itself in bitter opposition to the Labour Government. The hub of the Labour platform was nationalisation, and between 1945 and 1951 nationalisation was to be perhaps the central controversy of British politics. The Labour plan was to introduce into parliament bills which would remove the most vital sectors of British industry from private to public ownership. Almost inevitably, there was some misunderstanding over the word 'nationalisation'. Some dedicated Socialists believed that it would achieve the revolutionary end of the workers owning and directing the industry. No doubt several Conservatives feared the same thing. These hopes (or fears) were never realised. The workers found that they had merely changed a private board of directors elected by shareholders for a public board of directors appointed by and answerable to the government.

Even on nationalisation it was difficult for the Conservatives to mount a sustained attack upon the principle of the issue. Some industries, such as coal-mining, had been ailing for a long time: no legitimate argument could be used to oppose the transfer of the industry to public ownership. The issue for the Conservatives, therefore, became one of whether an industry had already proved itself to be viable under private ownership. On these grounds it was the nationalisation of road transport and steel that the Conservatives opposed most strongly. The issue of steel nationalisation became probably the most acrimonious point dividing the two parties—and one that was still central to much political thinking in the 1960s, no matter how out-dated. It became the symbol of the struggle over the types of economic structure Britain should possess. In any industrial society steel is central to the whole economy, and therefore Labour members considered its whole scheme of things would be judged by its success or failure in nationalising this key industry.

The argument was long and bitter. The Labour Government knew that although it could win in the House of Commons through its large majority any bill on steel nationalisation would be rejected by the Conservative-dominated House of Lords. Steel nationalisation therefore became involved in a constitutional debate. The Labour Party decided to reform the Parliament Act of 1911 in order to cut the delaying power of the House of Lords over bills from two years to one. It was 1949 before this action had been achieved, and this fact, together with the lengthy pre-legislative planning involved in steel nationalisation, meant that the government won control of the industry only at the end of a full constitutional term of office. By 1951 the Labour Party was in opposition, the nationalised industry had scarcely begun to function, and it was relatively easy for the new Conservative Government to carry through its avowed intention of de-nationalising steel without causing too much dislocation. This was the only issue on which the Conservatives took a definite stand. Every other act of nationalisation (except road transport) and Labour's whole welfare state system were not demolished by the new government. Indeed they even took pleasure in amending and improving them.

The actions of the postwar Labour Government and the transfer of power in 1951 had farreaching consequences on both parties. The Conservative Party was once again forced to move its position leftward and accept implicitly a government's responsibility to regulate and intervene in a large social and economic sector. Its effect on the Labour Party was perhaps somewhat more traumatic. Its span as a government in the late 1940s had been especially notable because it carried out to the letter its programme of 1945. In some sections of the party it aroused a problem which had no easy answer: what should the party do now? It had succeeded in lessening the economic differences between the middle and working classes, and it had rationalised in part the economic scene. To many it seemed that the party had achieved its socialist utopia: apart from continuing to care for its new creation, they had no plans for the future.

The party's dilemma was caused as much by its failures as by its achievements. Other areas of the party were disappointed because the promised utopia had not arrived. Its successes in lessening economic inequalities were counterbalanced by its failures to redress social inequalities. The nuances of education, speech and other less tangible social factors which help to maintain the British class structure had hardly been disturbed. Also, its nationalisation policies had disappointed many in the non-provision for worker cooperation in the management and direction of industry, and in the party's simple acceptance of nationalisation as the only possible way of reforming economic policy. This was probably more true of the British Labour Party than of continental Socialism as a whole. Instead of providing for an economic revolution, Labour policy was firmly moulded in the British tradition of governmental responsibility and action. The Labour emphasis on centralisation and bureaucracy as indispensable elements of economic policy tended to alienate from the party people who otherwise may have been more sympathetic to its aims. Though accepting many of Keynes's arguments, the Labour Party clearly ignored his warnings in these respects. Above all, in strictly applying those economic restrictions on the individual necessary to rebuild the economy, the Labour Party became tarred with the brush of austerity and high taxation. Despite these consequences, the postwar Labour Government was of some significance. Its willingness to use restrictive measures to save the economy, and so attract public opprobrium, undoubtedly facilitated the return of economic health. Exports were pushed up consistently and unemployment prevented. American aid was used to full advantage. It had political significance too. It brought the Labour Party into the mainstream of British constitutionalism. It was now an indispensable part of the British political scene; it was now undisputedly the only alternative governmental source to Conservatism. It meant, in other words, that the working classes were not pushed into a ghetto; they became accepted as a full and equal partner in the political community.

The failure of the British Labour Party to achieve a Socialist utopia, and the revelation that Socialist panaceas were fallible, had ramifications for European Socialism as a whole. From 1950 onwards Socialist parties in Europe, with the exception of Scandinavia, were generally out of favour with the electorate; they seemed to have no constructive alternative available. And with little sign of radical rethinking occurring, at least until the closing years of the decade, the Socialist parties seemed destined to remain in the wilderness for the foreseeable future.

France and Italy: The Experiment with Tripartism

We have already seen that in the first postwar elections held in France and Italy three mass parties achieved a clear superiority over all other political movements. Only one was a newcomer to the field, but in both countries Christian Democracy could claim to be in the direct descent of a long heritage of social Catholicism. Politically organised Catholicism had always been present because of the basic conflict in these two countries between Church and State. In Italy the new party was clearly a revival of the pre-Fascist Popular Party, which between 1919 and 1922 had attempted to fill the almost ever present vacuum at the centre of Italian politics. The other two mass parties were, of course, representative of the new traditional left, Communism and Socialism.

Although it had a great deal of sympathy with prewar political ideas, Christian Democracy appealed to the electorate as a new and renovating political force, with its political reforms firmly based on the two encyclicals, *Rerum Novarum* and *Quadragesimo Anno*, which criticised equally the materialism of capitalism and Marxism. Its conservative tendencies were submerged by the enthusiasm of its crusading left wing which was closely associated with the Resistance ideal. Part of its electorate looked to it, as a party based upon the universal concepts of Catholicism, as the only opponent capable of challenging Communism on all fronts. It set out to capture as much of the electorate as possible. Where Catholicism was not supported by a great percentage of the population, as in France and Germany, Christian Democracy deliberately avoided calling itself a party in order to prevent itself being stigmatised as a narrow sectarian grouping. Thus in Germany it was called the Christian Democratic Union (CDU) and in France the Popular Republican Movement (MRP).

Two distinct tendencies among the voters assisted Christian Democracy to achieve its striking electoral successes. First, many voters who were suspicious of Socialism and Communism were attracted to the party because of its acceptance of Resistance proposals for social reconstruction and moral renaissance. In France, the MRP also claimed to have the tacit support of General de Gaulle, who, however, never confirmed this; but the claim of association with the 'liberator' certainly attracted many voters to the party. Second, the French MRP and the Italian Christian Democrat vote was swollen by conservative support. With conservative parties banned or discredited, the Christian Democrats were the only major parties left in the field which were acceptable to these voters. In the short run, it strengthened the parties enormously in bargaining with Communists and Socialists about government formation and policy-making. But its true significance appeared only when the long-term effects were taken into consideration. Parties which are not based upon a comprehensive social philosophy with a cohesive economic base like socialism or strict conservatism, but rather upon ethnicism, religion or regionalism, have also possessed centrifugal propensities, with traditionalists and reformers always tugging in different, and quite often diametrically opposed, directions. This is especially true where socio-economic issues are concerned, and these tend to be more important and more numerous than other kinds of issues. This was a major problem which the postwar Christian Democrats had to face. The conservative support accredited them in these first elections only accentuated the dilemma and prolonged the finding of any comparatively straightforward solution; it weakened that control of the parties which had been offered to the reformers because of their Resistance role and their participation in the founding of the parties.

On the extreme left was Communism. Before 1939 it had really possessed only a nuisance value in Western Europe, apart from Germany. After 1945 its support in West Germany almost vanished, while elsewhere it increased substantially in strength. In France and Italy this increase was so great that the Communist Party became one of the dominating political forces. Mostly, the reasons for this emergence into a position of strength lie in the events of the war years. In the first place, the Communists naturally benefited from their active role in the Resistance: in many areas, notably rural districts, the Communists had been the sole resisters and after 1945 they remained perhaps the only significant political force in these areas. In addition, the Communists had been particularly successful between 1939 and 1945 among organised labour: in some instances it was soon clear that overall control of trade unions had passed to the Communists from the Socialists. Moreover, the Communist vision of a future utopia led many people to regard its method as the only one which could lift them out of the tremendous economic depression. For others, its ideology provided a comfortable haven where all problems could be given a satisfactory answer. Finally, its extreme position on the edge of the political spectrum attracted to it those people who simply wanted to protest against 'them'. For the workers and peasants in France and Italy, so often alienated from the mainstream of political life, a vote for Communism became the easiest way of protesting against the system. It has also been pointed out that Communism has thrived in Western Europe where the following factors still operate: a narrow-minded defence of private property; an over-rigid legal system; social groups agitating for special privileges when their political power had clearly declined; a widespread practice of deceit and secrecy among business interests; a clinging to antiquated tradition rather than accepting necessary economic and technological change; a poor and elitist educational system; and a concentration of ultra-conservative large landowners.[1] All these prerequisites are present to a marked extent in France and Italy.

Caught between these two political forces was Socialism. The Socialist parties of Europe were the traditional alternative to *laissez-faire* capitalism and nineteenth-century political liberalism. The failure of these forces in the prewar world, the Socialist refusal of compromise with Nazi and Fascist authoritarianism,

[1] Einaudi *et al.*, *Communism in Western Europe*, p. 7.

the fact that Socialists had been among the first groups to contest German occupation—all seemed to be clear indications that the time had come when Socialism would achieve its majority. After his release from a concentration camp, Kurt Schumacher, the German leader, sincerely believed that Socialism would be accepted by a large majority. Similarly, the old leader of the French Socialists, Léon Blum, who also had been incarcerated in a German prison camp, stated that 'Socialism is the master of the hour'. The Socialist leaders based their belief upon the social charters issued by the various Resistance movements: to a very large extent, in fact, Socialist and Resistance reform programmes were identical. In a way, therefore, Socialism would have had to attempt to become the nucleus of the proposed Resistance party, since it stood at the centre of the several political movements that had formed the Resistance.

This it failed to do. Resistance participants may have been inspired by Socialist ideals, but they had little sympathy for, and many had little in common with, the Socialist parties. Above all, they distrusted the monolithic structure and disliked the emphasis upon party bureaucracy and Marxist ideology. For their part, the Socialist parties were unwilling to abandon their strict adherence to Marxist doctrine or to slacken their party organisation. They were unable to make a strong attempt to attract other left-wing groups to form a broad radical party. In Italy, the Socialist Party was so closely tied to the Communists that it did not even consider playing this role: it was left to the ill-fated Action Party to make the attempt. Foregoing this opportunity, the Socialists retreated to their old hunting grounds bounded by the old organisational limits. In effect, they renounced Resistance proposals and returned to pre-war habits. The retreat was emphasised by the return of the old leaders from exile or prison camps, who took over the reins from younger men active within the Resistance: promotion to positions of authority could come only after a long apprenticeship within the party machine.

This act had serious consequences. It showed, in effect, that the Socialist leaders had not learnt any lessons from the past; and it put them at a serious disadvantage with regard to the other mass parties. Christian Democracy and Communism were in some ways relatively young movements in Western Europe. Both possessed a progressive image. The former in particular was led by younger men whose political beliefs had been forged almost entirely by their Resistance experience. Against these dynamic rivals Socialism appeared to be static, even retrogressive. The elections perhaps confirmed this, by hinting that the Socialist parties had done little to convert voters outside their traditional bases of support. Finally, there was the drawback of being caught between two dynamic mass movements. It may once have been hoped that Socialism could have played a broker role, throwing its weight first to one side and then to the other, and so ensure Socialist participation in almost every government. It soon became apparent, however, that having failed to draw the two extremes in toward itself it was under constant pressure in its role as outsider and suffered the danger of having splinters breaking away and allying with one or the other of its opponents. The Socialist parties of France and Italy have never been able to resolve this dilemma satisfactorily. Their history is an account of the struggle for supremacy within the party between maximalists (those seeking swift revolutionary change) and reformists (those agreeing to work for gradual change from within the system).

The dilemma still haunts them today. Mediation often involves compromise; this in turn can lead to abandonment of some principles. It was a difficult problem to tackle, for it could draw the parties into the centre, and leave the left-wing title open to the Communists by default. Either way the Socialist parties could not win. France and Italy show the two horns of the dilemma. In Italy where they clung to their left-wing title as champion of the masses and cooperated with the Communists, they found themselves accused of being fellow-travelling agents of Moscow: in fact it became increasingly difficult to pinpoint an independent Socialist course of action in Italy. In France the Socialists rejected Communist overtures, kept their freedom of action, and re-emphasised their loyalty to the Fourth Republic. Their concern for maintaining the regime led to Communist accusations that they had divided the working classes, reducing left-wing pressure to ineffectiveness. Caught between the two relentless pressures of supporting a constitutional system operated by non-sympathetic forces and of retaining their hold on organised labour against an ever strong Communist challenge, the Socialist parties in France and Italy spotlighted a problem which in some degree was common to European Socialism as a whole: like Alice's Red Queen they had to run faster and faster in order to hold ground already won. As long as a strong Communist party remained in existence, the dilemma could not be resolved with any satisfaction: absorption by Communism or a movement to the right were fundamentally the only two alternatives available.

Tripartism: Trials and Tribulations

In 1945 the dilemmas of Christian Democracy and Socialism did not yet need to be faced; the present still seemed optimistic. It was obvious that given the electorate's verdict the most satisfactory government would be one in which all three mass parties participated. Between 1945 and 1947 France and Italy were ruled by tripartite governments in which all three parties held ministerial office. The inauguration of tripartism raised hopes among optimists that the ideals of the Resistance might yet be realised. But the economic policies of the three parties were so divergent that any common formula for solving the immediate problems, which were basically economic, could not possibly be evolved. No other alternative was possible in France where the parties were equally balanced; not did it seem advisable in Italy where the Communists and Socialists tended to present a united front. The failure of tripartism to achieve a common economic policy illustrated the futility of any hopes of building a Resistance party. Governments were not divided into two factions: two cleavages consistently divided them, and because of the broad spread of differences within the Christian Democrats there were sometimes more than two. Generally the two Marxist parties were aligned against the Christian Democrats on economic policy, where issues usually revolved around state interference and control: the Christian Democrats favoured free enterprise, while the other parties advocated maximum government control. Where individual liberties were concerned, the Communists were usually isolated by the democratic alliance of the Socialists with the Christian Democrats.

These cleavages were constant and irreconcilable. The parties divided government administration among themselves. Each wanted to control its own share of government spoils without interference from its partners. The Communists were especially active in desiring to create their own state organisation within the official state. However, the mutual hostility of the parties prevented this tendency from overreaching itself. The most outstanding point about tripartism was that it was ever able to function at all. A complete stalemate and breakdown in the political system would certainly have occurred if it had lasted much longer than it did. Changes in the international climate and in the arrangement of domestic political forces allowed a way out of the impasse. Until these changes occurred, democracy in France and Italy could not hope to function in a healthy manner.

The first governments in both countries were still pervaded by the spirit of the Resistance. In France this was symbolised by the rule of General de Gaulle. Policy during this period was essentially formulated by de Gaulle, although he was assisted by his ministers, who were representative of all the Resistance parties, and by the Consultative Assembly. His policy was based upon his appreciation of the collapse of France in 1940 and the need to re-establish the country as a major world power. Hence his policy was primarily concerned with two general issues, the prosecution of the war and the reconstruction of the economy. De Gaulle was determined that France should offer as much assistance as possible in the remaining months of the war against Germany. This move was designed to help obliterate the humiliation of 1940 and to emphasise the value of a French military contribution. In this field de Gaulle did achieve his aim, most obviously in the decision of the Allies to allow France to participate on an equal status in the military occupation of Germany. More generally, France was allotted an important European and world role in President Roosevelt's blueprint of international affairs in the postwar world. In the economic area de Gaulle also achieved some striking successes. It was he who first launched an extension to the social welfare policy initiated by the prewar

Popular Front, thus laying a foundation for the future. It was intended to be a shrewd political manœuvre; by his policy de Gaulle hoped to lure the working classes away from their left-wing allegiance to participate as an essential part of the national foundation for a government of national unity.

Once peace was declared and it became 'politics as usual', de Gaulle became even more isolated from the country's political life. After the election of a left-wing Constituent Assembly it was obvious that the political state it favoured would be based firmly on the Jacobin or Revolutionary constitutional traditions. De Gaulle, on the other hand, favoured an authoritarian solution as the only means by which stable and effective government could be achieved in France. The war arrangement had been one of mutual convenience: politicians had accepted de Gaulle's leadership as the only one possible while the war lasted. De Gaulle had consistently refused to dabble in politics, consequently having no desire to be a part of parliamentary life. The gulf between the two widened steadily in 1945. In November there was a government reshuffle caused by the electoral successes of the three parties. But the argument between the two sides continued, de Gaulle favouring an authoritative executive, the parties advocating parliamentary superiority. The final break came immediately the parties could force their point of view because of their proved electoral backing. The issue was increased military expenditure, which the left-wing parties opposed. Seeing no way out of the impasse, de Gaulle resigned in January 1946, and retired from politics for the first time to his country home at Colombey-les-deux-Églises, there to wait for a call to office. For he was determined to form a government of his own liking only by constitutional means; for de Gaulle, a *coup d'état* was out of the question. A Gaullist takeover might well have succeeded, for, although out of favour with the dominant politicians who now regarded him as a man of the right, he was still the national hero of the ordinary Frenchman. With de Gaulle departed from the scene, tripartism in France began in earnest.

Italy appeared to be in a less favourable situation. Although allowed sovereignty over domestic affairs, the country was still treated as a defeated power and was refused parity with the

Allies. Moreover, there was no undisputed leader to assume office: leadership had to be provided by all those parties which had been represented on the Committees of National Liberation. The national link, which in France was de Gaulle, was in Italy provided by the Action Party and its leader, Parri. Like de Gaulle he had determined views on the future nature of his country; like de Gaulle he failed to bridge the gaps between himself and the others, and between the three mass parties; but unlike de Gaulle, he could command no national support. By the autumn of 1945 Parri and his few supporters were completely isolated in the government. Here, however, the left-wing parties were not so eager as their French colleagues to dispose of an obstacle. The strong Communist–Socialist alliance believed that their ends would be further advanced by a continuation of the governmental crisis. They were therefore reluctant to give Parri the *coup de grâce*. That was finally delivered by the increasingly influential conservative forces in November 1945. As the head of the largest single party Alcide de Gasperi, the Christian Democrat leader, assumed the reins of office. In that he governed with the sporadic assistance of the left, de Gasperi's first governments were of the tripartite formula; advances in one field meant concessions to the left elsewhere. The rise of de Gasperi was the strongest contrast Italy offered with France, despite the parallel development of the two countries between 1945 and 1947. The departure of de Gaulle meant the loss of a national leader and the opening of a period of comparative confusion and unrest; the rise of de Gasperi gave Italy a national leader with the will to attempt to impose on Italy a solution to its chronic economic problems.

Tripartism lasted for nineteen months in Italy, and for seventeen months in France. In Italy continuity was provided by the Christian Democrats and de Gasperi, who remained head of the government throughout the period. In France prime ministers came and went, the leadership alternating between the Socialists and the MRP. Ministers tended to stay longer in office, but continuity could not be guaranteed. A profound malaise was apparent throughout political life. The equal strength of the three parties meant that no common decisions could be arrived at, and that serious problems, where party attitudes were usually most

79

irreconcilable, were merely sidestepped and postponed for decision at some indeterminate future date. The strength of the parties was almost wholly devoted to winning partners in order to block opposition proposals. Almost without effort it became 'business as usual' as the Fourth Republic swiftly came to resemble the discredited Third Republic in the inordinate amount of time consumed by parliamentary intrigue and jostling for influence.

On the surface it appeared that Italy was faced with the same situation. However, de Gasperi was basically marking time during this period. No government could be formed without the support of the Christian Democrats. De Gasperi's problem was to make his party a nucleus that could attract sufficient democratic support to form a broad coalition of the democratic centre. To achieve this end the party had to move further to the right in order to attract those small parties that were hostile to Marxism. Once it was clear that they were unwilling to commit themselves to any positive action, de Gasperi aimed to free himself of the shackles of Communism and Socialism and to isolate the left from the centre of political life. A necessary consequence of this decision was the abandonment of the strict anti-Fascist policy of the Resistance alliance and the Action Party. Instead of permitting them to nurse their grudges which politically would sooner or later have manifested itself in the rise of a strong and rejuvenated neo-Fascist movement, de Gasperi wanted many of those individuals formerly associated with Mussolini's era to support him. In government services, therefore, such as the police and administrative bureaucracy, career officials who had served under the Fascist system were gradually brought back to replace the partisans appointed in the first instance by the Committees of National Liberation; at least it could be fairly certain that these replacements would be staunchly anti-Communist. De Gasperi also concentrated his attention on gaining the support of the business community who had been more or less ignored since 1944 and who lived in fear of a proletarian revolution. By these means de Gasperi gradually won the popular vote of confidence which he required if he was to pursue an independent course of action.

What, then, were the achievements of the era of tripartism?

That we can even ask this question indicates that the period, despite all its troubles, was not altogether without value. Given de Gasperi's basic political objectives, it is not surprising that little significant legislation was passed in Italy during these months; that came later when the premier felt that the basic outlines of Christian Democrat policy could be achieved without being radically altered or hindered by Communist and Socialist interference. For Italy the value of tripartism was that it disillusioned those who thought that the Communists could be responsible government partners.

In France, on the other hand, the list of actual legislative measures passed by the tripartite governments is quite impressive. Nearly all its legislation was concerned with those social and economic provisions demanded by the Resistance Charters. In 1946 France began to develop comprehensively de Gaulle's welfare state policy along lines similar to those being pursued by the British Labour Party. As in Britain, later conservative governments accepted the general principles of the measures passed during this period. Nationalisation and social security were greatly extended, and some 10 per cent of France's national income was channelled into these new services. Naturally there were many criticisms. It was attacked for being too extravagant, for spending too much money on an inflated bureaucracy administering the system, and for aggravating the serious economic situation, since the consumer paid in any case through substantial increases in prices and the cost of living. But in that the social security system did indicate that the government was willing to accept some responsibility for the welfare of the ordinary individual, it almost certainly prevented social discontent from being excessive and threatening the Fourth Republic itself. Above all, the tripartite governments overhauled the administrative structure and provided for a national economic plan: a national planning unit was formed under the prominent economist, Jean Monnet, to lay down the guidelines for France's economic development. But the plan was established because the government did not allow it to come before parliament and be bogged down in recriminations from all sides. The full advantages of the Monnet Plan took time to emerge, but by the 1950s it was clear that Monnet's office had contributed greatly towards economic expansion. No other country, not even Britain under a Labour government, was willing or able to indulge in such a long-term investment.

For eighteen months French governments limped along under the tripartite burden, while de Gasperi sought for an effective alternative. The climax of these developments came in May 1947. The break came first in France where the Communists were faced by an alliance of the other parties which decided to eject them from the government: an excuse was offered by Communist support for strikers in the Renault factory. The Communist leaders went into an opposition which proved to be permanent. At the time, however, they believed that they would shortly be returned in a much stronger position: it seemed impossible to them that French government could function satisfactorily in the face of Communist opposition. Their calculations proved wrong. The intensification of the Cold War contributed greatly to their permanent exclusion; it assisted the anti-Communist centre and right to grow in strength and determination. Later, the active interference of President Truman in the Italian elections of 1948 gave additional evidence that American foreign policy would assist the regime against collapse and would not tolerate a Communist takeover in France.

In the same month de Gasperi made his long-expected move against the Italian Communists. At last he thought he had found a broad base of support which would maintain a Christian Democrat government without excessive reliance on the Communists and Socialists on the extreme left or on the Monarchists and neo-Fascists on the extreme right. The break came because of dissension within the Socialist Party. A minority within the party had for a long time been unhappy about the close alliance with the Communists pursued by their leader, Pietro Nenni. Nenni had given no indication of changing this policy. Thus the reformist wing of the party, favouring working for gradual social change from within the system, broke away from the movement during the 1947 party conference in January to form an autonomous Socialist group. The new Social Democrats made it clear that they would basically support a democratic government, though at the cost of certain concessions. With this event de Gasperi felt that he could dispense entirely with the sporadic and unreliable support of the left, and so dissolved the cabinet for the fourth government crisis within two years. Unfortunately, no party was willing to join the Christian Democrats in a government. The latter were reluctant to rule alone: two important pieces of legislation—acceptance of the peace treaty and ratification of those sections of the constitution which gave a privileged position to the Catholic Church—had to be considered. De Gasperi did not wish his party to become isolated on these two issues. Consequently he had to come back to tripartism. Thus virtually the last governmental act of the Communist–Socialist alliance was to pass the peace treaty and approve the Lateran Pacts (favouring Catholicism)! Certain that the small parties would support the Christian Democrats, even if they would not come into the government, de Gasperi finally attacked the extreme left for obstructionism in a radio broadcast in April. The government again resigned. With tripartism now dead, the only solution was a minority Christian Democrat government. Again, like his French counterparts, de Gasperi had been encouraged by American assurances which seemed to pledge unstinting support for anti-Communist governments among America's European allies.

In Italy and France, therefore, the largest Communist parties in Western Europe were relegated to the role of an isolated opposition. Their dismissal emphasised the growing trend of conservatism, and hinted at the relatively impotent role the left (including the Socialists) would play in the politics of the 1950s. The Christian Democrats were left as victors. In Italy and Germany, and to a lesser extent in France, Christian Democracy was to play a decisive role in the policy formulation of the next decade. If the latent incompatibility of tripartism had continued, the result would have been chaos, which in fact was the end aim of extreme left-wing policy. The determination of the democratic centre and moderate left prevented this graver crisis from occurring. At the same time it gave rise to the threat of another danger: if de Gasperi's Christian Democrats or the French parties of the centre had failed in their resolution, the advantage would have gone over to the Communists. Democracy now had its liberty of movement but had simultaneously acquired sole responsibility.

G

The Communist departure meant the dropping of left-wing solutions on civil liberties and economic policy. State intervention in the economy became less widespread as ideas of free enterprise took over: support for nationalisation failed to sustain its first enthusiastic heights (this in fact had been true long before tripartism was summarily ended). Conservative support was now necessary, and the conservatives had their price.

In the wider world context, it suggested further evidence that the gulf between East and West was unbridgeable, even if it could have been spanned previously. France and Italy would now not only participate in the Cold War, but would be faced with a Cold War within their own boundaries. For it was almost axiomatic that the Communists would drop their 'do nothing' attitude during tripartism and switch to a more offensive campaign calculated to produce disruption and hinder government action. Finally, if any further proof were required, the end of tripartism illustrated the impossibility of Resistance dreams.

5 The Rebirth of Germany

Bonn is not Weimar.

F. R. Allemann[1]

The Allies had on the whole been very circumspect about interfering with the activities and rights of European governments. In France they had acted only in a liaison capacity and concentrated upon problems of supply. Even Italy, one of the defeated belligerents, had been allowed its own governments more or less from the fall of Mussolini, although the Allies did establish a Military Government to which the Italians were in essence answerable. But Italy had a free hand in domestic affairs, and after the signing of the peace treaty had complete sovereignty in foreign affairs. Germany, however, was classified as occupied territory and was placed under a Military Government. Austria, because of the complete nature of the *Anschluss*, was also placed in this category.

The Allied Debates on the Future

The Allies had for a long time been debating the problem of postwar Germany, although the Moscow Conference of foreign ministers in October 1943 had already taken the decision to try individuals classified as 'war criminals'. No one settled solution was agreed upon for some time. Several plans, some moderate, some severe, had been discussed. But by September 1944 agreement seemed to have been reached: Roosevelt and Churchill appeared to favour a plan proposed by Henry Morgenthau, the American Secretary of the Treasury. The Morgenthau Plan was to become notorious because of its extreme severity. In essence its solution for the German problem was to destroy entirely the country's industrial capacity. The Ruhr and other industrial areas

[1] *Bonn ist nicht Weimar*, Cologne, 1956.

were to be detached from the rest of the country and placed under international control, which presumably would be permanent; elsewhere the population was to exist, or even subsist, on a purely agricultural economy essentially eighteenth century in its outlines. In this way German aggressiveness was to be effectively curbed for ever.

Luckily for Germany and the Western world the Morgenthau Plan was eventually rejected, although the sentiment that had inspired the formula could still be detected in later discussions. Economically the Morgenthau Plan was completely unworkable; gradually the Allied leaders realised that an agricultural economy could not possibly meet the needs of Germany's large population. The plan was never openly repudiated. It quietly disappeared from official British and American circles. Churchill, already suspicious of Stalin's ambitions, had by the time of the Yalta Conference come down on the side of moderation. Roosevelt was undecided as to what formula to apply. The order finally issued was extremely ambiguous. It suggested severe economic restrictions, but proposed to allow the Germans sufficient freedom to make unwarranted violent unrest caused by foreign limitations. It permitted the Allies to pursue an austere policy reminiscent of the Morgenthau Plan, but included sufficient scope for such a policy to be amended and modified if Germany had to be utilised in any future struggle against Communism—although few apart from Churchill had begun to think along these lines.

Russia, on the other hand, had a clear attitude toward Germany. The sole preoccupation of Stalin was to destroy Germany completely and, as a corollary, to commandeer as much as possible of German industrial plant and material for reparations. For the Russians the ideal situation would be to start a Communist revolution in their designated occupation zone, or better still throughout the whole country, which would result in a people's democracy similar to those to be imposed upon Eastern Europe. If this proved to be impossible, Stalin would have been quite happy for something akin to the Morgenthau Plan to be adopted. Anything that would destroy German militarism and remove its threat from Russia's western borders was acceptable. Moreover, the Russians had definite views about Germany's eastern frontiers.

They requested that a substantial area of land be ceded to Poland, firstly to compensate for the 1939 invasion of that country, and secondly to commit Poland more closely to Russia and to allow the Poles to forget that Russia had already extended its frontier westward at the expense of Polish territory. These proposals met with some sympathy in the West, for the territory so claimed was part of the historic heartland of Prussia: many of the Allied leaders held 'Prussianism' responsible for German aggressiveness, and the destruction of Prussia as a political and historical unit was part of their policy.

These Russian demands failed to win acceptance at the 'Big Three' conference at Yalta, being deferred for a later decision. The Yalta meeting has been one of the most criticised events of the war: Roosevelt in particular has been charged with selling out to Russian imperialism. The divergencies apparent at Yalta, which had not appeared at the earlier Teheran meeting, were due simply to the fact that the Allies had by now moved on from strategic and military points to discuss postwar political developments. However, as far as Germany is concerned, the criticism should be redirected to the later Potsdam Conference of July 1945.

It was at Potsdam that the West accepted Russia's demands for reparations and boundary changes. It was agreed that Russia should receive compensation in the form of ten billion dollars, and that the German eastern frontier should be temporarily fixed on the Oder–Neisse line. This meant that some nine million Germans would come under Polish rule. The Allies never consented to the Oder–Neisse boundary being the permanent solution: it would be a temporary Polish administration and the fate of the area was to be decided by a later peace conference. But as far as Russia and Poland were concerned the matter was settled: the Oder–Neisse line was recognised as the *de jure* boundary between Germany and Poland. To emphasise this point, the vast majority of Germans were expelled from the region to join the flood of German refugees expelled by Czechoslovakia from the Sudetenland who were seeking accommodation within Germany. The German population of the Oder–Neisse territories was only one million in 1958, compared to a 1939 population of nearly ten million. The refugee and expellee problem was to be one of

87

the most serious to be faced by Germany in the postwar years.

It is perhaps of no little significance that at Potsdam Stalin was the only remaining representative of the wartime alliance. President Roosevelt had died, and had been replaced by Harry Truman; after the verdict of the British electorate Churchill had yielded the premiership to Clement Attlee. Being relatively inexperienced, the new Western leaders may have conceded more to Stalin than might otherwise have been the case. But it must be emphasised that the Potsdam concessions were in the line of previous wartime conferences, particularly that held at Yalta. Truman and Attlee closed ranks to refuse the further demand of Russia that the Ruhr industrial complex should be divorced from the rest of Germany and placed under a joint Allied authority. Their refusal indicates how far the West had moved from the Morgenthau Plan; the granting of Stalin's request would have given Russia incalculable advantages in any attempt to foster Communist influence and propaganda.

It was at Potsdam that the Allies settled the general outline of their policy toward Germany. In general, they wished to delay the re-establishment of a national German government for as long as possible. Having no clear idea of what the future German state would be, they agreed to concentrate upon the policy of the 'four D's'—demilitarisation, denazification, decentralisation, and decartelisation. The main principles enunciated were as follows:

local self-government shall be restored throughout Germany on democratic principles and in particular through elective councils as rapidly as is consistent with military security and the purposes of military occupation;
all democratic political parties with rights of assembly and of public discussion shall be allowed and encouraged throughout Germany;
representative and elective principles shall be introduced into regional, provincial and state (*Land*) administration as rapidly as may be justified by the successful application of these principles in local self-government;
for the time being no central German government shall be established. Notwithstanding this, however, certain essential German administrative departments, headed by State Secretaries, shall be established, particularly in the fields of finance, transport, communications, foreign trade

and industry. Such departments will act under the direction of the Control Council.[1]

The Allies had thus decided upon a military occupation of Germany and to take upon themselves the responsibility of governing the country. Even if this had not been the case, the Allies would still have been forced to impose their authority on postwar Germany. No German alternative was available. The invasion and defeat of Germany had not brought about only a military collapse; the entire political and administrative structure created by the Nazis also disintegrated almost overnight. Only local administrations were still capable of functioning, but even at this level there were large areas where local mayors and their officials had abandoned their posts. This was especially true in the east, where local administrators, along with many troops and a substantial portion of the population, fled westward before the Russian armies in order to reach territory captured and adminis-tered by the western Allies. As far as government was concerned, therefore, Germany was a blank cheque; the Allies could write in whatever price they chose.

The Military Governments

After hostilities had ceased the Allied forces moved into their previously demarcated zones: American troops, for example, were pulled out of Thuringia and Saxony since these areas were to be part of the Russian zone. For administrative purposes Germany was first divided into three zones, each subject to the authority of an occupying power. Later, Britain and America agreed to admit France as an occupying power and gave it a small zone out of their own territory. The Russians were to govern eastern Germany; Britain was given the north-western zone, and America the southern zone plus the port of Bremen for harbour facilities. France was allotted a small zone bordering her own territory as well as the already disputed area of the Saar. The city of Berlin was excluded from this arrangement, and was similarly divided into four zones. The city raised numerous problems by

[1] B. Ruhm von Oppen, ed. *Documents on Germany under Occupation 1945–1954*, London, 1955, p. 44.

being in the heart of the Russian zone. This arrangement was adopted because of the symbolic importance of Berlin as the capital of Germany. It was planned that reconstruction of a national government and administration would allow central administrative agencies to be established in the city, thereby creating a nucleus around which some degree of unity of the future German state could be attained. Coordination of activities within the four zones of Germany was to be achieved by the Allied Control Authority. A similar body, the Allied Kommandatura, was established for coordinating the government of Berlin.

Austria was also treated as occupied territory. The Allies had agreed in principle to the independence of the country, but because of its close ties with Germany since 1938 military government appeared to be inevitable; thus Austria was also divided into four zones, while Vienna was treated in a similar manner to Berlin. There were two important differences between Germany and Austria. The first and most obvious was the minuteness of the latter compared to the former. The rump of the old Habsburg Empire could never present a serious threat to peace or to the major powers, provided the country was stable internally and not too closely tied to a major power bloc. It was therefore relatively easy for the Allies to agree to the creation of a fully sovereign Austrian state if the latter pursued a neutral course and if this neutrality was guaranteed by the major powers. The second difference was that internal administration had not collapsed in Austria. In 1945 there was already in existence a central government in Vienna. This had received its original powers from the Russian authorities, but was also accepted immediately by the West. The groundwork had therefore been prepared. Furthermore, Austria proved to be unreceptive to Communism. The Communist Party lost strength steadily and soon disappeared from governing circles. Stalin did not seem prepared to force the issue in such an unimportant country, despite the 1948 Communist *coup d'etat* in Czechoslovakia. Austria was therefore in an advantageous position with regard to independence. The government, moreover, was a semi-permanent coalition of the only two significant parties, the People's Party and the Socialists (until 1966 a unique arrangement in European politics), which in every postwar election have gained 90 per cent or more of the votes cast. In its particular circumstances, Austria presented a united front to the outside world on the question of military evacuation and the granting of sovereignty for a neutral state.

In Germany the Allied Control Authority never really succeeded in getting off the ground. Although it had been agreed that matters affecting the whole of Germany were to be dealt with by the Authority, it became increasingly difficult for the four occupying powers to agree on what should be classified as all-German concerns. Moreover, a unanimous decision was necessary in the highest organ, the four-man Control Council; it meant that each occupier possessed a veto on unfavourable policies. In each occupation zone the military governor had supreme authority; he was answerable only to his own government, which usually held views distinct from those of the other Allies on what was to be done in Germany. The tendency of the zones to become independent 'states' was strengthened by the practice of withdrawing issues from the Control Council when unanimity could not be obtained.

The Allies began to pay the penalty for not clarifying in greater detail their future course of action before the war ended. In particular France and later Russia held divergent opinions. France was obsessed by the need to keep Germany weak and divided. Hence French governments tended to drag their heels on reconstruction except in the case of the Saar where they had designs for the eventual incorporation of the territory into France. Russia held quite different views about the meaning of democracy from those of Britain and America. The Russian plans were for a people's democracy dominated by Communists susceptible to Russian control. Ideally, Stalin would have preferred Communist superiority to be displayed through free elections. In accordance with this view, four political parties were licensed in 1945 by the Russian authorities: Communist, Social Democrat, Christian Democrat, and Free Democrat. In the only all-city elections in Berlin in 1946 the Social Democrats won a convincing victory over all other parties; the Communists went down to an ignominious defeat. Thereafter Russian policy changed its course:

the use of Russian force would be the only way to a German people's democracy. The Social Democrat Party in the Russian zone was forcibly merged with the weaker Communists in a new Russian-directed party, the Social Unity Party (SED). A major step had been taken to retract Eastern Germany from Western influence and establish it firmly behind the iron curtain.

Russian economic policy was also different from that of the West. The United States and Britain tended to give top priority to the reconstruction of the economy: from 1946 onwards their main emphasis was upon the need to integrate zonal economies. Russia, on the other hand, emphasised the need for reparations in both theory and practice. Whole factories and industrial material were dismantled and transported to Russia. Railway lines were uprooted for use elsewhere. The irony of this last action only appeared when the Russians began to fashion a sovereign state out of their zone. The East German economy then needed as much help as possible, but previous Russian policy had made transport and communication facilities almost non-existent. Moreover, in the first postwar years Russia had completely disregarded the Potsdam provisions by confiscating current East German productions as 'reparation exports' for Russian use. The Russian zone was operated as a separate and independent economic unit, as was the French zone for a while, again flouting the Potsdam agreements which had stated that current German production should not be overtapped and that Germany was to be treated as only one economic unit for purposes of foreign trade.

Nevertheless, the Allied Control Authority did achieve a limited success through a rather imposing administrative structure that it had established. In the three years of its existence it passed 125 legislative provisions. Much of this legislation was concerned with the agreed objectives of denazification, demilitarisation, decartelisation, and democratisation—particularly the first. Since the problems facing the Authority were of a very complex order, its performance is perhaps all the more laudatory.

The Allied honeymoon did not last long. As the conflict of national interests among the Allies became more apparent, Russian and to a lesser extent French obstructionism deprived the

Authority of much success. Eventually Marshal Sokolovsky, the Soviet commander, walked out of the Control Council in March 1948. The Allied Control Authority could no longer function. Three months later Russia refused to participate any longer in the Allied Kommandatura in Berlin. So far as Germany was concerned, the Cold War had started in earnest. The Western Allies were therefore forced to provide an alternative arrangement for administering their own areas. In the West the occupation was thereafter in the hands of the tripartite Allied Commission for Germany. At its head was the coordinating body of the Allied Council. High Commissioners replaced the Military Governors when civilian control superseded military control. Underneath the Allied Council was an extensive network of administrative committees and working parties, which administered German affairs apart from those of local government.

Further developments in Europe made the Allies afraid of Russian expansionist aims and desirous of Germany as an ally. Early in 1948 there was a successful Communist coup in Czechoslovakia. And in June, only two days after Russia had walked out of the Berlin Kommandatura, the Soviet Military Government announced the commencement of the Berlin blockade in an attempt to close the only remaining chink in the Russian iron curtain. America retaliated by building up a vast air lift to maintain the western sectors of Berlin as a viable economic unit and to illustrate its determination to throw a barrier against Russia's drive westward. The air lift had to be maintained until May 1949, when Russia abandoned the blockade as an unsuccessful tactic. In addition to the factors mentioned in Chapter 3, the Soviet tactics were also in part a retaliation against the Western decision to reform the German currency, a scheme designed to stabilise economic life.

The Soviet walk-out from the Berlin Kommandatura occurred during a six-power conference of Western foreign ministers in London. The meeting had been convened because Britain and the United States had already (perhaps somewhat belatedly) reached the conclusion that it would be futile to await Russian concurrence for the establishment of a native government for the whole of Germany. The Berlin episode only helped them to

93

crystallise their decision. At the London conference the Western Allies agreed in principle upon the amalgamation of their zones and to the creation of a central German government covering all three. It was eventually agreed that the new German state should be based upon a written constitution drafted by an elected constituent assembly approved by the Allied representatives in Germany and confirmed by popular consent. The Allies would retain some control over German affairs, particularly in the field of foreign policy. The relationship between the Allies and the new German government in such matters was formalised by the Occupation Statute, signed by the interested parties in Washington in April 1949. Under the statute, the Allied Military Government was replaced by the Allied High Commission. Further agreements in following years extended the areas of legitimate German government and lessened Allied rights in Germany. Finally the Paris Agreements, signed in October 1954, officially brought to an end the period of occupation of Germany: the Federal Republic of Germany was now a fully sovereign state. The Western Allies still retained their full occupation rights in Berlin, and today these are the basis of the Allies' justification for their military presence in that city.

After the conclusion of the war the Allied occupation forces had to attend to the immediate needs of the German people. The whole German administrative machine had stopped functioning. The German population was deprived of the priorities of food, shelter, and utilities; these had to be provided by the Allies. To facilitate the establishment of lines of supply one of the Allies' first preoccupations was with reconstructing German government and administration at the local level. Such re-establishment, of course, fell into line with the official Allied policy adopted at Potsdam. The pressing economic situation, however, and the shortage of experienced military staff probably caused the Allies to move in this direction earlier than would have been the case if they had followed only their own inclinations.

The search was concentrated upon key community leaders who were both efficient and untainted by Nazism. Since Nazi control and influence over German life had been extremely widespread and efficient, such men were difficult to find. Many local government officials were automatically disqualified because of their association with Nazism. Furthermore, many German opponents of Hitler's regime had been incarcerated for long periods in concentration camps and were too weak, both physically and mentally, to undertake the onus of local government reconstruction. Others who were willing were nothing more than enthusiastic amateurs. Nevertheless, local leaders were eventually found to fill the most important jobs, although increasingly the Allies had to abandon their strict interpretation of Nazi complicity and denazification. In the cities the Allies appointed lord mayors, mayors in the towns and villages, and county officials in rural areas. In turn these head officials assisted the Allies in recruiting staff for lesser local administrative posts. When a network of local administrative units had been established, the same process was adopted for the reconstruction of political institutions at the higher level of the district, until finally the pyramid could be topped by the creation of regional (*Land*) institutions.

These states, or *Laender*, were a revival of the traditional German form of government. Some, like Bavaria, were, apart from a few amendments to boundaries, historical entities with long and proud traditions; others, for example North-Rhine Westphalia, were artificially created by the Allies mostly out of remnants of the old Prussian State which the Allies had set out to destroy. Previously, the vast size and strength of Prussia in relation to the rest of Germany had caused a serious imbalance in the country's stability. Thus in establishing these new *Laender* the Allies sought for a more equal distribution of population. The premierships of the *Laender* were given the title of minister-president. To them the Allies appointed men of confirmed anti-Nazi convictions. These states therefore became the centre of German political life in the absence of a national government; they attracted ambitious politicians and become the focal point of all serious discussions on the nature of the new Germany.

Throughout the period of reconstruction the Allies gradually released more authority to German officials, but even by 1948 the country was still greatly decentralised. The first unifying move had been made in November 1945, when the Americans established a Council of States in their zone. The council consisted of the ministers-president of the four states established in the American zone. It was not intended to possess complete authority over the whole zone; rather it was intended to act as a coordinating body for the state governments in the field of interstate matters which could not be handled competently by individual states. Nevertheless, the Council of States did tend to develop some characteristics of a zonal government.

The first steps toward unification had been taken, but these were still very far from the resolutions taken at Potsdam. The decision to treat Germany as a single economic unit had been flouted blatantly during the first year of occupation. Economic affairs were handled on a zonal basis; interzonal trade was treated as if it was being conducted between independent states. Such a state of affairs was clearly unsatisfactory, and in many ways added an extra burden to the already heavy responsibilities of the occupying powers. Finally, in June 1946, the United States invited the other occupying forces to merge the economies of their zones with that of the American zone. In the event, only Britain was willing to accept the invitation. The agreement was signed in December, and plans for the joint administration of the two zones were laid for an opening day on 1 January 1947. The new economic unit was named 'Bizonia' and became the real starting point of the development of the future West German State. The Council of States of the American zone was naturally extended to embrace the four states of the British zone. German joint executive committees were created, each committee to have one representative from each state: committee members were always the heads of the relevant state ministries. Although policy was formulated by these committees, implementation of the policies could be carried through only by the state governments.

However, where particularist sentiment was strong, as for example in Bavaria, state cooperation with Bizonia decisions was far from forthcoming. Furthermore, the rapid deterioration in 1947 of the food situation caused additional difficulties for the successful functioning of the Bizonal Economic Administration. Some reform was clearly called for. Thus in 1947 an Economic Council was established. The Economic Council consisted again of one representative from each of the component states. This representative was selected not by the state government, but by the state legislature. The new council was to serve in a legislative capacity, while administrative agencies were established to supervise the execution of Economic Council decisions. A further rationalising revision occurred the following year, which enabled the Economic Council to compel the states to comply with its decisions. Since one difficulty facing the bizonal authorities had been that judicial enforcement of bizonal decisions had rested with the individual state courts, a German High Court was established in 1948 at Cologne with both original and appellate jurisdiction. The work of the Economic Council is important in that it was here that the non-Socialist coalition had its first successful experiment.

Thus by the time the Western Allies decided at London to press on with the re-establishment of a democratic German national government in their own zones, a complex structure of political and administrative institutions had already been founded. A similar set of institutions also existed in the Soviet zone, but these will not be mentioned here, being outside the field of this study. It will suffice to say that since 1946, when the SED first made its appearance, the whole pattern of Soviet policy had been to fashion the emerging institutions to serve the interests of the German (and hence the Russian) Communist leaders.

The German View of Independence

In Western Germany it was clear by 1948 that the emerging pattern of political institutions was developing along traditional German lines. In the Economic Council a bicameral structure had already appeared, with a 'lower house' based upon the principle of popular representation and an 'upper house' representative of the constituent states. An executive body of the cabinet variety, responsible to the legislature, had also appeared. An independent judiciary with definite powers had been established. Finally a clear-cut division of legislative and executive powers between 'national' and state governments had also emerged. It is significant that this was roughly the outline of the governmental structure of the still nascent Federal Republic, and that it was on the whole based on traditional German ideas on government apparent in all the stages of Germany's erratic history (except, of course, the Third Reich).

The reaction of most Germans to the total collapse of the Nazi regime had been one of massive withdrawal from any form of political activity. Political reconstruction was not their concern. Many people had identified themselves emotionally with the 'thousand year Reich' and its programme of national glorification; they felt themselves unable to bridge the gap to the harsh realities of the postwar years. The utter disintegration of the Nazi Reich was 'accompanied by an intense regionalisation of opinion and a shift of personal identification from the national to private interests. Communications between the occupation zones, between the new states, and even between cities for a while almost came to a complete standstill.'[1] The years immediately following the German surrender were dominated by the chaos caused by the chronic shortage of food and shelter; inevitably the struggle for mere survival occupied the exclusive attention of most Germans.

Nevertheless certain Germans were concerned with the need for political and social reconstruction and with the particular form the reconstruction would take. Gradually the Allies permitted groups and associations to become active: trade unions, for example, were some of the first associations the Allies encouraged to re-emerge. This process culminated with the licensing of political parties. Politically interested and active Germans operated from these bases. German administrators and politicians had been incorporated into the governmental structure created by the occupation forces: there was, in fact, a strong relationship between the development of new parties and the spread of German-directed administration. By the time of the London conference state governments were in office in all the *Laender* of the three western zones. Members of these governments were invariably also members of the licensed political parties.

The revived parties were representatives of traditional con-

[1] P. H. Merkl, *The Origin of the West German Republic*, New York, 1963, p. 28.

servatism, liberalism, Christian democracy, socialism, and communism. Two mass parties, the Social Democrats (SPD) and the Christian Democrats (CDU), soon achieved an undisputed superiority over the rest of the field. Right-wing parties had been too closely associated with Nazism, while Russian activity in the Soviet zone had done much to discredit the Communists. The origins of the CDU lay in the old Centre Party of the Empire and Weimar. However, whereas the Centre had been a purely Catholic party, the founders of the CDU wished to break out of this narrow sector, and, by attracting as much Protestant support as possible, to establish a broad non-denominational political movement. But the new party still had its strongest roots in Catholicism and its leaders were predominantly Catholic. Konrad Adenauer was to become the dominating personality of the party and of the new republic. He had served as Lord Mayor of Cologne in the 1920s, but had retired from politics and had carefully dissociated himself from the Nazi regime. After 1945 he came forward, by an astute 'takeover' technique, to lead the CDU, first in the British zone, and then in the whole of Germany. From chairing the Constituent Assembly he went on to become the first chancellor in Germany's second experiment with democracy.

The Social Democrats were one of the oldest parties in Germany and had kept hope alive during Hitler's interim period by maintaining a party organisation in exile. Their leader, Kurt Schumacher, had waited out the twelve years of Nazi rule in a concentration camp. This experience had so conditioned him that he inspired the party with an optimistic faith for its future, and also caused it to change from its traditional pacifist attitude to one of more intense nationalism, for Social Democracy was the sole true representative of Germany. He provided a wind of change in the SPD which had had a tradition of leaders conditioned by long years of service in the bureaucratised party machine, yet in the long run failed to dislodge the roots of traditionalism. Political discussions on the future of Germany tended to revolve round the positions adopted by these two parties.

When the Allies called upon the ministers-president to set in motion the machinery for forming a constituent assembly to

H

consider the drafting of a new constitution, the Germans themselves had already put forward several suggestions about the nature
of the new state. The collapse of the Third Reich had left a total
vacuum that was extremely conducive for and receptive to new
ideas. The reaction against Hitler meant that the new ideas were
dominated by a democratic spirit and Christian principles. The
return to fundamentals was linked to a close examination of the
lessons offered by German history. The most important influence
upon the deliberations of German politicians during the occupation was that of traditional forms of government. Needless to say,
the Nazi Third Reich was almost universally condemned. The
Weimar Republic, too, came in for its share of condemnation,
but German attitudes here were more equivocal. It was recognised
that the theory behind the Weimar Constitution was a worthy
one: many leading politicians felt that with certain new safeguards, reflecting the distrust of mass democracy, the Weimar
Constitution could be used as a basis for the future German State.
Centralisation was suspect. In many states, particularly Bavaria,
separatist sentiments were extremely popular. Some Bavarians
even proposed applying for membership of the United States;
similarly, some traditionalists in Hanover advocated incorporation with Britain.[1] Germans came to believe that a return to a
traditional form of German federalism would be an ideal form
for the new state, and that it would meet with Allied, especially
American, prejudices. There was hardly any mention of German
Realpolitik, but a wide acceptance of the 'pan-European' democratic tradition of the 1848 Frankfurt Constituent Assembly.
Germany had previously been conditioned to obey 'father state',
a lordly figure which had a life of its own and which alone could
determine what were, and protect, basic freedoms; this image no
longer existed, or at least did not exist to the same extent:

The political history of Germany had been dominated by the successive absorptions of the various claims to human freedom piecemeal
into the structure of monarchical government without undermining
the independent authority of that government. . . . The state in Ger-

[1] Comparable ideas existed elsewhere. Some leaders of the Sicilian Separatist
Party in Italy, for example, advocated annexation of Sicily by Britain. In Belgium
a Walloon political movement wanted Wallonia to become part of France.

many had become both the actual organisation and the ideal symbol for the compatible integration of these areas of individual freedom into the established order of political government and social hierarchy. ... It was this primal association between freedom and the traditional [authoritarian] state that the Nazis destroyed. ... Despite the widespread rejection of the Nazi experience in post-war Germany, one condition that has carried over is the bankruptcy of the state as a liberalising institution. Dominant now is an attitude which views the state as a morally neutral, purely utilitarian organisation of public power.[1]

Thus by the time the new Parliamentary Council met at Bonn to consider a new constitution, the German delegates themselves had found a fairly flexible framework of ideas which they felt could be operable in the new Germany. They had accepted the need for a parliamentary, democratic, and federal regime based upon traditional German ideas on organisation. It is a mistake to emphasise too heavily the role of the Allies in this process. It is true that the Basic Law which came into effect in 1949 reflected much of Allied policy for the future Germany, but it is true that it reflected even more so German views on the subject. Opponents of the Basic Law have often used Allied interference as a whipping block. Prejudice has been easily aroused by this means, but in practice Allied interference was never diametrically opposed to German views. Their suggestions and vetos merely gave extra support to one of two sides already formed in the council debates: furthermore, such situations were rare.

The Parliamentary Council set up by Allied recommendations first met in Bonn in September 1948, shortly after France had agreed to combine its zone with Bizonia. Politically the atmosphere was tense: the Berlin blockade was already in full swing. The economic outlook, however, was much brighter. In June, a much needed currency reform was inaugurated which, by limiting the supply of money, reforming the debt structure, and progressively removing financial controls, destroyed the black market and put the German mark on a more stable footing.

The participants had previously been nominated by the various state legislatures and were all representative of the licensed parties.

[1] L. Krieger, *The German Idea of Freedom*, Boston, 1957, pp. 468–70.

The party composition of the council was as follows: CDU twenty-seven; SPD twenty-seven; Free Democrats five; other parties six. Adenauer was elected President of the Council; as such he became the leading German representative at the many discussions and negotiations with the three Allied governors. The parity within the council between the two leading parties gave rise to many awkward situations. The smaller parties (except the Communists) tended to lean more favourably to the CDU, but this support was offset by disagreement within the CDU itself, still largely a loose confederation of state parties. By the end of October it was clear which were the most controversial issues: the administration of finance and the problem of federalism, in particular the role of the upper house. Many SPD members followed the suggestion of their leader, Schumacher, that the new state should be 'as federalistic as possible and as centralised as necessary'; the CDU, on the other hand, desired a more decentralised form. On the whole the debates were settled by compromise, with a tendency to favour the CDU position. This was again a break with the doctrinal past: the willingness to compromise was a rejection of the previous axiom that not more than one party or view can be correct.

After eighteen months the final draft was approved by the council. The emphasis upon federalism existed not because the CDU had more success in the bargaining process, although this may have had some weight, but because the whole nature and mood of postwar German government at that point was federally inclined. No central government existed to exert pressure upon the council, while all existing powers were in the hands of fully-operating state governments. Furthermore, the new draft constitution was not going to be ratified by popular approval, where centralist forces could perhaps gain some support, but by the state legislatures which were already jealous of their acquired powers and loath to see them pass into the hands of a central government. There was not, as in 1919, an extremely bitter fight between central and regional forces: federalism, to a greater or less extent, had been endorsed by all pro-democratic groups, both in the Parliamentary Council and in the state and local governments. But above all these emphases were not accompanied by the hope of an optimistic future. Germany was merely concerned about forgetting the past: the constitution 'is not the reflection of a positive enthusiasm for a better future as much as it is the expression of a deep revulsion against a distasteful past'.[1]

It had already been agreed that the new constitution should not be known as such. The delegates did not wish the new state to possess a fully sovereign character. They felt that this would only emphasise the division of Germany and make reunification even more remote. Thus they agreed that the constitution would be known as the Basic Law: a constitution could be ratified only by the whole of Germany. In voting upon the Basic Law the council took individual articles separately, obtaining rather different majorities. Finally the council approved the Basic Law as a whole by fifty-three votes to twelve. The opposition consisted of six delegates from minor parties and six of the eight delegates of the Christian Social Union (the Bavarian organisation of the CDU). The most vocal opposition came from Bavaria where a form of confederation was favoured. Bavaria, in fact, was the only state to reject the Basic Law (for being too centralised), but with the qualification that Bavaria would nevertheless accept a majority decision.

The Parliamentary Council enacted electoral provisions for the first postwar general election. This was held in August 1949. With a high turnout, the CDU won 139 seats, the SPD 131, the Free Democrats 52, while the remaining 80 seats went to smaller and regional parties. A federal convention was held to elect the first Federal President who then submitted the nomination of Dr Adenauer to the parliament as Federal Chancellor. After lengthy negotiations with some of the smaller parties, Adenauer was able to form a coalition government. With all these actions completed, Germany had, as the Federal Republic of Germany, its second chance to function as a parliamentary democracy. Its future operations would be extremely important and significant, for judgments would be made by comparing it, not only with the past, but also with the German regime set up in the Soviet zone by Russia in retaliation to the Western Allies' policy. As the Cold War intensified, the Federal Republic was placed under even

[1] Merkl, *The Origin of the West German Republic*, p. 176.

more pressure to become a committed partner of the Atlantic alliance—a course that would give severe headaches to some of its western neighbours. The transition to independence was formalised by a special ceremony held on 21 September 1949, at the headquarters of the Allied High Commission. With this ceremony, the occupation of Germany ended in practice and the Federal Republic formally began to operate. The date became yet another, and it is to be hoped the last but one, significant landmark in the tumultuous history of Germany.

6 The Cold War and the Atlantic Alliance

From Stettin in the Baltic to Trieste in the Adriatic an iron curtain has descended across the continent.

Sir Winston Churchill, 1946

The early months of 1947 are the latest possible date by which we can say that wartime camaraderie had completely evaporated. The West had now to accept definitely that consultation with Stalin's Russia was impossible. The years 1947 and 1948 strengthened the conviction of the Western Allies that Soviet Russia was probing for signs of possible weaknesses on their part preparatory to a major ideological and possibly even military advance westward on the European continent. Guerrilla warfare in Greece, Communist attempts at political and industrial sabotage in France and Italy, the arguments over Germany, the Communist coup in Czechoslovakia, the Berlin blockade—all these events followed swiftly on one another's heels. Whether they were all part of a calculated grand design or not, the end aim, the securing of Russian hegemony in Europe, was never in doubt. If any further proof was needed, this lengthy list of quasimilitary assaults gave added emphasis to the point that the democracies of Western Europe were not yet economically or militarily self-sufficient. The fall of Czechoslovakia, for which the West was largely unprepared because of the desire to see it as a cultural bridge between East and West, underlined the dangers. Some form of American guarantee or intervention on behalf of Western European independence was more or less necessary, for the security of the United States as well as that of Western Europe. A Russian victory in Europe would have given Communism control of one of the largest industrial concentrations in the world and would have left the United States virtually isolated within its own continent.

Check and Stalemate

The catalyst which could be said to have provoked America into positive action was Russian infiltration in the eastern Mediterranean. Communist guerrillas were again attempting to gain control of Greece. Simultaneously, Russian pressure on Turkey was increasing: the Soviet demands were for the Turks to admit Russia as an equal partner in the control of the Black Sea Straits. This would have given Russia a naval outlet into the Mediterranean. Russia further demanded that Turkey allow it to lease naval and military bases in the Straits which would then be used for 'joint defence purposes'. Elsewhere, Russia was still interested in Iran, was strenuously supporting the Yugoslavian claim to Trieste, and was suggesting that it should receive the trusteeship of the former Italian colonies of Tripolitania and Eritrea. The Greek civil war was not therefore an isolated occurrence in the eastern Mediterranean. A Communist attempt to control Greece had already been prevented by British troops in 1944. When the uprising broke out again in September 1946, the sagging Greek Government called for Britain's assistance and the fulfilment of its role of policeman of the Mediterranean. This new Communist insurrection was particularly effective first because it benefited from widespread discontent with the rather extreme right-wing government, and second because of the close proximity of supply bases across the Greek border in the Communist states of Albania, Bulgaria, and Yugoslavia. The fate of Greece could not be ignored by the rest of Western Europe. The Communist drive could be regarded as the first stage in an outflanking movement which later would have first Italy and then France, politically two of the weakest links in the Western armour, lying in its direct path. If this had succeeded the Allied presence in Germany would have become irrelevant: Russia would very largely have been the master of Europe.

It soon became fairly obvious that British military support was the sole prop of the Greek Government. But Britain, the only serious power left in Western Europe, was itself exhausted and not powerful enough to bring the war to a speedy end. The longer it dragged on, the less likelihood there was of Britain imposing a satisfactory solution—or indeed a solution of any kind. Early in 1947 the economic situation within Britain determined a reduction in British military strength: the United States was therefore informed that Britain could no longer fulfil its obligations in Greece and would have to withdraw no matter what happened. Only the United States could occupy the vacuum which would be caused by even a partial British withdrawal from Greece. President Truman therefore accepted responsibility for the area. In March 1947 he outlined what was to be known as the Truman Doctrine.

The doctrine was a pledge of American support for 'free peoples who are resisting attempted subjugation by armed minorities or by outside pressures'. Stressing the interrelatedness of the democratic world it emphasised that these attempts at subjugation did concern America, that world peace was necessary for American security. The Truman Doctrine marked the opening of a new, more aggressive phase in American foreign policy. In European affairs this manifested itself in a deep concern for the political and economic health of the Western democracies. Previously the United States had been hesitant, and often reluctant, to intervene abroad. As a first indication of the new guarantee American military missions were sent to both Greece and Turkey. American military aid went to Greece to modernise the equipment of the government forces, while military advisers helped them plan a systematic campaign against the Communist guerrillas.

The Truman Doctrine was above all a pledge of military aid and an indication of America's political relationship with the old continent. But quite obviously American protection of Western Europe by itself was basically a squandering of resources in that area. It would be much better and much more certain of success if the European democracies were on a sound economic footing; then prosperity would help diminish internal opposition and dissatisfaction, a fundamental source of Communist support, and would contribute toward Europe's own military capacity to defend itself. But this the Truman Doctrine did not set out to do. It was with these factors partly in mind that George Marshall, the American Secretary of State, issued in June 1947 the first general outline of the programme for economic recovery in Europe known as the Marshall Plan. The Marshall Plan, when finally adopted by the American Congress, was not intended to be part of the Cold War armament in that the American offer was not limited to those countries already unofficial members of or favourably disposed toward the American alliance. It could be considered to be a weapon of the Cold War first in that it was almost certainly taken into account by American officialdom that the offer would be rejected by Russia and its satellites, and second in that its generosity would be interpreted as a counterblow to wean Eastern Europe away from strict Communist control. Either way, the United States would appear as the magnanimous benefactor, while the Soviet Union would be accused by the world of self-centred intransigence. The only proviso the United States attached to this scheme was that the recipient nations should coordinate their economic activities to achieve the greatest benefit possible from the promised American aid.

In general, Western Europe welcomed the Marshall Plan wholeheartedly, with Britain taking the lead. The acceptance of the proposals in Eastern Europe was much more doubtful. Most were suspicious of the American offer. Poland and Czechoslovakia, however, expressed interest and willingness to participate in the programme. The Soviet Union itself was hostile to the plan, regarding it as a mere variant of the Truman Doctrine, and eventually forced Poland and Czechoslovakia to retract from their former willing position. Certainly it is difficult to see how the Communist bloc could have welcomed Marshall Aid in the light of the implications of the Truman Doctrine issued only two months earlier. It was clear that no Communist-led country subject to Moscow control would be allowed to associate with the West even to the extent of accepting 'unconditional' American aid.

The Marshall Plan was therefore limited to Western Europe. A new body, the Organisation of European Economic Cooperation, was formed by the recipients to help the administration of the Marshall Plan and the channelling of its funds to the most appropriate objectives. The Economic Recovery Programme (to give its correct title) illustrated once again the impossibility of bridging the gap between East and West and of creating an all-European cooperative effort. Through the Soviet Union's intransigence and later belligerence, the Marshall Plan came to have a different meaning. When financial aid first started to appear in Europe under its auspicies in 1948 it was already apparent that to all intents and purposes the plan was the economic complement of President Truman's expressed political intent to organise the West in an ideological alliance against the Soviet Union. The United States, therefore, had an alliance in political and economic terms; the military element was to appear later in the North Atlantic Treaty Organisation.

The Communist ideological offensive during these crucial years was not conducted in different areas at different times: several fronts were simultaneously in operation. In Germany and Greece the Communists were obstructed by the presence of British and American military forces. Elsewhere these were not present, thereby offering a possibility of success. This was especially true of France and Italy which, besides possessing the only significant Communist parties in Western Europe, were the least stable of the democracies: they were the weak link in the Western chain. In May 1947 Communist attempts to gain control by working from within the political system had come to an abrupt end when the parties were expelled from the governments. Isolated on the extreme left and quite often treated as pariahs, the Communists switched to a more aggressive policy of trying to immobilise the system from without. In the late 1940s this was a promising line to take: economic and social stability had yet to be achieved, and the Communists, as the principal consistent opposition, could hope to benefit from the discontent generated. In France and Italy until 1950 around 75 per cent of Marshall Aid could not be used for investment: it was needed to halt the downward slide of already extremely serious conditions. The prime agent of the Communist assault was to be the trade unions. The Communists had succeeded in providing the dominant leadership of the unions during the war. Afterwards they used the purges to dispose of people within the union federations who might have proved an obstacle to their plans. The union federations were a readymade instrument because historically they had not become involved in the political system: they had preferred to retain their independence and had developed the concept of the general strike as a weapon of direct action against the system. Traditionally, therefore, trade unionism had not operated to gain benefits for the workers from within the system, but had in essence been dedicated to the disruption and destruction of the system. In this they conformed closely to the projected Communist course of action.

In September 1947 the relationship between the major Communist parties in Western Europe and the Soviet Union became clearer when the latter re-established the old Third International. The name was changed from Comintern to Cominform, implying that the new body was no more than a clearing house for reciprocal information. But during this period the French and Italian parties were severely criticised for being too lax in the prosecution of their war against capitalism and bourgeois democracy. The result was that a more vigorous line was advocated within France and Italy by Thorez and Togliatti. Anti-Nazi patriotism was dead: in its place was a resolution exemplified by the following statement by Thorez to the French parliament in February 1949: 'If the Soviet army came to pursue an aggressor on our soil, the workers and the people of France could not act toward the Soviet army otherwise than the workers and the people of Poland, Rumania and Yugoslavia'.[1]

In France Thorez and his associates set out to wreck the national economy in November 1947. Through their control of the largest trade union federation they issued a call to the French working classes to rally round a revolutionary general strike and paralyse all major industries and communication networks. As non-Communist workers sometimes appeared reluctant to support their confrères, waves of violence and intimidation accompanied outbreaks of deliberate sabotage. The young Fourth Republic had to face its severest test. President Auriol strongly denounced the Communist activity. The government, including the Socialists, decided to meet the crisis by matching force with force. It announced that workers who persisted in prolonging the strike might well be deprived of all social security benefits. Since the

[1] Quoted in S. Neumann, ed., *Modern Political Parties*, Chicago, 1956, p. 123.

unions were not sufficiently wealthy to finance a long strike or to offer the workers any guarantee that they would replace the substantial benefits available under the existing social security system, this was a very serious threat. In addition, the Socialist Minister of the Interior did not hesitate to use army and police forces where necessary to re-establish law and order. The Communists were too weak to persuade the workers to withstand this double counter-attack. It was clear that they did not possess the resources to utilise the revolutionary situation to maximum advantage unless the government's will to resist had wavered. Within a month, many workers had returned to work, and on 10 December the general strike was called off. For the time being the crisis had been averted. The strike had caused a serious disruption in French production, but as soon as Marshall Aid money began to flow into the country the national economy and the franc began to stabilise themselves.

Having failed momentarily in France the Communist focus in Western Europe switched to Italy. Here the aim was not so much to cripple the country by strike action as to win power constitutionally through victory in the general election due to be held in April 1948. Communist hopes were high because of the proven electoral strength of the party in Italy and because of the example of the successful coup in Czechoslovakia in February. The Italian election campaign of 1948 still ranks as the stormiest in the country's history. The Communist campaign benefited greatly from the consistent support of the Socialists who under Nenni's guiding hand preferred to join a People's Bloc popular front rather than attempt to participate in the political system and help it to function. Opposing the People's Bloc were de Gasperi's Christian Democrats who led an alliance of the parties of the centre and the moderate right. The militancy of the Communists was counterbalanced by the militant role adopted by the Vatican, whose actions during this campaign were at times rather excessive. One of the more serious consequences of this was that, although helping to buttress the regime against a Communist takeover, it tied the Christian Democrats very closely to official Catholic opinion. Clerical domination was to loom as a leading issue in the 1950s and the party still has not succeeded in completely dissociating itself from confessional accusations. President Truman also weighed in and made it clear that the United States would not tolerate a Communist government in Italy. It was the first time that the American Government had actively sought to intervene in a European electoral contest. In the event Western fears proved to be unfounded. De Gasperi gained a convincing victory. The Christian Democrats alone won a majority in the Chamber of Deputies, although gaining only 49 per cent of the popular vote: wisely, de Gasperi sought to continue governing with the aid of his smaller allies. The People's Bloc, on the other hand, failed to break out of the 30 per cent barrier which was to be the high watermark of their efforts in subsequent elections. The Italian election was something of a relief for Western Europe. It was one of the first visible signs that international Communism could be halted.

The main Communist onslaught had been broken. Although an uneasy peace was not obtained for at least another year, those factors tending toward check and stalemate were already apparent. In July 1948 a Sicilian student attempted to assassinate the Italian Communist leader, Togliatti. When the news leaked out, spontaneous strikes broke out in the northern cities. The Communists, on the whole, were embarrassed by and unwilling to take advantage of the spontaneous action of their supporters. The Italian Government gave every indication of a determination to dispel the insurrectionary atmosphere by force; the Communists, on the other hand, knew that they did not have the means to transform the strikes into an effective revolution. These 1948 strikes had two consequences. First, they revealed in stark clarity the wide gulf between revolutionary utterances and the Italian Communists' real ability to act; and second, they weakened slightly the Communist grip on the unions as first Catholics and later Social Democrats broke away to form their own union federations. The strikes, therefore, fizzled out almost as swiftly as they began. Similar events occurred in France. A summons in the autumn of 1948 from the Communist leaders for a strike in the coal mines as a protest against the Marshall Plan failed completely. The workers were extremely reluctant to strike, and it was only a pale imitation of the revolutionary atmosphere of the previous year.

When the Communists called off the strike after eight weeks, over 80 per cent of the miners had already decided to return to work.

As 1948 drew to a close the Communist offensive had been contained by resolute Western action. In summing up the year's achievements, the Soviet leaders could see only a run of failures after the success in Czechoslovakia. After 1948 the Communist parties in France and Italy were no longer in a position to challenge seriously the constitutional regimes. Their approach was essentially negative: although no longer able to seize control, their size and presence could prevent the political system from firing on all cylinders. Ironically, the Communist presence and attitude was one of the fundamental premises for the movement of governments toward a more conservative expression.

No new constructive ideas were forthcoming; retreating to their own fortress the Communist attitude seemed to be 'what we have we hold at any price'. The price was to be a sacrifice of dynamism and mobility and a risk of appearing absurd in later economic situations when clearly Western Europe was enjoying great prosperity. This was particularly true of the more rigid French Communist Party. Communism became, if anything, more conservative than the conservatives. Their disciplined mass following could not be used for revolutionary ends, as a revolutionary situation and the Communists' own ability to utilise it became ever more remote. On the other hand, the Communist leaders did not dare to loosen their hold on their disciples. The result was that Communist activity more often than not was primarily concerned with retaining discipline, no matter how fantastic their outbursts and propaganda appeared in the light of solid economic facts. This drop into stagnation caught the parties in a hopeless dilemma. Committed to preserving a rigidly negative policy as the one having the least risk for Communist solidarity, they ran the gauntlet of having to answer to Moscow and the Cominform for failing to maintain efficiency and for allowing 'deviationist' and 'Titoist' tendencies to appear within the parties; at the same time Western pressure to neutralise them at least in the event of a war with Russia meant that a more active policy might endanger the party's security and existence, while increased Soviet pressure for greater activity in case of a war against the West handicapped any appeals to patriotism and encouraged dissidence among the rank and file. During the 1950s Communist movements were stretched further on the rack by the post-Stalin profession of competitive co-existence, and by the tensions generated by the consequent relaxation and modernisation of Russian life and policy, especially by its most tragic expression, the 1956 Hungarian uprising. The Sino-Soviet disagreements of the following decade and the invasion of Czechoslovakia in 1968 served to increase their agony.

By the end of 1948 the United States was stepping up the European Recovery Programme. The blockade was failing to drive the Allies out of Berlin. Short of open war with America the Russian ideological advance could not expand any further westward. But if open war was inadmissible because of American nuclear superiority, expansion would have to rely on the victory of internal Communism; and as we have seen, the possibility of this was becoming increasingly remote. Further east, the outflanking moves of Russian policy were also failing. The American guarantee and presence had stiffened Turkey's adamance, while the Greek Communist guerrillas were being steadily driven back until late in 1949 they finally surrendered. The latter's cause had become greatly weakened by the decision of Marshal Tito to break from the Soviet bloc and pursue a neutralist policy of national Communism. Yugoslavia's expulsion from Moscow's harmony of nations had deprived the Greek Communists of their essential supply line and base; thereafter they were fighting essentially a rearguard action.

Overall, the Cominform never became the force that it originally was intended to be. Its influence in European affairs west of the iron curtain was negligible, and consequently it was officially brought to an end in 1956 long after its value had expired. Thus, although the world situation was still tense and the atmosphere still black, the beginning of 1949 showed more promise and hope for Western European security and economic advancement than any Western political leader would have dared to hope for one year earlier.

NATO: The Military Alliance

As a further safeguard against Communist expansionism toward
the Atlantic, Western Europe moved early in 1949 toward the
formal military alliance that had already been implicit in much of
Western thought and action during the previous two years. The
Truman Doctrine had been only a generalised expression of an
American pledge to any individual country, while the Western
European nations themselves had advanced little further in the
military sphere than organising mutual aid treaties with one
another, such as the 1947 Treaty of Dunkirk between Britain
and France. These were, in any case, relatively few and unco-
ordinated. The greatest advance had been the 1948 Brussels
Treaty negotiated by Britain, France, and the Low Countries.
This treaty for collective self-defence was useless in that it was
specifically designed to thwart 'a renewal by Germany of an
aggressive policy': the real need now was a defence against Soviet
Russia, not Germany. Furthermore, arguments were already
appearing to suggest that the fledgling West German state should
be fully committed to the Western ideological alliance. On the
other hand, the Brussels Treaty was regarded by Bevin as an
interim measure until there could be constructed a collective
security system incorporating the United States.

What was required was a military and defensive equivalent of
the Marshall Plan and OEEC. Thus in April 1949 the representatives of twelve nations signed the Atlantic Pact. Under its terms
the United States and Canada agreed to enter a military agreement for the mutual defence of Western Europe. The European
nations concerned were Britain, France, Italy, Denmark, Norway,
the Netherlands, Belgium, and Luxembourg. In addition two
nations which had not been directly involved in the Second
World War, Portugal and Iceland, were signatories of the pact.
During the 1950s the new North Atlantic Treaty Organisation
was extended to embrace Greece, Turkey and the new state of
West Germany. Anti-Fascist feeling, especially in Britain,
debarred Spain's entry: Sweden and Switzerland preferred to
maintain their traditional neutrality, while Finland and Austria
were subsequently bound by international agreement to observe

the same course. Those who had desired a definite American commitment in Europe had had their wishes realised, for its 'essential novelty in 1949 lay in the fact that it brought the North American continent—the United States and Canada—into close association with Britain and Western Europe'.[1]

The new Atlantic alliance was not intended to pursue an aggressive policy; it was purely a defensive agreement, and was part of the wider American scheme to contain Communism on a world scale. Under the terms of the agreement the member states promised to provide military forces in all three armed services according to their means: the crucial element of the treaty was stated by Article Five of its charter:

The Parties agree that an armed attack against one or more of them in Europe or North America shall be considered an attack against them all; and consequently they agree, that if such an armed attack occurs, each of them, in exercise of the right of individual or collective self-defence recognised by Article 57 of the United Nations, will assist the Party or Parties so attacked by taking forthwith, individually and in concert with the other Parties, such action as it deems necessary, including the use of armed force, to restore and maintain the security of the North Atlantic area.

It was basically no more than an extension of the previous type of treaty that two nations would sign. At first glance, it would seem that commitment did not mean a firm guarantee of action. Nations need only take such steps as they deemed necessary, whereas the Brussels Treaty had guaranteed automatic military assistance: this clause had been included at the insistence of the United States, which did not want involvement without discretion. Since the United States would be the dominant party, and since American aid, both military and financial, was desired by Western Europe, the latter had to defer to American wishes on this point. Moreover, there was nothing in the agreement which specifically forbade members from decreasing their military and defence expenditure, or even from using NATO forces for other tasks. Both happened in the following decade: Britain's defence policy in the 1950s meant that it never gave NATO the required number of troops, while France's NATO contingents were usually

[1] Royal Institute of International Affairs, *Atlantic Alliance*, London, 1952, p. 1.

engaged in colonial struggles. The treaty was not particularly concerned with creating a formal structure of institutions: defence was its primary purpose. But in practice the degree of commitment was quite strong. Institutions did spring up extensively as it was discovered that the alliance could operate most satisfactorily when a complex structure of organs was in existence that provided for continuous consultation among the member states. The working of these institutions, despite many drawbacks, was such that it could later be suggested that NATO might well be an adequate base upon which one could establish European integration.

A common European army, or Atlantic army, was not the intention. Each country would provide its own battalions subject to orders from the NATO chain of command. Obviously, the dominant partner, in the sense of supplying the largest numbers of essential supplies and troops, would be the United States. Therefore it was logical for an American to become the overall commander of the alliance. Among the European nations, France promised to supply the largest ground contingent and was given the regional command of the central sector. The core of this new grand design for the protection of Western Europe was to be the defence of West Germany, seen by the West as the most obvious European target of the Soviet Union. For this reason American troops were to be stationed permanently in Germany and were to become the nucleus of an overall Allied force in West Germany that would eventually be built up to some fifty armed divisions. Given the acknowledged superiority of Russian conventional forces, the Allied commitment in Germany could not by itself hope to defeat or even halt a future juggernaut. It could, however, play a major rearguard action. In essence it was little more than a symbol of the Western determination to wage an all-out war rather than permit West Germany, the gateway to the west, to became a Russian satrap. For the whole of NATO strategy was built upon a belief in the superiority of American air power and an American monopoly for some time to come in nuclear weapons. The NATO ground troops in Europe were therefore primarily a second line of defence. According to the dominant way of thinking, the only war possible in Europe would be a total nuclear war. Until it could achieve parity in atomic weapons with the United States, Soviet Russia would not launch a full-scale assault on Western Europe: this would be a suicide course. In addition the Americans believed that Russia did not possess the level of defence necessary to check American air power striking deep in the heart of Russian territory. This strategic design lasted for only a few months. When Russia exploded its first atomic bomb late in 1949 America had to admit that Russia could achieve nuclear parity sooner than had been expected. Finally, when war broke out in Korea in 1950 signs were distressingly clear that the Soviet Union might very well be prepared to risk the conse-quences of total war. Even if one rejected this assumption, the main alternative was equally distressing. Although it could be suggested that, having been baulked in Europe, Russia was merely changing the arena of conflict, one implication was that war in Asia or elsewhere could place defence priorities upon Western Europe that the still fragile economies might not be capable of weathering. In other words, it might still lead to an economic collapse that could benefit only Russia.

In itself, the Atlantic alliance could not provide an ideological basis for a Western European political, social, and economic federation. But taken together with the Marshall Plan it did encourage trends in this direction. During this period official American opinion had taken a positive stand on European union and attempted to promote and encourage all movements and ideas directed toward this end. President Truman and his adminis-tration became more closely involved in European affairs than any other American government before or since. Before, American foreign policy was influenced and checked by isolationist ten-dencies: in any case, Europe would not have welcomed anything resembling American 'interference' in its own affairs. Afterwards, the Eisenhower administration retracted somewhat from a close involvement in Europe, while during President Eisenhower's term of office Europe was becoming stronger and more sensitive about its independence, so that it was advisable for American foreign policy in Europe not to pursue a too blunt approach.

As a first step toward the establishment of some form of European union, Truman and his advisers hoped to see a comprehensive coalition of moderate parliamentary forces governing the European democracies. This hypothetical coalition was termed the 'third force' (as, for example, the erratic third force coalitions in France upholding the Fourth Republic against threats from the two extremes of Communism and Gaullism). And it was hoped that this would lead Western Europe away from close contact with Communism, but at the same time that it would prevent the reaction swinging so far as to encourage a return of the excesses of right-wing authoritarianism.

Western Europe At Home

During the closing years of the decade this policy of the United States and the efforts of the European governments themselves appeared to be winning the battle for Western Europe. Signs of stability were already apparent. Economically, Marshall Aid and government policies had put the countries on a reasonably sound fiscal basis: the worst problems seemed to have been overcome, at least temporarily, and some sort of control had been asserted over inflation. Politically, the outlook was bright. Except for France right-wing authoritarianism remained weak (and in France it flourished as a danger only because of the charismatic and unifying figure of de Gaulle); at the other extreme Communism had been checked and isolated.

European governments, therefore, appearing to be masters in their own homes, could spare some attention for a consideration of their relationships with other nations. Rapport between the major continental powers was high because of this relative stability and because governmental policy was directed and heavily influenced by men who, all internationally oriented, possessed basically the same general political beliefs. The ideological bond was that in Germany, France, and Italy, the men primarily responsible for the direction of foreign policy were all Christian Democrats and were therefore affected strongly by the universal nature of Catholicism.

In West Germany Dr Adenauer embarked upon his career as Chancellor, which was destined to be the longest in German history. In 1949 Adenauer was not firmly in the saddle as the

Christian Democrat leader. The party still reflected the factionalism caused by its decentralised federal origins. But as Chancellor, Adenauer had a great advantage over all his CDU rivals. Adenauer's was a strong-willed nature, and he combined this with the possibilities for strong rule which the 1949 Basic Law offered the Chancellor to create for himself a position of leadership which could rarely be effectively challenged from within Germany. In Italy, Alcide de Gasperi occupied much the same position. After his success in the 1948 election de Gasperi headed a coalition of Christian Democrats and three small democratic parties. The decision of these parties to enter the government rather than merely lending it their support in the Chamber of Deputies was forced upon them by de Gasperi's electoral triumph and by their fear of being isolated from all the larger political movements. Such a coalition was also advisable from the smaller parties' point of view in that it helped de Gasperi to remain more or less at the centre of the wide range of political attitudes contained within Italian Christian Democracy, to maintain a centrist policy line, and to continue in his efforts to present Christian Democracy to the electorate and the outside world as a political movement that was not merely a subordinate appendage of the Vatican. De Gasperi was able to maintain this quadripartite Italian version of the 'third force' for five years. The high degree of consensus which it engendered enabled the government to attempt a positive legislative programme and to consolidate the efforts of reconstruction. France, on the other hand, was in a less advantageous position in that the old game of creating and then immediately afterwards baulking and defeating governments had resumed full sway. However, with Communism and right-wing authoritarianism still held at bay the choice of governments had to come from the relatively narrow sector of the third force, the moderate parties of the centre and the democratic right and left. The French MRP occupied a central position in this sector, and thus was an indispensable element of any French government during this period. Part of the reasonably successful prosecution of a fairly consistent French policy, at least in foreign affairs, lay in the fact that the MRP, in the shape of only two of its leaders, Georges Bidault and Robert Schuman, provided the foreign minister of the Fourth Republic for the whole of the first post-war decade apart from only one or two extremely short periods. Schuman, by far the more influential of the two, had also served briefly as head of the government before moving to the Foreign Office, but it is for his activities in the latter post that he is chiefly remembered.

This common ideological background meant common views on domestic and foreign policy. In domestic affairs, only de Gasperi and Adenauer were sufficiently strong and headed their governments for a sufficient span of time to impose their formulae upon their respective countries. Christian Democracy, born largely out of the experiences of Fascist rule and its consequences, still possessed a strong reforming wing, of which Adenauer and de Gasperi had to take cognisance. However, the views of both these men were steadily becoming more conservative, and this corresponded to a similar trend within their parties as a whole. Nevertheless, the Christian Democrat leaderships did focus their attention upon urgent social problems.

Adenauer in Germany bowed to pressure from Catholic trade unionists and his own left wing for legislation that would allow the workers to participate in the direction of their industries. Adenauer and his government colleagues were extremely reluctant to embark upon a novel course of action so remote from their own fundamentally conservative inclinations. Persistent pressure, however, from the social reformers in the CDU and from the opposition Social Democrats, coupled with the threat of strike action by the metal workers' union, easily the most powerful in the country, proved to be too strong, and the government had to divorce their action from their sympathy with the employers' associations, who were opposed to the whole idea. The result was the 'codetermination' law of 1951 which stated that organised labour should have representatives on the managing boards of the iron, steel, and coal industries. Codetermination was a hallowed principle of German trade unionists; it could trace its history back to 1849. After 1945 it had been helped by the Allied determination to break the large German cartels and by the British Labour Government which, sympathetic toward the idea, had already permitted the experiment to begin in its occupation zone, which included the Ruhr, Germany's largest industrial complex.

In practice the scheme was never as successful as appeared possible on paper. The managements adapted themselves to the new situation fairly easily. Open conflicts between management and labour were comparatively rare, but where they did occur, the management usually won because it maintained a united front, while the labour representatives were often divided. More often disputes of this nature were avoided through the development of techniques for merely postponing or circumventing the problem: this type of action succeeded because the two sides had tacitly agreed to divide rather than share power and responsibility. Organised labour was given its own bailiwick in which it was supreme, and it was expected not to intrude in those sectors of administration reserved for the management. Above all, co-determination failed to achieve the precise level of success expected of it because of the problems of finding suitably qualified workers to act as labour representatives on the directing boards and because of reluctance on the part of some capable workers to assume this new post and responsibility when it was offered to them.

The following year proposals were made to extend the practice of codetermination throughout the whole of German industry. It had proved to be a not very great threat to the employers. In fact, some argued that having workers' representatives on the directing boards gave extra advantages to the employers. At any rate, the conservative opposition to codetermination, now possessing greater political strength, was not as vehement as in 1951, and actually worked to obtain a codetermination law that would reduce further the official powers of the labour representatives: this was the general impact of the new law of 1952. Nevertheless, the fact that labour was now represented on managerial boards was significant; gradually these representatives acquired some knowledge and appreciation of the problems involved and were in a stronger position to work for industrial concord between management and labour. As for the main objective of organised labour, that codetermination would prevent industrial finance and influence being appropriated for disapproved political objectives, only an examination after an appreciable period of time has elapsed can give a good indication of success or failure.

The most pressing social problem facing West Germany was that of the poverty-stricken individual. The so-called German miracle of economic expansion had begun only slowly in 1949 after the Allies had carried through the much needed currency reform the previous year. A large percentage of the native population had lost most of their possessions during the war, and this deficit had not yet been made up. In addition the West German authorities faced the problem of assimilating the German expellees from Poland and Czechoslovakia, and refugees from Eastern Germany. To help the dispossessed, the Adenauer government passed an 'equalisation of burdens' law. The purpose of the law was to impose a temporary additional tax on those who had escaped severe losses in the war. The proceeds were to be re-distributed on a large scale to the less fortunate in an effort to equalise the amount of personal discomfort, to help the economy to gain greater strength, and to assimilate the refugees into the society and so prevent them being attracted toward extreme political solutions and ideas. This policy of social equalisation was a typical expression of Christian Democratic ideas on how to diminish disparities between social classes.

Similar ideas were pursued by de Gasperi in Italy to cope with similar problems. The special instance here was massive agrarian depression. In rural Italy, poverty and unemployment were virtually the only permanent characteristics of the society. Remedies had been demanded by the Resistance, and again had been part of de Gasperi's 1948 election manifesto. But the immobilist tendencies of the Italian system had so far prevented any positive action. By 1949, however, the Christian Democrats were ready to present a draft programme. The first stage took a further year before it was ready to be put into action. This stage planned for one million acres of land belonging to large estates that was not already being used at all or to its full extent to be appropriated by the government for redistribution to the peasants who would be allowed to buy the land over a period of thirty years before becoming the fully legal occupiers.

The act only scratched the surface of the problem; it did not even approach the scope demanded by the Resistance or the level originally planned by de Gasperi. It was hailed, none the less, as the beginning of a programme of social justice in an attempt to lessen the gap in living standards between the landed gentry and the peasants, and between the industrial north and the rural south. Socially, it may have been a progressive move; economically it was negative. Although intended to cut the economic gulf between the relatively prosperous north and the backward south, it did not prevent this gulf from widening further. In addition, by distributing the land in small lots to individual families, it did nothing to assist a trend toward large-scale agriculture, which was necessary if the agricultural economy was to be viable in the modern world. Originally, it may have shown that the Christian Democrats were at least willing to tackle a problem that for long had bedevilled Italian politics, but it was virtually one of the last positive actions taken by the Christian Democrats. It soon became submerged in petty party jealousies and squabbles as the Christian Democrats struggled to maintain some form of inner cohesiveness. In the event, less than one-half of the land included in the programme (known as the Southern Italy Fund) was actually given to the depressed peasants. The whole project foundered in the determination of elements within the Christian Democrat Party to direct it without any outside interference: the public works programmes implicit in the plan would be crucial political factors and local politicians wished some influence over who was appointed in their area and how much finance would be directed to it.

No comparable legislation was passed in France. Governments changed too often, and a party's influence within the governments waxed and waned too rapidly for any long-term or serious problems to be broached. This deficiency, admittedly grave, was not as serious as might first appear. France had already seen important legislation passed under the late tripartite governments, and in the Monnet Plan had an overall economic scheme which West Germany and Italy still lacked. The plan was only changed by the new third force to accommodate what few general principles they could all accept and the general outline of economic recovery demanded by the Marshall Plan. Robert

Schuman, therefore, who only had eight months as prime-minister, was unable to stamp his individuality on any far-reaching legislation. If this had been his only important term of office, Schuman would be remembered only as an average leading politician of the Fourth Republic, but he was later able to direct the French Foreign Ministry for five years. During this period he was able to plan French foreign policy on a long-term basis. He conceived French foreign policy as being only part of a wider scheme of European union, and it is in the field of European union that Schuman put forward his claim to be remembered as a leading European statesman.

The Schuman Plan

Schuman was well qualified to attempt some form of reconciliation among European nations. Born in Lorraine he had naturally been a German citizen before 1918 and hence spoke German fluently: during the First World War he had even served in the Kaiser's army. De Gasperi possessed a similar background. His origins lay in the German-speaking South Tyrol, and when that region belonged to the Austro-Hungarian Empire he had been a representative in the Austrian parliament. German, therefore, was a common language of the three leading continental statesmen. To balance the picture, Adenauer had been accused in the 1920s of being pro-French; he had been suspected of favouring the French claims for annexing the Rhineland. Now he saw West Germany's greater need as being accepted as an equal by the other Western democracies. The most dramatic way of achieving this acceptance would be a *rapprochement* with the traditional enemy, France. And this could best come about by German support of the schemes for European cooperation and union.

During this period an impetus toward such schemes was given by the fact that governments were no longer forced to concentrate their attention solely on domestic economic problems. The first two years of the Marshall Plan were achieving the desired results. The United States during this period gave eight billion dollars of aid to Western Europe; the lagging European economies could not fail to respond to such a stimulus. By 1950 the West

German miracle was under way. Italy and France, which had had the most severe problems, had pushed their production outputs up until at long last they stood above prewar figues. Overall, production in Western Europe rose by nearly one-quarter; in this massive increase in productivity, the steel industry, the basis of any industrial society, was looking particularly healthy.

The administration of the Marshall Plan through OEEC was giving Western Europe a first lesson in European cooperation. Those people, such as the veteran Italian Foreign Minister, Count Carlo Sforza, who favoured closer forms of European integration, were encouraged by the success of both the administration of the Marshall Plan and its results to press on with their own proposals for further cooperation. It was Robert Schuman who cut through all objections and hesitations. In May 1950 he made the dramatic suggestion that coal and steel resources in Western Europe should be pooled and jointly administered by the nations and a supranational authority. The draft of the Schuman Plan was the basis of all future discussions on how European integration should be organised. The plan also suggested that all tariffs in these heavy industries should be gradually eliminated. In April 1952 representatives of the six nations—France, West Germany, Italy, the Netherlands, Belgium, Luxembourg—who were to become the nucleus of future integratory moves in Western Europe signed a treaty which formally established the European Coal and Steel Community (ECSC). The treaty allowed a transition period of five years, at the end of which the formula would be fully operative. The transition period was necessary both to iron out problems and differences that would inevitably arise and to allow the industries within each country to rationalise themselves and to come to terms with the new and radically different situation. The ECSC is important in that it marks the first significant step toward European union that went beyond being merely consultative and national in character.

7 Integration: The Postwar Beginning

Tacit and intellectual consent are insufficient if we are to build Europe. We must have results.

Paul-Henri Spaak[1]

As we have seen, the idea of European unity received a major impetus during and immediately after the Second World War. Its previous long story of failure seemed to be offered its best yet opportunity of coming to a successful conclusion. Between the world wars several organisations had worked for European unity. Perhaps the most notable of these was the Pan-European Union founded by Count Coudenhove-Kalergi in 1922. The period, however, was still dominated by the concept of the nation state, and these movements were forced to labour in the wilderness.

The Opening Gambits

The turning point came around 1943. The various Resistance movements were about that time developing suggestions and plans for the postwar future, among which schemes for European unification occupied a prominent position. After the war private movements proliferated. In Britain, for example, there was the United Europe Movement; in France Edouard Herriot, who in 1930 had written a book called *The United States of Europe*, headed the French Council for Europe; while in defeated Germany several groups combined to form the Europa-Bund. Internationally, the European Union of Federalists was established in 1946, to be superseded two years later by the European Movement which enjoyed the leadership of Winston Churchill, Léon Blum, and Alcide de Gasperi—a disparate mixture of Conservatism, Socialism and moderate Christian Democracy which nevertheless emphasised the widespread appeal of the ideal. There were,

[1] Council of Europe, *The First Five Years*, Strasbourg, 1954, p. 22.

naturally, differences of opinion between those of right- and left-wing inclination, but these tended to be overruled by the general desire to have the conception practically adopted.

The motivations for seeking an integrated Europe were equally various. Germany, for example, supported the idea because democratic politicians saw it as the most obvious road towards acceptance by their neighbours as an independent and responsible nation. Italy, the other defeated Axis power, supported integration because it might help to check the political instability caused by a large Communist party, and because the opening of broader economic markets might help to decrease substantially its permanent labour surplus. But for most countries, the crucial question was whether or not Britain would become a committed member of any European organisation. Scandinavia was unwilling to enter any commitments without Britain, while France and the Low Countries regarded British partnership as indispensable for ensuring some form of security against a recurrence of German militancy and against the threat of Soviet dreams of European hegemony. There was above these narrower national reasons the wider implications of the war. Russia and the United States had developed into 'super-powers' against which the nation states of Europe could not hope to compete unless through an effort of maximum cooperation. War-time devastation implied that economic cooperation was advisable, if not imperative, if the proposed reconstruction programmes were to be successful. The importance of Britain in this respect can be illustrated by economic statistics. After 1945 British steel production, for example, was more than two-thirds of the combined total of the other future OEEC members, while Britain's coal output nearly equalled that of the other OEEC states. There was contained within the optimism of the immediate postwar years a grain of scepticism concerning the value of a comprehensive international organisation.

One difference between 1919 and 1945 was the European attitude toward international organisations. There were many in 1945 who doubted the ability of a world organisation to succeed; in 1919, on the contrary, enthusiasts had hailed the League of Nations as a panacea. However the concept of regionalism was regarded as possessing a great amount of validity. Protagonists of European unity argued that integration on the continent was realistic and inherently valuable, as well as being an important foundation for and a major step toward a world organisation. Finally, there was the threat of Soviet Russia. It is perhaps a truism that countries and people who might otherwise stay apart flock together when confronted by a common external danger. This danger is the catalyst which serves both to define Europe as an entity (no less now than in the past) and to create within it some general working principles. Communist Russia has since 1945 been an admirable catalyst; its role in the development of European integration, although negative, has been considerable. Some evidence of this attitude of expediency toward European union still remains, and at this point it may be remarked that European integration, especially political union, will never achieve a properly stable basis until it dispenses entirely with this negative or defensive impetus. The latter undoubtedly has fulfilled an important short-term function; its long-term effect could be catastrophic.

In 1945 the United States, by virtue of overwhelming military strength, wartime participation, and recognition of its global responsibilities, may have been a European power, but was not and could not be a European nation. It could encourage integratory moves, but not lead them directly. During the hostilities Britain had provided the European lead, and because of her wartime role she was recognised as having the reasons and the opportunity to bring about some kind of unity. And both inside and outside Britain the hopes of the European federalists were focused on the charismatic leader of wartime Britain, Winston Churchill.

It was accepted that during the war Churchill had become an ardent federalist. While leaders of prewar pan-European organisations, like Coudenhove-Kalergi, were forced to spend the war in captivity or exile, Churchill kept the flame of union alight. It was he who in 1940, just before the total collapse of France, had dramatically proposed an Anglo-French Union (which was turned down by the French Government). Throughout the war he returned to the theme of pan-Europe. In March 1943, for example, he gave a broadcast which emphasised the need for a

Council of Europe with an effective network of working institutions beneath it; these even included a common military organisation. Consequently the federalists were shocked and disheartened by the result of the 1945 British general election. Although Churchill might still agitate for union there could be no guarantee that the new Labour Government would display an enthusiastic interest in this field.

Churchill did continue to argue for European integration. A major break through the barricades of traditionalism occurred in September 1946, when Churchill, speaking at the University of Zurich, ranged widely through the whole field of unity, arguing that it was imperative to establish a United States of Europe. Churchill's speech was important in that it was his most significant discussion of pan-Europe since losing the British premiership. It had the results of spurring the federalists to greater efforts, of stimulating existing bodies to increase their activity and to seek more converts, and of inspiring the creation of new organisations. Besides those national organisations already mentioned, there were also several movements in which membership was defined not by nationality but by the profession of a particular political conviction or ideology. For example, there was the Nouvelles Équipes Internationales which worked among Catholics in France and Belgium. Similarly there was the Mouvement Socialiste pour les États Unis d'Europe which was active in France, Belgium and Luxembourg, though this organisation met serious competition from the non-party but socialist-inclined European Union of Federalists which had branches in France, the Netherlands, Belgium, and Italy. As indicated earlier, the most significant difference between these groups and their prewar equivalents was that the former enjoyed considerable sympathy among parliamentarians in several countries, as well as occasionally counting government ministers among their membership.

The British Labour Government watched these proceedings cautiously. The burst of enthusiasm was too strong to be denied entirely. Still under the aegis of Churchill, the various organisations agreed to establish an International Committee of the Movements for European Unity in December 1947: this committee was directed by Duncan Sandys. Its object was to make arrangements for a congress of all those interested in federation to impress observers with the vitality and practicality of their cause. In due course the arrangements were made, and the Congress of Europe was held at The Hague in May 1948. The Congress was an impressive display of the widespread interest in the ideal. There were 663 delegates from sixteen European democracies, as well as observers from Canada, the United States, and Eastern European countries (most of these, however, were refugees). All political inclinations except Communism and the extreme right were represented; many influential political leaders were also absent. The Congress itself was too unwieldy and too disparate to achieve any practical measure of success, but it did emphasise the interest in unification and justify its meeting by suggesting ways in which the movement could be carried forward and the ideal translated into reality. It was at this point that British leadership, now represented solely by Churchill, his associates, and his previous utterances, began to disappear from the federalist movement.

Churchill himself had not been notably concerned with translating the general principle into practical realities. He had been, perhaps deliberately, rather ambiguous. His speeches had not been concerned fundamentally with 'Britain cum the Continent', but with 'Britain and the Continent'. Like most British politicians he had seen European unity as a valuable ideal. But Britain did not have to be part of this unity; it could only be associated with it. The fundamental British attitude had already been summed up nearly twenty years earlier, when Churchill himself had written: 'We see nothing but good and hope in a richer, freer, more contented European commonalty. But we have our own dream and our own task. We are with Europe, but not of it. We are linked, but not compromised. We are interested and associated, but not absorbed.' Until the 1960s this was the reality of an intransigent British attitude.

And yet the various movements—brash or hesitating—towards integration in the late 1940s all looked to Britain for leadership, and all revolved around the hope that Britain would be absorbed. On the other hand, British political leaders concentrated primarily on what Churchill had called their own dream and their own task. This had two parts. First, there was the commitment to the Commonwealth, and second, there was the 'special' Anglo-American relationship which had flowered to its fullest between Churchill and Roosevelt. It is a mistake to regard the development of European communities as the outcome of a continuing argument between Britain and the continent; yet in a way it is a simple but effective method of analysing the subject since Britain was the leading spokesman for a particular point of view. Both views had protagonists in the countries which desired closer union, and even among British politicians and those who followed Britain—in Scandinavia, for example—there were several divergent views. The essence of the debate, in general terms, was whether people desired a European community or a broader Atlantic community that would include the United States and hence, it was argued, would be a more effective organisation in the ideological struggle against Communism. In this formative period of European union the role of Britain was crucial, for it was the only major protagonist caught between the diverging claims of the Atlantic and the continent.

The official British policy was to establish a number of mutual aid pacts with other European democracies. The first and in the event the only such pact was the Treaty of Dunkirk of March 1947, signed by Britain and France. Although the pact provided for bilateral economic assistance and cooperation, its justification was primarily military. The Treaty of Dunkirk was primarily designed as a military alliance against any future German aggression. As such, it was a totally inadequate instrument to deal with the realities of the postwar world.

By 1948 the time seemed more propitious for attempting to pull Britain into a pan-European orbit. The Labour Government, which had been further hostile to British involvement in union, first because it might hinder what the party might in future consider to be necessary economic controls inside Britain, and, second, because its markedly anti-Communist nature might make accommodation with the East more difficult, appeared to be more willing to listen to European overtures. It had finally rejected the hope of a working arrangement with Soviet Russia. In the House of Commons the Foreign Secretary, Ernest Bevin, declared that further steps should be taken. This may have inspired some pro-federalists to hope for a renewed British leadership, but the farthest Bevin wished to go was an effective interlocking system of bilateral treaties along the lines of the Treaty of Dunkirk. However, with Germany still an occupied country, only France could enter into a defensive treaty with Britain with some semblance of a claim to equality; for the rest, the onus would be on Britain.

The extension of Dunkirk came in a slightly different context. Bevin negotiated with France and the Benelux countries to enter into a cooperative arrangement. The result was the Treaty of Brussels signed in March 1948 by Britain, France, the Netherlands, Belgium, and Luxembourg. The Brussels Treaty was seen by Britain as a practical basis for cooperation, but not union; at the same time Bevin reiterated his warning against what he regarded as excessively ambitious hopes of integration. The Brussels pact was basically of a military nature, again with Germany specifically stated as the possible antagonist: in this area it was to be overtaken and absorbed by the creation of NATO. But it also contained provisions for 'economic, social, and cultural collaboration'. The general direction of its affairs would only be an intergovernmental arrangement, being handled by a committee of the foreign ministers concerned. It seems clear that the British leaders, at least, did not envisage an institutional body, yet some form of organisation proved necessary to enable its functions to be carried out.

Bevin saw the Brussels agreement gradually being widened, eventually to cover the whole of Western Europe, but each step forward would have to be thoroughly tested and the overall character of the structure at every stage would be one of intergovernmental cooperation, not supranational authority. However, there were already signs that the Brussels organisation was running away from the British idea. The enthusiasm which was aroused by the Hague Congress was one indication that the British attitude was in danger of becoming somewhat isolated. At the Congress ideas and views ranged from those wishing a weak form of confederation to those demanding the establishment of a fully sovereign supranational authority. Even within the anti-federalist forces the British idea of a close association with the United States and American leadership of an Atlantic alliance faced opposition from those who argued for a 'third force', or a cooperative European military arrangement without American involvement; in 1946 General de Gaulle had already made it clear that he favoured this path.

Despite British disapproval, ardent federalists of the European Movement hoped to be able to utilise the Brussels agreement as a springboard for their ambitions. They were assisted by the changing international atmosphere. The increasing intensity of the Cold War had made the United States even more desirous of a stable and effective European partner; an integrated Europe was seen as being capable of achieving this level. Before 1939 America had been hostile to integration as being injurious to the American economy. By now official British policy was moving into total opposition. It is perhaps ironical that Britain was mainly responsible for releasing a tiger which later proved un-controllable. It again resorted to its previously tried formula of proposing a counter-resolution that would serve as a compromise. The formula was to suggest that European foreign ministers should form a semipermanent committee that would meet at intervals to discuss problems of a common concern, except economic problems which after April 1948 were the province of the OEEC, and defence which would be the province of the pro-posed military body that became known as NATO. It was clear to the pro-Europeans that Britain had not renounced its convic-tion that anything more than a purely intergovernmental system of cooperation and consultation would be undesirable.

But the force of opinion against Britain and its supporters (notably Ireland and Scandinavia) was gaining strength. By October 1948 Britain yielded to the pressure for a European Assembly to the extent of reluctantly endorsing the establishment of a study commission on the subject. An Assembly was regarded as a major step toward full integration, but its supporters were still desirous of British participation. In order both to placate and lure British opinion the study commission issued a report in January 1949 which suggested that a new organisation could and should have both a consultative and debating assembly and a council of ministers: in this way national governments could be brought into the supranational field. After further discussion Britain agreed to the proposal. It was finally settled that the ministers should discuss affairs in private, but that Assembly debates would be public. These discussions were the nucleus of the Council of Europe.

The British idea was still, in Bevin's words, to ensure that the proposed structure would be 'as little embarrassing as possible'.[1] In view of the past it is not surprising, and in view of the future it is significant, that Britain still tended to remain aloof from Europe and to consider itself the link *par excellence* between Europe and the United States. It is important to stress that these developments were not simply a confrontation between Britain and the continent, but whereas federalist sympathies were widespread on the continent, they gained little foothold in Britain, which by virtue of its importance was the leading Western European opponent of supranationalism. Notwithstanding these events, in May 1949, one month after the establishment of NATO, the Statute of the Council of Europe was signed in London, and arrangements were made for the organisation to establish permanent offices in Strasbourg. Its supporters regarded it as a happy augury that on the same day the Soviet Union finally called off the Berlin blockade. With the federalist implications of its opening article, that 'the aim of·the Council of Europe is to achieve a greater unity between its Members for the purpose of safeguarding and realising the ideals and principles which are their common heritage and facilitating their economic and social progress', the new body became Western Europe's first postwar political organisation.

Political Association: the Council of Europe

In August 1949 the Consultative Assembly of the Council of Europe held its first session in Strasbourg. The ardent federalists immediately set out to make the new body a more effective organ of union than was apparent in its charter. To this end they had two objectives: first, to develop some semblance of supra-

[1] Lord Strang, *Home and Abroad*, London, 1956, p. 290.

national authority, and, second, to strengthen the Assembly in its relationships with the Committee of Ministers. For the creation of the Council of Europe had not in any degree diminished national sovereignty as represented by the ministers. The aims of the Council were to be achieved by 'discussion of questions of common concern and by agreements and common action in economic, social, cultural, scientific, legal and administrative matters and in the maintenance and further realisation of human rights and fundamental freedoms'. Defence was omitted because of its controversial nature, because of the NATO discussions, and because neutral countries—Sweden, Ireland, and later Austria and Switzerland—had become members. It will be seen that the aims are generalised. The article gives the Council a wide field of reference, but at the same time limits it rather severely, for it is to be expected that any international body would minimally agree to a framework of discussion and agreement. It was essentially a continuation of the traditional functional approach. The Council of Europe itself could not move forward to a supranational or federalist structure. This is not to say that it could not encourage efforts in this direction: in later years this became a primary function of the Council. Before we assess the achievements of the Council of Europe we should perhaps briefly examine its structure to see the drawbacks that did exist.

There are no surprises or novelties about the Committee of Ministers. It is basically little more than a conference of foreign ministers that meets twice yearly. Since 1952 it has adopted the practice of permitting deputies to fulfil a minister's functions: these have acquired a permanent nature, like United Nations' deputies, and usually attend to all business except that of a highly important nature. Most decisions on policy require a unanimous vote. This is extremely important in that it has given reluctant members, particularly those sceptical about closer union, the right of a veto. There is, however, an important loophole which allows members to pursue a policy without requiring the assent or co-operation of the remainder. This loophole was not used directly until 1956 with the creation of a European Settlement Fund. And it is significant that the most radical innovations initiated by the

Six, for example the establishment of ECSC, have been carried out outside the framework of the Council of Europe and its Committee of Ministers. Further, the Committee is in no sense of the word an executive body. Its powers in no way approach the scope of its functions. In relaying decisions to the member national governments it can only recommend; its decisions are authoritative only when related to its internal organisation. Thus it can be seen that the Committee of Ministers is not a novel institution. Nevertheless, even within its limited situation, it possesses a great degree of flexibility, leaving members to go their own way whenever national reasons dictate a strictly national path.

The Assembly, on the other hand, has been a much more radical and imaginative body. Since 1951 its membership has been determined by the national parliaments, although other methods are possible. It is still possible, for example, for direct suffrage to be applied to enable the Assembly to become a true European parliament. One interesting point is that more or less from the outset delegates displayed some tendencies to congregate in party groupings in debates rather than along national lines. In view of the behaviour of the assemblies created later by the members of ECSC and EEC this behaviour is interesting and was the first pointer to the possibility that national differences could be submerged and 'European parties' established. Again, the Assembly does not possess powers which match its functions. The basis of its existence is essentially deliberation. It can only offer recommendations to the Committee of Ministers and cannot bind the latter in any way. It has, however, achieved some success in winning more control over its own affairs and it did gain the right to discuss questions of European defence. The essential point is that just as the Committee of Ministers is not a true executive body, the Assembly is weakened by not being a true legislative body.

Partly because of the restrictions on action and scope, the relationship between the Assembly and the Committee of Ministers has usually been rather uneasy and strained. This was also precipitated by the divergent attitudes of the two bodies which reflect their different bases. The Assembly has been composed of people who are interested in Europe and the idea of unity, while the ministers have first and foremost been members of national governments to whom they are primarily responsible. The Assembly has been prepared to initiate radical ideas about which the ministers have often reserved grave doubts: initiative has been juxtaposed with traditionalism and disinterest. Despite the introduction of a liaison committee in 1950, little common ground appeared between the two sides. All this has frustrated the Assembly whose major proposals have involved the idea of a greater European unity.

The frustrations and tensions exhibited by the Council of Europe can only be attributed to its structure and the political forces that determined it. The design had been influenced greatly by the negative British attitude. The pro-Europeans on the continent had reluctantly compromised as much as possible in order to ensure that Britain came into the organisation. Britain's willingness to compromise had been far less marked. The end result was that the Council of Europe was in no position to advance by itself the concept of European union to any great length.

The complete failure of federal projects within the Council was evident by the time of its second session, held in 1950. This had several farreaching effects. First, the British entry into the Council had led many to accept that Britain was prepared to move further along the European path. They were soon disillusioned: Britain still refused to accept anything above a loose intergovernmental structure. The effort to placate Britain therefore came to an end. Henceforth attempts to achieve a modicum of unity would take place more or less regardless of the British attitude. Second, it tended to downgrade the Council of Europe. Support for it declined fairly rapidly, particularly in France, when it was seen that the Council was turning into a regional version of the United Nations Assembly and Security Council. Many former ardent supporters were willing now to regard it only as a symbol of European unity and of better things to come. They argued that the Council had value and power only as an instrument of and sounding-board for public opinion.

The Council of Europe still exists and within its limited terms of reference has reason to be proud of the work it has done since its inception. It has always been active in the field of European integration. It has sponsored other European organs, such as the European Convention for the Protection of Human Rights and Fundamental Freedoms in 1950. After the creation of ECSC, which it endorsed, it saw an outlet for its creativity in proposing European authorities to cover other economic and social sectors such as transport in 1953, civil aviation in 1954, and agriculture in 1955 (although this latter body was organised within the confines of OEEC, since Switzerland and Portugal, who were not members of the Council, were participants). It has similarly exerted itself to establish working relationships with other international organisations, so much so that the Council of Europe became a kind of central clearing house for cooperation and coordination. Other European organisations—OEEC, Western European Union (WEU), ECSC—as well as several United Nations bodies send reports to the Council of Europe. The first serious danger to it came with the creation of ECSC outside its boundaries, since there was a possibility that the six participants might well decide to sever their membership of the Council. This danger happily did not arise. The ECSC nations continued to appear in the Council, and it still remains an organisation in which nearly all the democracies of Western Europe are represented. Because of this last fact it possesses value as a forum for ideas and national views, and it is this which has probably done a great deal to prevent it being completely submerged by later unifying developments. Perhaps the major significance of the Council of Europe rests in the fact that it was the first European organisation with a political flavour to be established. As such it is an important milestone on the road to the closer association of the Common Market principles. The European Union of Federalists, whilst recognising its shortcomings, emphasised this particular value of the Council: 'The first session of the Council . . . marked at the same time a beginning and an end. It marked the beginning of a real and organic cooperation between the nations of Europe; it marked the end of the illusion that the aim of European unity can be achieved without political machinery on a supranational level.'[1]

[1] European Union of Federalists, *From the Powerless Consultative Assembly to a European Pact*, London, p. 4.

Economic Cooperation: OEEC

At this point a few words should be spent on the first postwar efforts to integrate and rationalise the various European economies which reached fruition one year before the Council of Europe was established. But first it should be mentioned that the honour of being the first postwar economic arrangement, indeed the first postwar integrative organisation of any kind, belongs to Benelux, the economic grouping of Belgium, the Netherlands, and Luxembourg. The agreement to come together as an economic unit was made by the exiled governments during the war. This decision was put into practice in 1946, and two years later the first fruits of the war-time agreement were apparent with the removal of customs duties and the establishment of a common external tariff. When the wider OEEC structure began to operate Benelux was treated as one country. By 1958 it was reported that Benelux trade had tripled in value.

This type of decision and planning could be introduced without much difficulty into such a compact, relatively homogeneous unit as the Benelux states. The obstacles facing the introduction of such a scheme over the wider area of Western Europe, however, were tremendous. Yet the creation of the Organisation for European Economic Cooperation was an ambitious step in this direction. The roots of OEEC lie in the havoc caused by the Second World War and the quite obvious postwar conclusions that pressed with ever more urgency upon statesmen that the nations of Western Europe could not achieve the necessary degree of economic reconstruction and stability by their own efforts.

The upshot of this conclusion was the decision by the American Government to offer financial assistance to the whole of Europe. On 5 June 1947 George Marshall, the American Secretary of State, made this offer public in his famous Harvard speech. Immediately Bevin and Georges Bidault, the French Foreign Minister, invited their Russian counterpart, Molotov, to attend discussions on the American offer. The Russians declined the suggestion. They wished for each country to negotiate a bilateral economic agreement with the United States, whereas the essence of the American offer was the stipulation that the administration of the relief programme must be collective in order to achieve the maximum benefits. As the Cold War intensified, there was no alternative but to leave the Soviet Union out of the reckoning. Britain and France therefore invited all other European states, with the exception of Germany and Spain, to attend a conference in Paris. Apart from the Russian-dominated states in the east, only Finland did not feel free to accept the invitation. Thus representatives of only fourteen nations appeared in Paris in July to consider the American proposal and construct a comprehensive list of European resources and requirements to cover the period from 1948 to 1951. Before dispersing they agreed to meet at intervals to review the situation and to establish a permanent administration to organise the programme. France and Britain, in deep economic difficulties, initiated the plans. In April 1948, in Paris, OEEC came into being.

Its first and immediate preoccupation was with the European Recovery Programme. Its task was to discover a method of dividing American aid among the member states in such a way that the maximum cure possible would be achieved. OEEC was basically reluctant to undertake this task, for no matter what was decided some members would receive less than others. From the outset, therefore, there was a possibility that the functioning of OEEC would never get off the ground. However, the European states had to make some decision if American aid was to be forthcoming. The United States had made it clear that it did not wish to draw up the details itself; the responsibility had to be Europe's. Under persistent American pressure the states eventually found a formula with which everyone, some albeit reluctantly, agreed. The formula was that the financial aid would be distributed among OEEC members according to their trade and payment deficits. Those states which possessed a low standard of living but had very small deficits suffered most by the arrangement. But OEEC, with American encouragement, survived this first hurdle to pass on to a wider area of activity.

The basic responsibility for the successful operation of OEEC belonged to the nations themselves; the organisation itself was primarily concerned with cooperation and coordination. Thus, like the Council of Europe, it was only a first step in the movement towards integration, being essentially an intergovernmental body. But the nature of its task necessarily demanded some permanent institutional organs to enable it to perform its function satisfactorily. The focus of OEEC and its governing body was its Council, which possessed one representative from each member government. This body had the power to determine questions of general policy and overall administration. Its decisions were obligatory on the members, but only because a decision became a decision when everyone had participated in its formulation and agreed to adhere to it. On the other hand, OEEC could not force any decision on a recalcitrant member. Any state had the right to go its own way on any one issue by ignoring or vetoing OEEC suggestions, or by pleading special circumstances. Thus again it was made obvious that OEEC was not a supranational body. But it was definitely more than the Brussels Treaty from which, like the Council of Europe, it had partly drawn its inspiration.

The OEEC Council could not hope to function successfully in a vacuum. It constructed a complex network of subordinate committees and boards which, often composed of experts, performed specialised functions. Council recommendations were nearly always based upon reports prepared by these organs. As the work load of OEEC began to grow, it was forced to decentralise. The result was the establishment of several separate but related agencies, of which the best known and one of the most successful is probably the European Payments Union set up in 1950, which, by enabling intra-European debts to be cancelled out, eased the pressure on scarce monetary resources which was one factor hampering the expansion of European trade.

On paper the OEEC structure did not appear to possess a great number of possibilities. Undoubtedly it had its drawbacks and liabilities, but it succeeded far beyond the level that a first glance might suggest. As an example of mutual cooperation it could hardly be bettered; the right of a veto, for example, was very rarely exercised:

It was an organisation based wholly on voluntary cooperation by states, yet, by the use of small groups of technical experts, by the technique of questionnaire, analysis of the replies of States and 'confrontation' within the committees, that is to say cross-examination of

State representatives on those replies, the Organisation was able to impose a general standard of concurrence in its activities which is indeed impressive. It was a bold Member State which pursued an economic policy at odds with the rest.[1]

The acceptance of the principle of voluntary cooperation undoubtedly helped OEEC to sidestep many of the economic difficulties with which it might have been confronted. Also, in order further to assist it in its tasks, in its formative years it developed a valuable relationship with the Council of Europe. It is probable that, considering the political situation and attitudes of the late 1940s, no better way could have been discovered of administering Marshall Aid. OEEC further proved its value by going beyond the implementation of the European Recovery Programme, and by inspiring individuals to consider close schemes of integration. The founders of the ECSC and Common Market undoubtedly learnt some important lessons from the functioning of OEEC.

It had its limitations. Its work was mostly concerned with the removal or diminution of quota restrictions on European trade. This could not prevent trade being distorted or prevented by other discriminatory methods. Furthermore, it concentrated on easier problems (for which perhaps it can hardly be blamed), but it did mean that increasingly progress became slower as only the most difficult problems remained. Again, it concerned itself more with short-term problems than with the more important long-term difficulty of attempting to settle the problems of economic growth and development.

Economically, this is perhaps one reason why the founders of ECSC and the Common Market preferred to do just that rather than work through the organs of OEEC. But OEEC worked well within its field of reference. Its ability to tackle other problems was handicapped by the conditions surrounding its inception. Although the United States desired a maximum degree of economic unity and France especially saw advantages in establishing some degree of supranationality, Britain drew back from this extended plan, desiring only economic cooperation, not integration. In this the British view was endorsed by the smaller nations which feared the possibility of total subordination to their larger

[1] D. W. Bowett, *The Law of International Relations*, London, 1963, p. 168.

neighbours. Cooperation won over unity. Although OEEC may have developed primarily as 'a conference of sovereign states in permanent session',[1] this statement, though accurate, does not give full justice to the value of the organisation. Its true value lay in the foundations it established for the future. While several nations were unwilling to accept economic integration, OEEC played a major role in driving home the realisation that European economic systems were mutually dependent, not independent, and that they prospered or failed together.

OEEC survived for twelve years. In many ways its demise was a matter of regret. Strictly speaking, it did not die. In December 1960 it was transformed, with all its organs remaining intact, into the Organisation for Economic Cooperation and Development (OECD). The United States and Canada, which had only been associate members of OEEC, now became full members of OECD. The change of name reflected the different purpose and situation. OEEC had been constructed initially to handle the Marshall Aid programme. While it went on to fresh fields, it remained limited to Europe. The United States was concerned with the economic split between the Six and the Seven that was developing at the end of the decade. OECD was intended to counteract this and to concern itself with the long-range problems of economic development both inside and outside Europe. With the entry of Japan in 1964 it was no longer even an Atlantic organisation.

[1] Political and Economic Planning, *European Organisations*, London, 1959, p. 54.

8 The Korean War: Its Impact on Europe

The attack upon Korea makes it plain beyond all doubt that communism has passed beyond the use of subversion to conquer independent nations and will now use armed invasion and war.

President Truman, 1950

In 1948 Western European interests had been submerged in the concern and anxieties caused by the intensification of the Cold War and the possibility of global escalation in which the continent would be the first to be destroyed. Although still overwhelmingly present, this danger had receded slightly by the early months of 1950: with some semblance of order in their own houses, the European powers were able to spare time to consider methods of closer economic, and perhaps even political cooperation. This period of relative optimism abruptly came to an end in June 1950, when war broke out on the Korean peninsula.

The wartime Allies had been unable to agree on a satisfactory solution for the former Japanese 'colony'. The favourite compromise solution, partition, was accepted. The artificial boundary of the Thirty-eighth Parallel had been a constant source of dissatisfaction between the two Korean states, one Communist and one democratic. Since it was the state of South Korea that had been invaded by the small, but well-trained Communist forces of North Korea, the Truman Doctrine was speedily invoked, and the United States resolved to send as much aid as possible to South Korea.

America sought approval from the United Nations for its action. The United Nations approved the establishment of a United Nations force in South Korea under American command. The approval was possible only because previously the Russian delegate on the Security Council had walked out and refused to participate any further in Council discussions; since he had not yet returned, the Security Council was not faced with a Russian veto on the Korean question. Although some Western European and Commonwealth nations sent small contingents to Korea under the United Nations resolution, the defence of South Korea was primarily the concern of the United States, which supplied the vast bulk of money, supplies, and troops.

The Korean War was not simply an isolated war in a remote part of Asia. It was the first open conflict between Communism and the West; previously, as for instance in Greece, Communist aggression had been carried on by internal insurrection and guerrilla warfare, and not by the invading armies of a foreign state. It merely emphasised that periods of relative tranquillity, as the previous months had been, could be no more than an uneasy peace. The Soviet Union had not renounced its ambitions of further conquest. Having been baulked by decisive countermeasures in Western Europe itself, it had turned to examine the more fluid situation in Asia.

The immediate fears were that the Korean War would escalate into a global conflict in much the same way as the Spanish Civil War had been the prologue to the Second World War. For Western European governments the dilemma was whether to press for a speedy expulsion of the Communist forces from the southern half of the peninsula, or whether, by so intensifying Western aid to South Korea, the resulting hardening of the bipolarity between West and East would provoke armed clashes elsewhere—particularly, of course, in Europe. The first reaction of the democratic governments of Western Europe was an increase in confidence in their American ally. Despite American pledges of support, such as the Truman Doctrine and NATO, there remained a lingering suspicion that in the last resort the United States might not be prepared to take a firm stand and might retreat back to 'Fortress America' and the old American condition of isolation. But the determined American response to the new wave of Communist aggression seemed to indicate that the United States could be relied upon to uphold the Truman Doctrine. It was felt, therefore, that the new Atlantic military alliance would be a satisfactory deterrent (or at least the best available in existing circumstances) against a Russian invasion of Western Europe.

This confidence and relief soon changed into fear as the Korean

War entered into a different and more dangerous stage. The preponderance of American military strength was soon sufficient to force the invaders back across the Thirty-eighth Parallel. The United States, however, did not stop there, and in turn invaded North Korea. This crossing of the Thirty-eighth Parallel, coupled with the acknowledged pressures from certain official quarters within the United States for a full-scale attack on the North Korean supply lines which lay in Manchuria, now part of Communist China, provoked Chinese intervention. In theory, these men were 'volunteers' helping their North Korean comrades; in practice, they were well-equipped units of the Communist armies of China.

The Chinese intervention caused a second world crisis. The fears in Europe of a direct clash with Communism on the continent itself, which had been allayed by the initial American successes, now became very real. The governments of Western Europe were reluctant to become further involved in the Asian conflict: they saw little need to intensify Russian hostility in Europe as a direct consequence of a war in which they were not closely involved. The only exception to this general mood may possibly have been France, whose military and economic resources were already being strained beyond their present capacity by the losing battle to control French Indo-China.

Military Consequences

It was inevitable, therefore, that the war in Asia would affect the policies and internal affairs of the governments of Western Europe. The most obvious consequences were military. The Korean War had imposed an extra demand upon American financial resources and had at the same time intensified the Cold War. The United States, therefore, faced with an allocation problem, began to think in terms of military aid rather than economic aid. For Western Europe, this switch of direction in American policy meant, first, that the whole nature of Marshall Aid was changed; it became closely related to a military, rather than an economic, build-up in strength. Second, and more significant, American assistance was now primarily made conditional upon the promises and actions of the Western European governments to strengthen and enlarge their own military forces.

At the same time the United States undertook a review of its defensive commitments. Where Europe was concerned, it arrived at the conclusion that in the event of a military confrontation with the Soviet Union on the continent the present strength of the Atlantic alliance, expressed through the North Atlantic Treaty Organisation, was insufficient. The United States, moreover, saw no need why it alone should be called upon to meet the deficit. If this could not be met by the present European members of the alliance, then America argued that the most obvious method of strengthening NATO would be to permit West Germany to rearm. With increasing persistence, the United States Government demanded that West Germany should be brought into the Western defensive alliance with its own military forces.

Yet another of the decisions of the wartime Allies was therefore revised by the force of postwar exigencies, although pressure for West German rearmament had in fact begun before the outbreak of war in Korea. The Allied agreement had already been flouted in the Soviet zone of Germany, where the Russians had begun to develop a 'people's police force', which, despite all protestations to the contrary, was clearly intended to be the nucleus of an East German army. Many West Germans felt that this would be a prelude to an invasion of the Federal Republic: but it would be a 'liberation' movement, as technically only Germans, and not Russians, would be involved. The parallel divided nature of Korea and Germany was an obvious point. Worried about this situation, Dr Adenauer had already suggested that West Germany should be given the opportunity to defend itself, and that the surest way of winning the West German population to a massive commitment to Western democracy was to give them an equal share in the responsibility of defending Western Europe. Otherwise, he argued, many Germans might well opt for the attractions of a neutral, but unified Germany: this could be nothing more than an illusion for it would only be a matter of time before an unarmed and isolated Germany passed totally into the Soviet sphere of control.

Although it was becoming increasingly obvious that a West German military contribution to NATO would be invaluable, especially as the other European countries could not by themselves achieve the new levels of armament set by the United States, this American demand still appeared to come as something of a surprise to Western Europe, particularly to France. In the 1940s France's primary objective had been the prostration of Germany. Various French governments had attempted to detach the Saar from Germany by integrating its economy with the French economy, and were still hoping that the Saar would eventually become an integral part of France. French claims to the Saar had always been disputed by West Germany: in the volume of Dr Adenauer's memoirs on foreign affairs, for instance, the space devoted to it ranks second only to the Russian threat. Franco-German relations were, therefore, not altogether on a cordial basis. A rearmed Germany, by providing a threat to French security, merely served to arouse all the old fears.

But to all West Germany's neighbours, the idea of a German military force only a few years after Hitler's armies had been driven out of their territory was utterly repugnant. On the other hand it was obvious that the United States meant to stand by its latest policy—and Western Europe was still completely dependent on American aid. A total economic and military withdrawal by the United States from Europe would leave it extremely vulnerable to Russian hegemony: indeed the outcome would probably never be in doubt. Although Truman's government had already admitted that it was in America's best interests to participate in a European defensive and economic alliance, many Europeans feared that withdrawal was a distinct possibility. Therefore the problem facing the European governments was not to oppose the American proposal adamantly, but rather to find some compromise which would dilute the dangers of a strong Germany army. The memories of German military strength and efficiency in the nineteenth and twentieth centuries were still too powerful to be ignored. The shackling of a German military contribution to NATO would have to be achieved by placing it under non-German control. Moreover, whatever course was adopted would have to receive the blessing of Germany's traditional enemy, France, for it to have any chance of operating successfully.

It was the French Government which eventually offered a novel way out of the impasse. Taking ECSC as the example, it suggested that there should be a pooling of military resources, or, in other words, a European army. In this way there could be no distinct German army under a separate German command. This idea was the basis of the proposed European Defence Community (EDC). Once again, because of the reluctance of Britain and the Scandinavian countries to become too closely involved with any creation that suggested the abrogation of national sovereignty, its application was limited to the six nations who had established the ECSC.

Representatives of the six nations met in Paris in May 1952 to sign the treaty establishing the EDC. All that remained was the ratification of the treaty by the individual parliaments of the countries concerned. At first glance, it seemed that Schuman's vision of European unity being established gradually by the creation of a number of supranational bodies, along the lines of the ECSC, and binding the national economies closer together, was one important step nearer realisation. Superficially EDC followed this pattern, but its fundamental implications were different. ECSC consisted of six equal partners. The European Defence Community had been suggested and was designed as a means of preventing German parity in the military sphere, which the original American demand for a West German military contribution, almost certainly within the boundaries of NATO, had implied. The plan was for the other five members of EDC to allocate only a proportion of their armed forces to the European army: a substantial percentage of French military strength, for example, was tied down in Indo-China. The German contribution to EDC, on the other hand, was to be the total sum of German military resources.

This limiting specification did not altogether allay the fears in Europe of the possibility of a future German hegemony. The strong anti-German sentiment of Western European public opinion generally tended to delay the EDC negotiations throughout. In West Germany itself, opinions were deeply divided. After 1945 West Germans had developed strong neutralist tendencies. It was felt in many circles that the risks involved in rearmament were too great and that the American suggestion would make Germany the primary battlefield in any possible conflict. The opposition Social Democrats were opposed to the whole plan, fearing that by tieing West Germany closer to the Western ideological camp, it would jeopardise any opportunities that might arise for the reunification of the whole country. Adenauer and the CDU, however, were firmly in favour of EDC. Adenauer saw the reunification question as having only remote possibilities; besides, he believed that it could more easily come about if West Germany were in a position of strength, and not one of weakness. The most important issue was seen to be the acceptance on equal terms of West Germany by the Western world. Adenauer considered German participation in EDC, although on unequal terms, as an important step in the right direction. Moreover, Adenauer's government leaned more heavily on American support than probably any other Western European government. As mentioned previously, Dr Adenauer had already suggested several times that his country should be allowed to play an active role in the defence of the West. When the United States suggested German rearmament, Adenauer therefore also supported it because he wished to maintain a close German–American accord. Adenauer's views on the choice of reunification versus the Western alliance had also been endorsed by the Western leaders. Their 'final' decision on this subject was the result of the latest moves of the Soviet Union, which naturally was utterly opposed to the concept of EDC, and particularly to West German membership within it.

The Soviet Union had clearly not given up hope of attracting West Germany into its orbit: an armed West Germany tied to the Atlantic alliance would preclude this possibility indefinitely, short of total war. In March 1952 Russia reopened the German question by suggesting that the four wartime Allies should meet to consider the signature of a peace treaty with Germany and the consequent reunification of the country. The Russian proposal was designed not so much to appeal to the Western leaders, as to attempt to turn West German public opinion (which, to say the least, was not favourably disposed to the EDC at the outset) completely against rearmament. Two factors meant that the

Russians were bargaining from a relatively weak position. First, a treaty signed in 1950 between the newly established East German State and Poland had confirmed the Oder–Neisse line as a *de jure* boundary. This fact was ill-calculated to appeal to West German nationalists. The latter were one of the influential groups inside the Federal Republic at whom the Russian suggestion had been aimed, but they refused and still refuse, to admit that the territories east of the Oder–Neisse line were anything else than under the *temporary administration* of Poland. Similarly, the Russian note failed to convince West German democrats because of the deaf ear the Soviet Union consistently turned to all appeals for free elections in East Germany. After the 1946 fiasco (for the Communists) in Berlin, all elections had been 'managed' by the Communist leaders. Moreover, the United Nations had, after West German representations, appointed a neutral investigating commission which had been charged with the task of studying the election procedures in the two Germanies. The commission was naturally admitted to West Germany, but was denied permission to enter East Germany. If anything, this latest Russian move had, for the Soviet Union, the adverse effect of making West German public opinion more favourably disposed to the American suggestion and Adenauer's policies.

The Western leaders themselves placed no credence in Soviet sincerity. In their reply to the Russian suggestion, the foreign ministers of the United States, Britain and France clearly indicated that they thought it motivated entirely by the desire to wreck E D C. By implication also the reply demonstrated that the West had finally shelved indefinitely any faint hope of a *rapprochement* with Soviet Russia. This meant that German reunification could not possibly be given any hope of success. The American doctrine of containment, coupled with the obsessive fears of the West about the overwhelming superiority of Russian conventional forces, made the complete loss of one-third of the old German Reich to Communism less important than the desire to strengthen their own alliance with a rearmed West Germany. German militarism could thereby be supervised and checked. It could not, however, remove completely the suspicions of Germany's neighbours. For them, the fear of a world conflagration could after 1945 be caused by the now familiar 'German problem' instead of a possible German nationalist dream of European hegemony.

But at that time the concept of EDC was perhaps too idealistic to have great hopes of concrete achievement. In its implications for European integration, the European Defence Community was something of a paradox. Where diminution of national sovereignty is concerned, the renunciation of national control over national military strength, inevitably an extremely sensitive area, to a supranational body, should have had a solid background of integration before being introduced. For this reason, the EDC realistically should have been one of the last integrating communities formed in that chain envisaged by Schuman and his associates. Europeans reared on a tradition of nationalism had not yet grown accustomed to the idea of such close international cooperation and such a supranational authority.

Even if it had actually been put into force, the whole operation might well have run into such innumerable difficulties as to render the project unworkable. In any case, the French proposition had never been primarily intended to further the cause of European integration. The fundamental reason behind the collective French idea had been to prevent an independent German military force, and at the very best perhaps to delay any German rearmament by prolonging the preliminary discussions and negotiations. Astounded by the rapidity with which the idea was embraced by the other proposed members and the willingness to ratify it, French governments were extremely reluctant to put it forward for ratification in France and so perhaps allow EDC, about which many Frenchmen were unenthusiastic, to become a functioning entity. The governments, even if not themselves doubtful of the project, knew that they were not strong enough to force such a controversial issue through the immobilist National Assembly. From its inception until 1954 the EDC treaty was a sword of Damocles hanging over French politics, though it was but one of many—and perhaps not the most important one for France's health. The parties of the narrow centre sector, from which all French governments had to be drawn, were agreed only on the fundamental issue of preserving the Republic: they had reserved their rights to disagree on anything else. Thus there was a tendency towards immobilism. No controversial issue could ever hope to be dealt with satisfactorily, so governments merely tended to forget about them or postpone them until some indeterminate future date.

Political Consequences

The changed military emphasis in European affairs caused by the Korean War also had economic and political consequences. Naturally, the war had to be paid for, and Western Europe had to provide some of the payment. Moreover, the demand for increased Western European military strength created a correspondingly increased demand for military equipment and the necessary raw material. The war was a boon to manufacturers producing military equipment. Nevertheless, the economic consequences of the war in Western Europe were serious. Governments had to face the familiar dilemma of guns or butter. The demand for raw material outstripped supply. Prices rose steadily, and inflation once again began to spread through the whole economic structure. The Western European countries had by 1950 only just succeeded in pegging the inflationary tendencies more or less rampant since 1945—and that had required massive American assistance. Now they were confronted with the same problem. Progressive measures had to be delayed while means were found of keeping the old enemy in check. Rises in prices meant a rise in the cost of living of the individual; he in turn demanded wage increases, which on the whole could not be met. And as a result, discontent and unrest were generated which could be utilised as a basis of political action by groups opposed to parliamentary democracy. There was a real danger that in such an economic situation, the deprived individual might make a clear distinction between Communist aggression in far-distant Asia, and Communist support at home for what he considered a decent standard of living. And in the wings, waiting for a chance to set up its standard, there was always the shadow of right-wing authoritarianism.

It may seem ironical that the new American emphasis on increased military expenditure engendered by its analysis of the possible consequences of the Korean War should threaten the existence of that moderate Third Force in Italy and France which

American foreign policy in Europe had consistently attempted to stabilise and protect since early 1947. But this was indeed the case. However, the relative successes of the Western European economies prevented the dangers from becoming less remote.

The Korean War had less immediately obvious effects on the political systems of the four major European powers. In elections from approximately the middle of 1948 onwards, conservative political forces had increased both their confidence and their share of the votes at the polls. The British Labour Government's huge majority had almost disappeared in the 1950 general election. Conservatism had certainly not suffered a reverse in the Italian election of 1948. In France a strong new conservative alliance under the leadership of Charles de Gaulle, the Rally of the French People (RPF), had made sweeping gains in local elections.

The conservative revival had been an almost inevitable consequence of the regaining of political and economic stability. The reformist trend had been persistently decelerating since 1945. Certain social changes had been effected; people seemed satisfied with the ground already gained, particularly in the field of economic privileges and guarantees, and saw no need for any urgency for more farreaching reforms that might touch their immediate needs only remotely. The immediate postwar era with its emphasis on planning and reconstruction had tended to become tarred with the brush of austerity. After years of deprivation, people now regarded the time to be ripe for more consumer goods, all the more so because it was popularly claimed that the economies had at long last climbed out of the slough caused by the war. Nongovernment political forces, which generally included the conservative right, were well placed to appeal to these popular sentiments. Moreover the upthrust of Communism in 1947 and 1948 had caused a popular reaction. People moved to the right politically to be further away from any association with the extreme left. Those parties of the right, usually traditionally associated with patriotism and national pride, which had always been hostile to any dealings with Communism benefited from this reaction. Thereafter the Communist parties in Western Europe could attract only those completely disenchanted with the whole system. People gravitated to those conservative parties which desired to work the existing system in a much more efficient manner rather than to establish a thoroughgoing authoritarian regime.

The Korean War was only a contributory factor in this general movement towards traditional conservatism. Aggressive foreign policies and a determination to organise a country's military capacity to the best advantage have for long been considered by conservative parties to be their own prerogative. Certainly, leftist parties, especially Socialist movements, had and still have a tinge of pacifism in their makeup. The immediate appeal of conservatism, therefore, was that it possessed a long and successful tradition of prosecuting aggressive foreign and colonial policies in distant parts of the globe and that it was better equipped than its rivals to handle the current situation. Elections in Western Europe held between the outbreak of the Korean War and 1953 illustrated the growing appeal of conservatism to the European voter.

In France the National Assembly had by 1951 served its full constitutional term. All analyses of the existing political mood made it obvious that the new elections, to be held in June, would drastically reduce the dominating lead gained by the three mass parties in 1946. The moderate and conservative forces had gradually been gaining in strength, while further to the right there was de Gaulle's RPF with several outstanding municipal successes behind it. The 1951 election confirmed that, out of the multitude of French political parties, the number of serious political movements had increased from three to six. It also confirmed a movement of support to the right. This movement, however, was confined to the supporters of the centre and the moderate left. Despite the setbacks of previous years for international Communism, the French Communist party succeeded in retaining its voting strength. The main losses were those of the Socialists and the MRP. In supporting the system the Socialists had obviously run the risk of allowing Communism to make inroads into their support by appealing to the voters that they were the sole representatives of working classes still largely confined to a political ghetto. In 1945 and 1946 the MRP had clearly attracted many electors who normally would have voted for conservative parties. In 1951, though the MRP itself had moved to the right, these voters returned to their old allegiance towards conservatism, particularly toward the Radical and Independent (Conservative) parties. In addition, the young RPF attracted not only those on the right who disliked and opposed the Fourth Republic; in presenting itself as a Catholic party (by appealing to traditional Catholic principles) it also offered a direct challenge to the MRP. Nevertheless it failed to maintain the high level it had achieved in previous local elections.

The conservative trend again appeared in the British general election of October 1951. For eighteen months Attlee and the Labour Party had struggled to sustain an effective government on a majority of five. The Labour Government was not only faced with a strong Conservative opposition, but also by dissension within its own ranks. Early in 1951 Aneurin Bevan, the acknowledged leader of Labour's left wing, accompanied by two other ministers (one of whom was Harold Wilson), had resigned from the government over the new emphasis in policy on military and defence matters to the detriment of social services. The Labour Government could hope to function effectively only with a larger majority, and Attlee decided to seek this through a fresh election. The Conservatives were the victors by a majority only slightly larger than Labour's between 1950 and 1951. But it was sufficient for them not to dissolve Parliament for a further four years. Winston Churchill thus won his first election as a party leader.

In 1953 the parliaments of the other two major states of Western Europe, Italy and West Germany, also had run their constitutional course. After these elections conservatism again emerged in greater strength. The main losers in the new elections for the Italian Chamber of Deputies, held in June 1953, were as in France, the Socialists and the Christian Democrats. The Socialists lost votes here, not because they were full participants in the system, but because they had clung to their close alliance with the Communists. Moderates deserted them for the Social Democrats and the centre, while the more militant tended to be attracted by the more extreme Communists. On the other hand, the Christian Democrats, essentially a broad coalition of many diverse elements, suffered from the renewed popularity of right-wing parties. The Liberal party was becoming a staunch representative of the conservative propertied classes, while monarchism and neo-Fascism were attracting many more electors.

The West German Bundestag elections, held in September, seemed at first glance to present an entirely different result. Here the minor parties of all political persuasions had suffered the most serious losses, apparently clearing the atmosphere for a distinctive confrontation between the two mass parties. But the Social Democrats, as the only serious party of the left, remained more or less at the same level of support; they had still to escape from the traditional 'thirty per cent barrier'. It was the Christian Democrats who gained slightly, mainly at the expense of small conservative-minded parties. The West German election result may at first seem to reflect a different trend. Whereas in Britain, France, and Italy, conservative parties gained at the expense of more moderate and left-wing groups, the West German CDU was the only political party to increase its support. However, the argument still holds true generally. Elsewhere the swing to conservatism had expressed itself in a realignment of voting support. In West Germany this realignment occurred within the ranks of the Christian Democratic Union and its leaders. This trend was true of European Christian Democracy as a whole; in France and Italy also, the general attitudes of Christian Democratic leadership and policies were becoming more conservative.

This revival of conservatism throughout the political spectrum had inevitable consequences upon political leaderships and policies. During the early years of the 1950s measures of social reform—as, for example, codetermination in West Germany and land redistribution in Italy—had been opposed by conservative parties and interest groups with partial success. Their increased strength after the 1951 and 1953 elections meant that they could both influence the administration of any extant measures of social reform and prevent a successful repetition of any such measures in the future. Increasing national self-confidence, or rather national self-interest, which the conservative rejuvenation partly expressed, removed more or less completely any urgency that might have lingered on in the political arena of the need for European union as the best and only sensible means of reconstruction. Of all the nations of Western Europe, only these four—Britain, France, Italy, and West Germany—could, because of their importance, take a decisive lead in uniting Europe. But pro-European voices in government circles were becoming weaker or had been removed altogether. The British parties had never shown any great interest in becoming a member of a European federation. Previously some interest in and encouragement for a union on the continent had been forthcoming; now it was quite clear, if it was not earlier, that British party opinion had hardened into a conviction that union should stop at the type of consultative structure illustrated by OEEC and the Council of Europe. Owing to the fears and suspicions that still existed of a German design for Europe, West Germany was unable to take a direct lead in espousing union. Moreover, Adenauer's new coalition government contained a new party which, although small, was the avowed champion of the numerous refugees and expellees who had swollen the West German population and were not yet assimilated into society. Its leaders and, it was claimed, its supporters were primarily interested in German reunification and repatriation to their former areas of domicile in Poland and Czechoslovakia. The government's principal task, therefore, was a concentration of resources to accommodate and assimilate these people in order to prevent a possible regeneration of virulent right-wing nationalism.

France and Italy were faced with a different problem; but the result was the same. The 'conversation' of pro-European foreign ministers came to an end in mid-1952 when Count Carlo Sforza departed from the Italian foreign ministry. De Gasperi himself had to concentrate more on national problems either aggravated or caused by the party situation; yet he too was unable to overcome the changing nature of his own party. In France the new alignment of political forces after the 1951 election meant that the MRP, whose share of the vote dropped from 26 per cent to 13 per cent, lost its strong position within the narrow pro-Republic sector. Its leaders, therefore, could no longer demand such a large share of government offices (especially as its rivals or partners knew that it would be obliged to support the regime in any case) or attempt to force governments to pursue their own largely pro-European policies. The dismissal of Robert Schuman from the French Foreign Ministry in 1952 was a symptom of the changing nature and problems of French political life.

The problem facing France and Italy was one of strong latent or actual forces on the political extremes. Britain was not confronted with a strong ultra-right political movement, nor did the British Communist Party even present the threat of being a nuisance. Owing to the new variety of the German problem and the split personality of Germany, the Communist vote in the Federal Republic was negligible and on the decline. But even so legal steps were being taken to outlaw it; this process was to last five years. But for foreign nations, the greatest German danger was still seen to be a rebirth of Nazism or neo-Nazism. And fears had been aroused by relatively striking successes achieved in state elections in 1951 by a militant, openly neo-Nazi movement called the Socialist Reich Party (SRP). The government, sensitive about foreign opinion and prejudices on this matter and equally afraid of the potential impact of right-wing authoritarian appeals, reacted swiftly and requested that the SRP be banned. This was done in 1952 by the Constitutional Court which argued that under the relevant clause of the 1949 Basic Law the SRP both represented a threat to and did not accept the democratic principle as the basis of West German political and constitutional life and therefore should be outlawed. More specifically the SRP was charged with deifying Hitler, condoning Nazi mass murders, supporting the 'Fuehrer' principle, Nazi political beliefs, and the abolition of all other parties.

In France and Italy the democratic forces were unable or unwilling to pursue the same severe course of action. Instead both governments decided to modify their electoral laws in an attempt to retain control of governmental authority and to deprive dangerous or small 'nuisance' parties of parliamentary representation. This line had also been followed by the West German CDU, with the support of the Social Democrats. It could perhaps be argued that this action in France and Italy contributed somewhat to the reduction of their own support by presenting the opposition with emotional propaganda. But given the entrenched Communist position on the left and the rapidly increasing confidence of both traditional and radical conservatism on the right, reforming the electoral system in such a way as to favour themselves was probably the only alternative open to the centre government groups.

The Italian electoral system was based on the principle of proportional representation. De Gasperi and the Christian Democrats carried through a reform which would give a parliamentary bonus to large parties, and to a large coalition of parties more so. The new law proposed that a party or coalition of parties which managed to win an absolute majority of votes in the country would be rewarded by being given two-thirds of the seats in the Chamber of Deputies. The plan was clearly designed to manufacture a large Christian Democratic majority, which, after a pronounced swing to the right in the 1951 and 1952 local elections, was considerably questionable. As such, the manœuvre was labelled 'the swindle law' by its opponents. With the ultra-right isolated, and the Communist–Socialist fraternisation segregated on the left, only the Christian Democrats, in their quadripartite alliance with other small moderate parties (in de Gasperi's opinion, the only possible hope for stability in Italy), were left with a possibility of winning the requisite 50 per cent plus of the votes. The manœuvre backfired completely. The government parties had to spend most of the campaign period justifying the new law and never really made any positive appeals as they had done in 1948. The Christian Democrat alliance failed by the narrow margin of 57,000 votes to win the requisite majority. The law therefore was never put into practice. The immediate result of the election was a new search for a government majority. Some small parties, for example the Social Democrats, might be willing to uphold a centrist government in parliament but were certainly not willing to be part of the government. It turned out that a government majority could be obtained only by admitting the former discredited Monarchists into the ruling circle; and this de Gasperi did not want. Again, therefore, the Christian Democrats had to go it alone. But the new government failed to gain a vote of confidence when it presented itself for approval to the Chamber of Deputies; the Social Democrats and Liberals abstained, while the extremes voted against. The old de Gasperi magic seemed to have disappeared. This defeat was a portent of the end of de Gasperi's political career; it also meant an increase in the danger of immobilism, for, while the Christian Democrats by virtue of their size and position in the spectrum had to be included in any government, it was clear that de Gasperi had no crown prince with the ability to hold its many conflicting elements behind one consistent line.

The elections of 1945 and 1946 in France had also been held under a system of proportional representation. The centre parties had feared that if this system was retained for the 1951 elections it would result in a considerable number of seats being won by the Communists and the new Gaullist movement, the RPF. Local elections had indicated that Communism was retaining its high level of voting support, while in the 1947 municipal elections the newly formed RPF had astoundingly won 40 per cent of the poll. The French dilemma was to find a way of preventing these two parties from gaining a negative majority in the National Assembly. The new electoral law was, as in Italy, intended to put a premium on the ability of the several parties to form a coalition alliance with one another. Like the German and Italian laws, it moved away from the continental preference for an electoral system which gives justice to all shades of opinion, and approached the Anglo-Saxon idea which puts the highest premium upon achieving a satisfactory and stable government majority. In this way de Gaulle's RPF would be confronted with a larger alliance of the centre, while the Communists would be successfully isolated since the Socialists were partners, albeit reluctantly, of the centre.

The electoral law, severely criticised and with only a few apologetic defenders, was called the 'thieves' ballot' by the Communists. But it did have a limited measure of success. Whereas the Communists and the RPF, with less than half the votes, would have gained over 50 per cent of the seats if the old system had been retained, the new law caused Communist representation to be halved. However, it was replaced as France's largest party by the RPF. On the other hand, the law failed to provide the centre bloc with the strength it needed: these parties had prevented a negative majority in the National Assembly by their agreement to cooperate. But the area of agreement was extremely small, and because it was non-existent in the next elections of 1956, this law was of no value. It could be argued that the electoral law did prevent the RPF from making further inroads among the electorate. But probably the party's own volatile nature provides a more satisfactory explanation. It had risen too quickly and had already passed the zenith of its success. Held together only by the reputation and personality of de Gaulle, it was unable to retain the allegiance of voters simply by emphasising loyalty to the party. De Gaulle himself was unwilling to become involved in politics, and the period between 1947 and 1951 when the RPF was denied representation at the highest levels only soured him further. By 1951 he was already becoming disinterested in the RPF, and early in 1953 he abandoned it to a fate of disintegration and assimilation by other conservative movements. Releasing his followers from any pledge of allegiance to himself, he retired for the second time to his country home.

De Gaulle had realised that the 1951 election had produced a hexagon of major political forces which enjoyed approximately equal strength in the National Assembly. With the majority agreed that the RPF and the Communists should be excluded from the government, the remaining four groupings found it relatively easy to come together on the question of defending the Republic. The real gains in 1951 had been obtained by the Radicals and the Independents, both open representatives of conservative and traditional forces. Coupled with the increasing conservatism of the MRP, they became indispensable supporters of governments. In return for this support they naturally demanded deference for their views. The party which suffered most was the Socialist Party, now faced with the unpalatable alternatives of cooperating with a centre that was becoming more conservative in order to sustain the Republic, or of joining the Communists and RPF in a negative majority, so forfeiting all opportunities of positively influencing the government, and in the long run thereby destroying a constitution that was largely of its own making. Reluctantly the Socialist leaders agreed that cooperation with the conservatives was the lesser of two evils. The new nature of French government was best illustrated by the government headed by the Independent, Antoine Pinay. Conservative inclinations and the virtual impossibility of achieving any progressive ends in the French system led to do-nothing attitudes and policies, in which any issue that might possibly arouse controversy, such as the EDC proposals, was shelved indefinitely.

In this way France illustrated very clearly the different trends at work in Western European politics in the early 1950s. For many the success of the conservative revival was a great disappointment and a delay in their plans for further social reform. However, it was traditional conservatism, and not authoritarian conservatism, which had succeeded. In this sense, Western Europe was perhaps fortunate. The intensification of the Cold War had made several people look back favourably upon the authoritarian right of Hitler's and Mussolini's variety as a strong and avowed opponent of Communism. The threat from one extreme could very well have caused large numbers of people to seek refuge at the other extreme. This danger was cushioned and thwarted by the re-emergence of moderate conservatism. In West Germany the authoritarian right had failed in its comeback and had eventually been outlawed by legal measures. In Italy also it had made little headway. In both countries the flexibility of the newly created Christian Democratic movements had given the systems a stability they would otherwise have lacked. And in France, where the RPF was the strongest authoritarian challenger, the attempt had also failed. In fact, the lure of full participation in political life had proved to be too potent for many RPF deputies; they were, in any case, usually conservatives who had only used de Gaulle's name as an electoral convenience. Many had already deserted the cause and had joined the loose ranks of Independents and Radicals before de Gaulle eventually decided to sever absolutely his connection with the movement. But the four major states, after these first elections of the 1950s, seemed set firm for a period of rule by conservatism which at best would be benevolent and socially concerned, and at worst slothful and guilty of dangerous neglect.

9 Integration: Advance and Retreat

After the first Schuman Plan Authority has been set up, others will follow. Thus gradually, one after another, by the functional method, there will be set up various European Ministries, which will be responsible towards what will become a European Parliament.

André Philip[1]

I ... have pointed out ... that political and military integration are on a par with economic integration, but that to try to press on too zealously would have dangerous consequences and might well be doomed to failure.

Ludwig Erhard, 1954[2]

It was clear to the disciples of a united Europe that the Council of Europe and the OEEC could have only a limited application in this direction: neither satisfied the desires of the federalists. The alternatives available were either to reform the existing organisations or to create an entirely new range of institutions. The possibility of the first alternative was exceedingly remote. The participation of neutral countries and of anti-integrative states such as Britain in one or other of the two organisations was an effective barrier against reform. The second alternative, therefore, was the one to which the determined federalists turned. It was immaterial whether the opponents of union were utterly antagonistic or were hanging back to see if union could really work: the federalists were not prepared to wait. The green light was also given by members of the Council of Europe who were satisfied with the existing state of affairs. Many, perhaps, were certain that a closer union could not succeed. Nevertheless the pro-Europeans were ready to move into the second stage of development. All they were waiting for was the necessary impetus.

[1] Council of Europe, *The First Five Years*, p. 64.
[2] Ludwig Erhard, *The Economics of Success*, London, 1963, p. 155.

ECSC: Integration by Sectors

The men who offered the impetus were Robert Schuman and Jean Monnet. On 9 May 1950 the former made public the proposal which has since become popularly known as the Schuman Plan. Schuman considered that the next move towards closer integration would be best achieved by a compromise between the concept of functionalism as represented by the present institutions and the idea of federalism as urged by the more extreme pro-Europeans. The basic scheme was to integrate the economies of countries in only one sector or area of economic activity; afterwards, other sectors would be dealt with on the same basis until finally the dams holding back trade would be lifted over the whole field of economics. It was a sensible long-term approach and was also an attempt to resolve the question of a balanced economic development programme in Western Europe. It was believed that the difficulties surrounding political union would be more easily overcome by this arrangement.

The immediate proposal was that integration, that is the elimination of all trade barriers, should first occur in the coal and steel industries, the basic components of any industrial society. The choice of steel and the genesis of the scheme itself had been partly influenced by the publication of two reports. Five months earlier the Economic Committee of the Strasbourg Assembly had suggested an international steel authority to tackle the problems of the industry which, it argued, could not be resolved by the tried methods of cartelisation or national protective measures. Shortly afterwards, and just before the Korean War stimulated an increased demand for steel, the relevant section of the Economic Commission for Europe put forward the same idea as a way of rationalising the existing situation of great supply and little demand. The proposal was eagerly taken up by the Consultative Assembly of the Council of Europe. Britain had immediately expressed once again its misgivings about European integration in general and the Schuman Plan in particular, especially as the prime condition of entry was to be the abrogation of certain national rights to the control of a supranational executive authority. Nevertheless, Schuman's offer was open to the whole of

Western Europe, and it was hoped that as many nations as possible would feel free to join the new institution. Schuman himself had seen that European union could not be achieved until the mutual and traditional suspicions of European nations were allayed. Furthermore, with or without Britain, the key lay with a reciprocal friendship between France and Germany. In his speech of 9 May Schuman emphasised that these two states must become part of the new order.

Only the six countries which were to become known as 'Little Europe'—Benelux, France, Italy and West Germany—were sufficiently interested to enter into serious negotiations. These discussions took months to complete. Eventually the treaty establishing a European Coal and Steel Community was signed by representatives of the six nations in April 1951. Ratification took a further year to complete. One reason why ECSC succeeded relatively easily in escaping from the drawing board was the presence of Christian Democratic parties (not necessarily Catholic) in all six governments: in fact, during the crucial years 1950–52 only the Netherlands and France did not have Christian Democrat premiers. However, the ECSC proposals were supported by nearly all democratic parties. Their support was quite clearly for different reasons: only in the Netherlands can we say with any exactitude that the various parties—Socialist, Protestant, Liberal and Catholic—made a serious attempt to produce a composite Dutch national attitude. This agreement on ECSC was possible because of the vague and ambiguous terms of the treaty. All interpreted it in different ways, but every party thought it saw advantages for itself and its beliefs. It was essentially a temporary coalition of political interests which launched ECSC. There was no guarantee that this particular constellation would survive or would even continue to support the new structure. This interpretation can also explain the initial enthusiasm for and the later hostility toward EDC: it was introduced by a temporary coalition which disbanded before the new institutions could be established. All governments and nations have fluctuated in the degree of their support of ECSC. In recent years President de Gaulle and France have been most critical. Since its supply of oil from the Sahara made it less necessary for France to possess some kind of control over Ruhr coal, its spokesmen suggested in the 1960s that the ECSC High Authority could well have its powers greatly reduced or that it should be disbanded. The other member nations have opposed ECSC equally vehemently when it has seemed to affect adversely national economic interests.

The schedule contained in the treaty was for a five-year transitional period that would consist of two distinct stages. First, ECSC would have to face the problems of demolishing tariffs and the various other restrictions on trade. Only then could it move on to destroy private agreements, cartels, and the like to establish not just a common market but a free common market. It is obvious that an intergovernmental structure would not suffice to enforce this programme. What was required was a clearly supranational authority with the necessary powers to tackle both the immediate political problem and the long-range problem of economic development.

The institution established to oversee the problems to be faced was called the High Authority of ECSC. The High Authority was composed of nine members, elected for their ability as individuals, of whom not more than two could be from one member state. Their term of office of six years was staggered to provide continuity, with one-third retiring every two years. The High Authority was entitled to give a wide range of reports from recommended opinions to binding decisions: to help it in its task it possessed powers to punish those who disobeyed its decisions, and more positively to direct investments, and to control both prices and production of coal and steel whenever a shortage or a surplus arose. The major significance of the High Authority lay in its ability to control and direct the activities of the national coal and steel industries without being countermanded by the national governments. This was the fundamental supranational element in ECSC.

The High Authority was far from being a sovereign body. In order to make sure that no one element could control the ECSC, an elaborate system of checks and balances was introduced into the structure. The High Authority was not the only executive-type body in ECSC. It was paralleled by the Special Council of Ministers, introduced as a precondition for the participation of Benelux, which feared that ECSC and the High Authority might otherwise be used as instruments of French or German national interest. The juxta-position of the High Authority and the Council of Ministers was the traditional clash of interest between supranationalism and nation-alism. The ministers were members of the national governments and their task was to restrain the High Authority from being over ambi-tious by trying to integrate its attitudes and actions with those of the member governments. The national governments were them-selves partly restrained by the fact that they did not finance ECSC. This was carried out by the High Authority which obtained the necessary monetary resources by utilising its power to levy a tax on coal and steel production. The tax was paid direct to the High Authority by the firms concerned.

A second restraint upon the High Authority, though less potent or practicable, was offered by the third major institution of ECSC, its Common Assembly. The Assembly held another record in the history of European integration. It was the first international parlia-mentary assembly to possess powers which were legally guaranteed. From its inception it was intended to be the repository of ultimate control. This, however, did not materialise. The Assembly was still not a true legislative body. Its significance lay elsewhere, in the fact that legally it had the power to censure the High Authority by forcing it to resign as a unit. This drastic power has not been used, the Assembly preferring to influence the High Authority by more amicable methods. One further point about the Assembly was that it could be regarded as a serious rival to the Consultative Assem-bly of the Council of Europe to be the nucleus of a European parliament: as in the case of its rival, delegates were appointed by the national parliament, while its charter also contained provisions for the introduction of direct universal suffrage.

Two further checks upon any arbitrary action by the High Authority were offered by the avenues of legal action and public opinion. The Court of Justice of ECSC could rule on the legality of any High Authority action: the latter could be questioned in the Court not only by national governments, but also by private enterprise. This was yet another revolutionary move on the part of ECSC, being a significant departure from the traditional concepts of international law. Finally, there was the power of public opinion. Naturally, the force of this, as always, was relatively weak. At the

beginning ECSC moved cautiously rather than jeopardise opportunities of expansion of the European ideal by precipitous action.
This was reinforced by the tendency of national governments
not to handle unpopular decisions if they could be transferred
to the High Authority. While this meant that public responsibility belonged to the High Authority, it meant, on the other
hand, that the latter was to some extent strengthened in its
relationships with the member governments.

An assessment of the work of ECSC could not honestly be made
until near the end of the five-year transitional period. But by 1958
it was clear that the experiment had been an economic success.
Within this period the elimination of trade discrimination was
virtually completed. The net result was that international trade in
steel within the confines of ECSC had multiplied by 157 per cent,
steel output itself was up by 65 per cent while the coal industry
was successfully tackling the painful problem of modernisation.
No better justification for this experimental attempt at economic
integration could be given than the statistics for the first five
years, a comparison with the efforts of other countries, and an
attempt to assess what the coal and steel industries of 'little Europe'
would have been like without ECSC.

Yet ECSC was not just to be an economic body. The ultimate
aim of its founders, particularly Robert Schuman and Jean Monnet,
was the fulfilment of the dream of political integration. What,
then, had ECSC achieved in this field? It could justifiably be argued
that ECSC had not conditioned the European public to endorse or
agitate for a rash of supranational bodies, but perhaps this is only
a superficial assessment of the value of the Community. More
serious—and accurate—is the charge that it had failed to establish
any authority over national governments or national parliaments.
The latter had refused to bow down to the ECSC Assembly. In
this sense, therefore, the 'parliamentary' work of ECSC very rarely
had direct practical consequences.

Nevertheless there have been some beneficial aspects. First,
there were the developments within ECSC itself. Over the years
the two predominantly supranational bodies within the Community, the High Authority and the Common Assembly, had constructed an effective system of consultation—particularly successful

in the field of proposed expenditure. These two institutions formed a 'European alliance' against the threat of an overruling national interest. Far from utilising its right to restrain the High Authority, the Assembly was constantly urging it to move even further along the road to supranationalism. This tendency of the Common Assembly had one invaluable effect in that it disposed of possible accusations that supranationalism had an elitist character. By helping to give an air of democracy to ECSC it allowed the acceptance of the Community by left-wing parties and organisations, which at best may have been apathetic and at worst totally opposed to a 'Christian Democratic conspiracy'. The fact that the fourth main architect was a Socialist, Paul-Henri Spaak of Belgium (since popularly acclaimed as 'Mr Europe'), also helped Socialist parties to accept the new Community structure. While the Assembly's attempts to gain greater powers for itself usually proved to be abortive, it showed determination and imagination in its assessment of its responsibility for the future. Within it political orientations gradually came to be international rather than national in character. It can be argued that in the three major groupings of Socialism, Liberalism and Christian Democracy, ECSC had the nucleus of 'European' parties. This tendency was encouraged by the official recognition accorded to the three Assembly groupings: their administrative expenses, for example, were covered by the ECSC budget. Other organisations have also tended to coalesce on a 'European' basis. For example, the High Authority was assisted by a rather weak Consultative Committee. Although probably the most unsuccessful part of ECSC, the Committee possessed some value in that trade union representatives have preferred to place national commitments and prejudices second to the need to develop an integrated international trade union policy.

Second, there are the developments caused by ECSC. The Community had been a departure from the normal collection of ideas espoused by pro-Europeans. Since 1945 they had tended to argue for a federal system of government to be introduced in Western Europe. One feature of a federal system would be the single act of the abrogation of a lengthy list of national rights and powers to a federal or supranational body, whose precedence over the former national units would be stipulated by a constitution. By their very nature constitutions are apt to be rather rigid in construction and 'once and for all' in their application. ECSC is clearly not this type of institution. Its method of integration was to pursue the gradual relinquishing of the rights of national governments to the supranational High Authority. But until that stage was reached, certain acts of the High Authority could be vetoed by member governments. What was needed, therefore, was an atmosphere of mutual confidence. ECSC procedure was designed to produce this by devising a list of specific problems to be tackled by certain deadlines. As the barriers fell (but only when all participants were prepared) the success of the institutions could be utilised in arguments for moving on to a list of further commitments. The whole process was gradual but dynamic. Success tended to breed success and the willingness to look for fresh fields to conquer, particularly as the application of ECSC, besides solving problems, created many others—for example, the need to establish a common labour policy. It therefore paved the way for the creation of the larger (in scope) European Economic Community, although the fact that since 1958 the work of these two bodies, plus that of Euratom, tends to overlap in certain fields, has created even more unresolved problems. Some rationalisation was achieved in 1965 when the executive institutions of the three existing communities, ECSC, Euratom and the Economic Community, were merged into only one executive organ.

Finally, credit must be given to ECSC for the work it performed in helping to overcome the major divisive factor in modern Western European history, the mutual hostility between France and Germany. In one sense ECSC had been drafted as a solution to the Ruhr problem. The massive Ruhr industrial complex was West Germany's largest economic asset for the future: it also had been before 1945 the central factory of German militarism. What many people were looking for, therefore, was some way of ensuring that the Ruhr resources could not be used for the same purpose. An international coal and steel community was one means of setting minds at rest. The Ruhr, however, was not the only dilemma: there was also the disputed area of the Saar, then under French administration and integrated with the

French economy but claimed by the young West German State. The Saar population was predominantly German and it was hardly likely that German discontent over French control of the region would diminish or cease. The main economic activity of the Saar was coal and steel, and ECSC again offered the opportunity to ease existing tensions and prepare the ground for an amicable Franco-German *rapprochement* on the area as a preliminary to a much wider area of agreement. ECSC therefore fulfilled to the best of its limited ability Schuman's stipulation in 1950 that a prime consideration within Europe had to be the reconciliation of France and Germany. In March 1962 ECSC was offered a much wider scope when Britain, with its very large coal industry, formally applied for membership. But as with the Common Market discussions, French intransigence (on grounds of economic self-interest) prevented Britain's application passing beyond the negotiation stage.

EDC: the Misplaced Sector

During the initial negotiations over ECSC the international climate changed for the worse. Added to the anxieties of the Cold War in Europe, there was now the renewed threat of a third world war as conflict broke out in Korea. As we have seen, this new problem forced the United States to undertake a reassessment of its defensive and military commitments throughout the world, and that for Europe the net result was the demand by Secretary of State Dean Acheson in September 1950, at a NATO Council meeting in New York, for a German military contribution to the Western alliance.

The most obvious way of achieving this was to admit West Germany to NATO. But this was feared by most of Germany's neighbours and adamantly opposed by France, because NATO forces were essentially national armies, although under one integrated command. Hence there was a new impetus for the establishment of a European army, which had already been raised in the Assembly of the Council of Europe. France took the lead in drawing up plans for the European Defence Community, initially known as the Pleven Plan after the French premier who sponsored it. Schuman was again in the forefront of things and in November he emphasised that EDC was a better way of meeting the American request since it precluded the possibility of an independent German army. The plan passed its first test when Pleven persuaded the French National Assembly to accept the general principle in October. The next few months were taken up with the customary round of discussions and negotiations. The United States endorsed the scheme, and the NATO commander, General Eisenhower, was particularly enthusiastic. Britain also approved, but made it clear that British policy forbade participation, but not association. The negotiations of the six protagonists were completed in Paris by February 1951, but it was only some fifteen months later that the final treaty was signed: the delay had been occasioned by arguments over the conditions of German participation.

The actual structure of EDC was to be built along the lines of ECSC, although for obvious reasons the 'supranational executive', the Board of Commissioners, was to have considerably less leverage against the national representatives of the Council of Ministers. Otherwise the details of the treaty were significant only in so far as they concerned West Germany. The Federal Republic was to be the poor relation of EDC. It was to be allowed only twelve armed divisions, of which ten would be fully integrated into the European army and placed under non-German commanders; West Germany was not permitted any other military force bar these twelve divisions. It meant that West Germany was excluded from being a full member of NATO and denied the right of manufacturing nuclear weapons. Even if EDC had succeeded, it is difficult to see how West Germany, with a potential economic and demographic superiority in Western Europe, would have been satisfied for long with these biased arrangements. European integration in this or any other sector can never function correctly except on a basis of mutual trust and equal partnership. Furthermore, both the United States and Britain were asked to station troops on the continent. These were not so much a token gesture against the possibility of a Russian invasion as a further guarantee to France against a German nationalist revival.

Notwithstanding the many drawbacks surrounding EDC, there

was reason to believe late in 1952 that the movement toward integration had passed the critical point and could only go forward at a much faster pace: supporters believed that the creation of ECSC and EDC had finally consigned the old shibboleths of nationalism to a tardy grave. The first attempt to build a comprehensive supranational authority in Europe had ended in failure through the effort to incorporate Britain into the design. While a 'greater Europe' was now out of the question, it seemed probable that such a multi-purpose unit could be built by the 'little Europe' of the Six. EDC itself was a major step in the right direction, for the ECSC Assembly was to serve as a temporary parliamentary institution for EDC while studying the possibility of establishing a permanent and democratic assembly. The Consultative Assembly of the Council of Europe, although such a development would clearly diminish its own importance, was enthusiastic about the idea.

However, a principal cause of the new suggestions for a further advance was EDC itself. The dilemma it raised was summed up by Dr Adenauer on his first visit to the United States in April 1953, when he said that a unified European army was a completely illogical development unless there was a correspondingly unified European foreign policy. But again, a unified army and foreign policy could not exist in an institutional vacuum. The logical step therefore seemed to be the development of a comprehensive political community. The concept was strengthened by three major criticisms that had been levelled against the integration by sectors programme. First, there was the point already mentioned: that it was essentially an elitist concept of politics. Some kind of popular participation, and hence a democratically elected parliament, would be advisable. Second, even within the elitist structure, the amount of power available to European organs was considerably less than their burden of responsibility. And third, there was the possible danger that the policies of the various sectors might not coincide or might even be diametrically opposed to one another.

These were the basic factors which had caused the foreign ministers of the Six, in September 1952, to ask the ECSC Common Assembly to consider ways and means of creating a European Political Community, and to draw up a draft proposal of the structure within a period of six months. The Assembly did this as an 'Ad Hoc Assembly', incorporating extra delegates to bring the number up to the proposed EDC membership. At the end of the six-month period the president of the Assembly, Paul-Henri Spaak, presented its findings to the six foreign ministers. What had been drawn up was a draft statute for a European Political Community with a structure similar to that of ECSC and EDC. Since an EPC had been the ultimate goal of the integration by sectors programme, this was not to be just a third community, but nothing less than the beginning of a comprehensive European federation. ECSC and EDC were to be only subsidiary parts of the new EPC. To emphasise the nature of the new body, its name was shortened to that of the European Community. By mid-1953, therefore, 'little Europe' seemed to have demolished the final barriers guarding the road to full integration.

This, however, proved to be the high watermark of European union as far as the early 1950s were concerned. The pace and the enthusiasm dropped considerably when attention had to switch from abstract principles to general details until it appeared that total abandonment was probable. Only ECSC appeared to be strong enough to avoid the scrap heap. Several factors were involved in the withdrawal from the frontier of full integration. The international situation had improved with the ending of the Korean War under the Panmunjom armistice, and with the more relaxed relationship between the United States and Soviet Russia. Western Europe, moreover, was feeling more confident about its own defensive arrangements as NATO began to improve its own organisation. Apart from the need to possess a German military contribution, there appeared to be no military justification for EDC. Above all, there was still the question-mark hovering above West Germany: no European nation was completely free from doubt about the wisdom of German rearmament.

The changed mood was reflected in the further discussions held by the foreign ministers or their deputies of the six nations of 'little Europe' in the second half of 1953. Meeting first at Baden-Baden in August, and later in Rome and The Hague, they did little to advance the scheme any further. In fact they did not discuss the topic in anything but general terms. Such a mood had serious implications, for it meant essentially a return to the pre-1949 situation where the major objective was to create a favourable climate for the establishment of European institutions—and hence where generalities were more important than details. The Six were not yet willing to surrender all sovereignty to a supranational authority.

However, the great argument of these years was not around EPC, but around EDC. For EPC stood or fell with the ratification or rejection of EDC. The one-year-old EDC treaty had not been ratified by anyone by the time of the publication of the EPC draft treaty. Only the German and Benelux governments retained their earlier enthusiasm for EDC. It was eventually ratified by the Low Countries in the early months of 1954. In March of the same year it was approved by West Germany after a prolonged battle in which the SPD took its opposition to the scheme to the Federal Constitutional Court. In Italy de Gasperi also faced strong opposition. The political extremes were implacably opposed, while many others thought that the Italian Government should bargain for a return of Trieste as the condition of Italian entry into EDC. De Gasperi may well have held the winning hand in the end, but the decision was never put to the test as Italy was waiting for ratification by France before committing itself to EDC. Thus the fate of the new ambitious structures of integration hinged upon the French attitudes.

As we have seen, France had never been basically enthusiastic about EDC, regarding it merely as the lesser of two evils, although it had been sponsored by Frenchmen. Pleven lost the premiership, and the new prime minister requested further concessions before ratification. Whether these were sincerely held beliefs or mere time-wasting devices was irrelevant: they had a most damaging effect upon the hopes of EDC and EPC. First, France requested the special privilege of being allowed to switch officers between EDC and overseas colonial duties without the prior approval of EDC. It was argued that this was necessary because, alone of the Six, France had global responsibilities. This modification, formally requested by France, might by itself have been accepted eventually by the other five, even though their first reaction was that it violated the treaty and would make it void. Equally injurious was the dominant attitude within the French National Assembly that before entering EDC France should secure a firmer pledge of support and closer cooperation from the United States and Britain. No French premier, relying always upon the unstable centre coalition for his majority, could afford to ignore this widely held sentiment. In essence, if actual British membership of EDC was out of the question, they wanted British troops which could not be removed simply by a decision of the British Government to be permanently stationed in Europe. The Assembly felt that this would offset the dangers of a possible German supremacy in EDC. The plea fell upon stony ground in Britain. It served first to discredit EDC and to confirm Britain's increasing anxiety over 'contamination' by supranationalism, and second to place a great strain on Franco-German relations, which were still bedevilled by the problem of the Saar. France also met with little sympathy in the United States, which was now committed to EDC. The only answer to the French request that America should help finance the Indo-China war and so ease the drain on French resources was Dulles's threat of an 'agonising re-appraisal' of American policy if EDC was not ratified.

The final nail in the EDC coffin was, paradoxically, the 1954 Geneva conference. France hoped that the more pliant Russian attitude would extend to Indo-China where France was seeking a peace settlement with the Communist leader, Ho Chi Minh. The French Government was therefore very reluctant to commit any action which would annoy the Russians. EDC therefore could not be ratified. On the other side, it was quite clear that Moscow had anticipated the French course of action and hoped that EDC, which it opposed and feared, would be defeated. All that was left was for a French premier finally to lower the coffin into the ground.

The first result was the ironical one of the creation of a distinct German national army within Western European Union and NATO—the very thing France had striven to avoid. The damage done to European integration was also enormous. The death of EDC automatically meant the destruction of the more ambitious EPC. Only ECSC was left and even it did not escape the shock-waves; Jean Monnet announced that, in order to pursue schemes of

European integration as a private citizen, he would not seek re-election as President of the ECSC High Authority. It was doubtful whether even such an influential individual as Monnet could achieve as great an effect as he could from within the supranational High Authority. Almost simultaneously, the most famous postwar Italian exponent of unity, Alcide de Gasperi, died. The forces of federation were in disarray, and at the time the most obvious conclusion to be drawn was that the whole momentum of European integration was grinding to a halt.

10 The International Détente

The possibility and necessity of peaceful coexistence. . . .

G. M. Malenkov, 1955

It has already been hinted that in 1953 the climate of international affairs altered considerably, and this necessarily affected political developments within Western Europe itself. The year 1953 saw a lessening of the acute tension which had marked the Cold War since its inauguration six years earlier. For Western Europe in particular the changed atmosphere meant that there was a reduction in the intensity of the feeling of the American and Russian presence in the area, influencing and in many ways directing political events and developments. The new climate also meant that the threat of the Cold War giving rise to a direct and actual military confrontation of the United States and Soviet Russia had receded, although the diminution of the danger could by no means be said to be approaching evaporation. The most prominent feature of the new status of the Cold War was summed up in the catch-phrase, 'peaceful coexistence'. The four events which probably formed the major contribution to this change were the ending of the Korean War, the American presidential election in November 1952, the death of Russia's dictator, Stalin, and the eventual production by the Soviet Union of a hydrogen bomb.

The Korean War was as yet the only open sore on the globe in which the two super-powers were in one way or another directly involved and committed. But by 1952 it had become clear that a military settlement in Korea would be possible only if a worldwide confrontation occurred; short of total war, the Asian conflict had degenerated into an uneasy but absolute stalemate with neither side willing to pour in its full resources. It seemed that peace by way of a negotiated settlement could not come as long as the Democrat Party occupied the presidency in the United States; the Russians were unwilling to negotiate with President Truman and what they called his 'war-mongering' party.

The Republican Party, after twenty years in the political wilderness, thus had a golden opportunity to use the promise of peace in Korea, which most Americans desperately wanted, in their 1952 election campaign. This chance, coming on top of their good fortune in obtaining Dwight Eisenhower, the commander of the Allied forces in the Second World War and later in NATO and the country's most popular military figure, as their presidential candidate, put the Republicans in an almost invincible position. After the expected victory occurred, Eisenhower proceeded to honour his electoral promise of negotiating a peace in Korea, emphasised by his symbolic trip to the wartorn country. After nearly three years of conflict, the result was the not unexpected one of a return to the prewar partition boundary of the Thirty-eighth Parallel.

In this way the result of the American presidential election helped to allay European fears that the almost xenophobic nationalism, in which the United States was seen to be submerged, would drag the old continent into an undesired world war. It was an erroneous impression; a few more years were to pass before the American fear of Communism left its state of delirium, epitomised for foreign observers by the witch-hunts of Senator Joseph McCarthy, for a quieter and more rational level.

The settlement of the Korean War was only one particular aspect of the changed emphasis in American foreign policy. More general and perhaps more important was the fact that the Republican Party had traditionally been less concerned about foreign relationships and close American involvement overseas. In many ways the Republicans, before the 1940s, had identified themselves closely with the 'isolationist impulse' which had a long and proud tradition in the United States.[1] Although a complete withdrawal from Europe and elsewhere was out of the question, the upshot of the Republican victory was a relative disinterest, and an accompanying greater reluctance on the part of the United States to intervene actively in European affairs.

It was not as if the United States had abandoned Europe. Indeed many European leaders welcomed this change in American foreign policy. For one thing, they felt that Eisenhower, who had twice

[1] S. Adler, *The Isolationist Impulse*, New York, 1961.

been their military commander, could be trusted not to treat the European commitment too lightly. On the other hand, with relatively stable economies at last, most Western European nations were on the verge of following West Germany into an economic boom and a period of prosperity. This greater economic independence was accompanied by a feeling that Western Europe should have more political independence, that perhaps the continent should dissociate itself to some extent from America's coat-tails, and a renewed confidence in a hopeful political future. If the United States had maintained the same high degree of involvement in European affairs as in the late 1940s, then almost certainly the mid 1950s would have seen several clashes of will between the two sides of the Atlantic. As it was, this disagreement was delayed until de Gaulle emerged in France as the champion of an old-fashioned pride in nationalism and resentment at dictation from an outsider.

Correspondingly, the possible dangers of a Russian advance westward in Europe, which had previously been checked by resolute American action and promises, seemed to recede sharply with the announcement from Moscow of the death of Stalin. In his last years the Russian dictator appeared to lose that shrewdness which had marked his long political career. In a state bordering paranoia, his suspicions and ruthlessness increased greatly, so that his lieutenants were never certain of being able to avoid accusations of treachery or of being able to ascertain what abrupt changes would occur in Soviet domestic and foreign policy. Because of this uncertainty, there was, as it were, a built-in fuse which at any moment could cause an explosion of Russian armies into Western Europe, notwithstanding the knowledge that the United States probably held an advantage in nuclear military capacity.

Stalin's successors appeared to be more aware of the dangers to Russia implicit in the concept of a nuclear war, and hence appeared to be more reluctant to pursue policies which could easily cause such a war. The so-called 'thaw' which would advance and recede regularly in future years according to the analysis by the Russian leaders of the current international situation, was not so much a renunciation of the messianic aims of Communism; rather it was an indication that the new Soviet leaders had acknowledged the possibility that their competition with the West could, given the existing military state of affairs, be won by safer methods.

This did not mean that Soviet Russia was willing to relax its hegemony in Eastern Europe, at least to the extent of jeopardising the basis of that hegemony. In June 1953 demonstrations in East Berlin turned into riots and a full-scale protest against the Communist puppet regime. The Russians held back until it was obvious that the rebellion, if successful, would reject Russian influence completely. Thereupon Russian military units swiftly moved in to re-establish authority. Similarly in Hungary in October 1956 demonstrations against the severity of the regime turned over-night into a revolt against the regime itself. Within a week it seemed to be successful, and it was reported that Russian troops were preparing to leave the country. But the new Hungarian leaders went too far (that is, for the Soviet Union); their intention of becoming a neutral state between the two power blocs threw out of balance the whole Communist security system as well as serving as a dangerous precedent. Again, after an initial period of hesitation and standing back, Russia eventually moved to quell the revolt in a very short space of time: the counterattack was aided by the fact that the West and other parts of the world were involved at that time in the Suez crisis and in no position to pay attention to Eastern Europe. But these two abortive uprisings, following the pattern of the Berlin blockade and all subsequent Berlin crises, pointed to two facts: while the Soviet Union may not have been willing to advance openly, it was certainly not willing openly to yield up any of its *de facto* control in Europe: and the United States was unwilling to advance beyond the iron curtain as long as this involved the risk of world war.

Nevertheless the new Soviet policy of peaceful coexistence with the non-Communist world did allow Western Europe to breathe more freely. Oddly enough, the knowledge that the Soviet Union possessed the hydrogen bomb produced the same effect. The news of Russia's thermonuclear status was received calmly in Western Europe, unlike the situation in 1949 when Russia's first atomic explosion was regarded as being almost a declaration of open war. The essence of the situation, as seen by European observers, was that Russia's technological advance, in destroying American nuclear (and therefore military) supremacy, brought with it stalemate. Neither side could ignore the risk of massive and instantaneous thermonuclear retaliation. Peace thus became imperative and, paradoxically, more probable.

The symbol of the new 'understanding' between East and West was the July 1955 summit conference at Geneva. Although no fruitful conclusions were reached—and only a supreme optimist could have expected any significant achievements to be gained— the conference was significant in that it was the first time since Potsdam, ten years earlier, that the American and Russian leaders had met face to face. The fact that President Eisenhower and Premier Khrushchev could sit at the same table seemed to indicate that the two sides had agreed that short of total war an 'unstable peace' was the only possible way out of the nuclear stalemate.

In the years following 1953 this changed situation clarified itself to some extent. Western European democracy, which had lived under the threat of war virtually since 1945, adapted itself readily to rather better conditions. Moreover, the new political vigour caused by the eclipse of both right-wing and left-wing extremism and by the new economic prosperity, the first for several decades, conduced to form an optimistic mood of self-confidence. On its feet at last, Western Europe felt for the first time that it was capable of holding its own in the changed postwar world (except, perhaps, for the colonial question). Consequently both the United States and Soviet Russia found it more difficult to direct or influence the course of political affairs in Western Europe. Only of government circles in West Germany could it be said, sometimes unjustly, that there was a strong willingness to accept American proposals or a perfect relationship with the United States: and West Germany's particular dilemma was unique as far as Europe was concerned.

The Military Scene: EDC, WEU and NATO

The purely military imperatives which had very largely dominated Western foreign policy during the previous years did not now possess the same urgency. The 'thaw' therefore inevitably affected the fate of the proposed European Defence Community, whose actual operation still awaited ratification by the French National

Assembly. The relaxation of international tension permitted France, the original sponsor, a way out of the dilemma that it had created for itself. Now it seemed clear that if the ED C treaty failed to emerge from the National Assembly, protests from France's allies, including the United States, would not be as vehement as a year earlier.

But there was another facet of the military problem. In American strategic circles, Truman's policy of containment had been dropped in favour of one of 'roll-back', which pleased the anxious American public for it appeared to suggest that the United States was now preparing to embark upon a more obviously aggressive foreign policy. The previous Democratic government of America had believed that the ideological mission of Communism was as important as the military aspect, and had therefore concentrated just as much on the political part of the Cold War; containment was essentially a policy which operated simultaneously on political, ideological, and military levels.

However, the new American Secretary of State, John Foster Dulles, who in many ways was more important than President Eisenhower as the architect of American foreign policy during this period, was convinced that the military aspect overwhelmed everything else, that the Cold War as played by the Soviet Union was nothing more than the latest example of the traditional game of power politics. His idea was that the United States should avoid another Korea, but where confrontation with the enemy was unavoidable the venue should be picked by the United States. From this thinking there developed the concept of 'massive retaliation'. These ideas are illustrative of one important flaw in Dulles's political make-up—a tendency to simplify affairs and rationalise the many hues of grey into a straightforward division between white and black.

Thus the effects of the policy of the new American Government were paradoxical. There was a tendency to remain more remote from foreign contact, especially in Europe, than its predecessor, yet paradoxically it was simultaneously attempting to give the United States a more progressive and aggressive image. Naturally this side of American policy was not calculated to appeal to Europeans: America's allies became, if anything, more anxious and more tense. Where EDC was concerned, to which the United States was fully committed, it tended to strengthen the opposition. This was particularly true in France where the opposition, of course, still had the opportunity to block the treaty. But no French politician would take kindly to American pressure or interference in France's domestic politics on behalf of EDC. Thus Dulles's accusation in December 1953 of 'dilatory manoeuvres' and the later threat of an 'agonising reappraisal' by the United States of her foreign commitments made it even more unlikely that a French Government would be able to push the EDC treaty through the National Assembly.

The French premier who eventually dared to bring the EDC treaty before parliament was Pierre Mendès-France. Mendès-France was a member of the Radical Party and was regarded by many observers as one of the few men capable of commanding a large amount of personal loyalty and of holding together a stable moderate–left coalition. His main objectives and interests were in domestic affairs where he desired to inaugurate a programme of economic reform. Before he could approach this more 'mundane' problem, two pressing crises crippling French political life had to be removed from the scene: the Indo-China War and the European Defence Community. As a result, Mendès-France first negotiated the end of the Indo-China War, and then, one month later, in August 1954, he brought the EDC treaty to the National Assembly, knowing that it would almost certainly be defeated. Since the original short-term justification for EDC had almost disappeared, and since the compromise had never really been acceptable to most French political leaders, Mendès-France did not even attempt to defend it. It was simply introduced into parliament without comment as a hindrance which had to be disposed of before other business could be tackled: the vote was not even upon the treaty itself, but upon whether the treaty should be discussed.

The refusal of the French National Assembly to ratify EDC was the burial ceremony of the treaty. It meant a serious setback to the hopes and ambitions of the European federalists: at the time it appeared that the movement for European union had been set back for several years by the French action. It also created a gap in the Western defensive system. Since the original request, the

United States had based its conception of the defensive alliance of Western Europe upon the increase in strength which a West German military contribution would give. Some alternative therefore had to be found. The search took the Western nations a remarkably short time to complete. All else failing, they eventually fell back, with British encouragement, upon the 1948 Treaty of Brussels, the defensive pact against the revival of German militarism signed by Britain and four of the proposed members of EDC. Britain had refused anything but a close association with EDC, but felt that the new proposed structure was sufficiently diluted of supranational overtones to allow her to enter without endangering her freedom of action.

Britain had originally objected to the EDC proposals for several reasons. Looking at the wider implications of an Atlantic community, it had been argued that EDC would adversely affect the successful overall integration of NATO. Britain had also suggested that the time lag between the proposal and the actuality would be too great, since a West German military contribution was essential at that moment. On top of these objections, and far more important, were the British suspicions of being pushed into a federated Europe and of being left to hold the burden of European defence because the United States was seeking to lighten its own responsibilities. At the time of the original proposal in 1950, the British Labour Government had also been wary of participation in a structure dominated by Christian Democrats and very uncertain about the advisability of German rearmament. But the overwhelming shadow of Soviet Russia forced Britain to swallow several scruples and move closer to Europe and American demands. In 1955 it was the British Prime Minister, Anthony Eden, who took the lead in salvaging something from the wreck of EDC. It was an excellent opportunity to bring forward again the British counterproposal that West German rearmament could best be achieved and supervised within NATO itself. Konrad Adenauer, who saw rearmament as an indispensable part of his own policy, quickly fell into line behind Eden, and the others followed shortly thereafter. In order to soften any possible clash between France and West Germany, it was agreed that British participation in the new body, which was to be called Western European Union, would involve the stationing of troops on the continent unless a majority of the Brussels powers consented to their withdrawal. British participation was also seen by the other signatories, especially France which had wanted Britain's counterweight within EDC, as a further check against the possibility of the new organisation being dominated in the future by Germany.

An independent structure for the new organisation was out of the question. It was too weak to support one, and in any case Britain would almost certainly refuse to commit itself to anything that smelled of supranationalism. Rather than leave the new treaty out on a limb, it was decided that its interests would best be served by incorporation within NATO, of which all the signatories were members. At last, therefore, the United States had achieved its aim of levying a German military contribution; while the West German Chancellor, Adenauer, had moved another step forward in his ambition to have West Germany fully accepted as an equal partner with the other democracies in all international agreements. Ironically, the new treaty established what France had most desired to avoid—the creation of a German army.

Apart from advancing German claims for equality the new WEU structure achieved no significant results. Indeed its impact was negative. The development of Russian nuclear strength had very largely invalidated most of the original concepts behind NATO and other defensive schemes for Western Europe. Now it was clear that a conventional type of war with a primary and extensive deployment of ground troops, especially by Russia, had become more remote. Thus the original cause of the demand for German rearmament had disappeared or at least had greatly diminished in urgency. Again, NATO had not been strengthened by the new agreement, for that military body had been forced to reconsider its role and organisation. Until some new strategy for the defence of the West was found, no one could say whether NATO had been strengthened, or even whether it would survive in its original form.

European Union: New Departures

Events had conspired to make Europeans more aware of Europe

as an entity. There had been a constriction of political activity by the West European democracies. First, there had been the realisation, painful at times, that they could no longer hope to play the same political and international role as before. If the failure to combat Communism without American help in the late 1940s had failed to teach them this lesson, then the uprisings in East Germany and Hungary and the abortive Suez expedition of 1956 were rude and strong reminders. Second, the growing surge of nationalism in Asia and Africa precipitated the end of the colonial system. Henceforth European influence in these areas would be primarily economic, not political: again, therefore, in the geographical sense, there was a withdrawal back to Europe. Apart from the settler problem facing Britain in Kenya and Rhodesia and the even more acute crisis facing France in Algeria, the process of withdrawal appeared to be progressing fairly smoothly. Other areas of the world gained the spotlight. In 1956 while Europe showed indignation and fury over the ruthless crushing of the Hungarian uprising, the rest of the world refused to shift its attention from the Suez crisis. Furthermore, the all-pervading menace of the Cold War had waned. America and Russia were no longer explicitly implicated in Western Europe, leaving Europeans with a greater sense of independence.

Taken together, all these factors allowed more time to be devoted to national problems and to the future of Europe itself. And since in a period of prosperity national problems tend to appear less important and their solutions less urgent than during periods of depression or tension, these also tended to be forgotten or set aside. By more or less remaining the sole occupant of the field, European union became once again a major focus of discussion. Unlike the situation in 1945, these discussions did not have to start from scratch. Despite the failure of EDC, there was a wide array of international cooperative organisations in which the Western European democracies were involved: the Council of Europe; Western European Union; OEEC. But above all these there were, for the ardent federalists, the working examples of Benelux and the Coal and Steel Community, while in 1952 the Scandinavian countries had in the Nordic Council attempted a further venture into the field of supranational coordination and cooperation.

But the state of health of European harmony depended above all upon the nature of the relationship between France and West Germany, the two old enemies. The EDC treaty, or rather the French reluctance to ratify it, had been one bone of contention between the two countries. Another had been the future of the Saar province, a fairly important industrial region sandwiched between the two states. The Saar population was predominantly German, and in 1945 the Allies gave France the task of administering the region. But the Saar had never been part of the French occupation zone; instead the French intention was that it would be fully integrated economically, and ultimately politically, with France itself. This task was supervised by proconsuls, who played much the same role as the governors of the French colonies. However, no German politician would or could admit that this was the final or right solution for a Saar settlement. Negotiations between the two countries seemed only half-hearted as neither appeared willing to compromise, and other states were decidely lukewarm about the French hopes.

Eventually another proposal was put forward by the Council of Europe Assembly. This was that the Saar province should be given 'European status', in other words, that the Saar would be a nucleus of the future integrated European state. As such it would have separate representation in existing European organisations. But again this was inadmissible to West Germany, which demanded that the Saar should be given an opportunity to join the Federal Republic. After much haggling, this 'European' solution was agreed upon by the two protagonists at the same time as the Paris Agreements. It could be said that the fate of the Saar was settled by a 1955 referendum in the province where the proposal of European status was decisively rejected. A positive vote in this referendum had to be given if the Europeanisation of the Saar, and its inclusion as a separate unit within WEU, was to succeed. France at last seemed resigned to accepting the fact that the Saar was primarily German and wished to revert to being part of the German State. In any case the various plans of French politicians had never interested their electorate, which had always been quite apathetic about the Saar. With the issue of the Saar settled, relations between France and West Germany could become much more cordial. Thus, despite the defeat of ED C and the failure to manœu-vre the Saar into being a European province, the pro-federal forces had not suffered a complete reversal. The gloom had been more than dispelled by the fact that the two strongest continental powers could now sit round the same table without the atmos-phere being clouded by areas of serious dispute.

This was the Western European climate in which the most serious forward move toward an integrated union was to occur in 1957—the idea of an overall European Economic Community. Before the launching of the Common Market is discussed, some time should be spent examining the internal political structure and events within the major national protagonists.

11 The Death of Colonialism

A wind of change is blowing through the continent.

Harold Macmillan, 1960

The granting of independence to their colonial territories by the European powers had already been forced upon them in the immediate postwar years. During the 1950s the pace of independence accelerated so swiftly that very few colonial areas remained by the end of the decade. And most of these colonies had already been promised independence. The stampede for independence naturally had considerable effects upon the internal deliberations and functioning of the colonial powers themselves, whether they had decided to grant independence or to maintain, by force if necessary, effective control over their colonies. And later the withdrawal of the Western European nations from their colonies also influenced political life on the old continent.

If we look for an explanation of the great upsurge in both strength and numbers of political movements in Asia and Africa agitating for independence in the postwar years, we find that the Second World War itself had been the major catalyst. The Arab world, South-East Asia, and parts of North Africa—all colonial areas—had become involved in the global conflict. Nearly everywhere this involvement had been against the wishes of the native political leaders.

Apart from Japan, the protagonists had been Europeans. The two power blocs had constructed military strategies for these areas without considering either the desires of the native leaders or the effects and repercussions involvement might entail. For example, the largest colonial territory in the world, India, had been brought unwillingly into the war by Britain; the recognised Indian national leader, Mahatma Gandhi, had not been a party to this decision. The crucial area of the Middle East was taken over and occupied to prevent its capture by the other side. Iran, in theory an independent nation, was occupied by British and Russian forces to prevent its oilfields falling into enemy hands. The country was partitioned between the two powers and to the native population it would certainly seem that they governed the two areas absolutely in accordance with their own wishes. The position of the French colonies revealed the completely passive role of the local populations. The French colonies became involved in the conflict only if the local French civilian and military rulers declared their allegiance to de Gaulle's liberation movement; if, on the other hand, the local commander preferred the Vichy regime, then that colony usually remained on the sidelines as a spectator.

The war defeated colonialism, for repeated military reversals in the early years of war not only drove the European nations out of some of their colonies, but also hurt their prestige severely. It also meant that if any return was possible after the war, the colonial powers would have to rebuild their old structure of authority from the foundations upwards. The fall of France in 1940, and the dilemma which de Gaulle and Pétain presented to French colonial garrisons, underlined the inherent weaknesses of French military authority which until then had been successfully concealed behind a reputation. Similarly, the Japanese advance into South-East Asia revealed the weaknesses in the British and Dutch colonial structures in this area, while also implying their existence in other colonial territories.

These lessons, which the more perceptive of the local nationalist leaders were swift to realise, held true at the war's end. Throughout large areas of South-East Asia, for instance, the local population did not witness a triumphant return of the colonial power by virtue of a military victory over the invaders. Japanese forces were still occupying most of the former colonial territories when the atomic bomb compelled their leaders to surrender. Moreover, the most dominant 'liberating' power was the United States, with its marked anti-colonialist bias.

European Attitudes

The decisions of the Allies on the postwar arrangements meant that Italy lost its colonial possessions—just as the German colonies had disappeared after 1918. Now only five colonial powers remained: France, Britain, the Netherlands, Portugal, and Belgium. Where these powers had been ousted in the early years of the war, they returned in an attempt to take over where they had been compelled to stop.

The policies and plans of these powers for their colonies varied greatly. Generally speaking, the two major powers, France and Britain, faced the problem with the most realism: at least they accepted the need for making concessions to the local political movements. The three smaller nations adopted a much more intransigent attitude. So far as they were concerned, the old rigid structure should be maintained; concessions would be made only as a last resort. For all five powers the major problem they had to face after the war was whether they had the military capacity to sustain their authority completely over a colony where even a minority of the population, by various means, actively opposed their continued rule. At first the European nations were reluctant to admit their insufficiency in this matter, but in nearly every instance the answer had to be in the negative.

The Netherlands had only one important colonial area in its East Indian possessions, but the produce of these islands was an important asset of the home economy. The Dutch had decided to re-establish the old pattern of colonial control in the Indonesian islands, but of all the colonial powers, they were in the weakest position. Control over the colonies had been ended by the emphatic Japanese victory; in addition, the Netherlands did not have the military strength to reassert authority over the area after the war, nor did it possess the resources to wage a drawnout war against local guerrillas seeking national independence. Belgium and Portugal had been more fortunate. Strict supervision was continued as part of the policy of preventing the development of an educated native elite. The continuation of this intransigent policy was possible because their African colonies had not been disturbed in any way—apart from the new demand for the uranium deposits of the Belgian Congo. It was only toward the end of the 1950s that Belgium and Portugal were faced with the threat of colonial insurrection. Demands for independence have so far failed in the largely undeveloped Portuguese territories, but Belgium was forced to leave the Congo in 1960. The Netherlands was never given an opportunity to develop any comprehensive plan for a form of association with its Indonesian colony. And feelings were so bitter after independence that close cooperation was out of the question. Belgium did belatedly switch from its paternal attitude to envisage a complete union between itself and the Congo. Opposed by Congolese leaders, it could never have been a practical proposition. Portugal's scheme was to regard its colonies as an integral part of Portugal: in theory, therefore, they were not colonies, and requests for independence would be regarded as internal dissension or as demands for secession.

When we turn to consider the attitude of Britain and France toward the colonial problem, we find the existence of a more enlightened opinion. These two powers did recognise in part the new postwar urge for independence, and did attempt to counter it by discovering ways of retaining the closest possible links between the mother country and its colonies. On the whole, the more flexible approach was adopted by Britain. Before 1939 Britain had already created a form of international organisation which permitted the country to retain a close association with the independent dominions of Canada, Australia, New Zealand, and South Africa. It was only natural that this Commonwealth scheme should first be considered as worthy of extension to the colonies. It is reasonably safe to say that the Commonwealth scheme was the most popular, since most political leaders in Britain accepted the fact that a return to the old system could not last indefinitely. The Labour Party was firmly committed to proceed with liberation as quickly as events would permit. The Conservatives, on the other hand, were divided in opinion. Churchill himself had stated that he did not intend to preside over the liquidation of the empire. Faced with a strong imperialist wing which did not see colonial independence as inevitable, the Conservatives argued for a much slower rate of liberation.

The argument was settled by the 1945 elections. The new Labour Government immediately set about winding up Britain's suzerainty in the colonies. By the time the Conservatives returned to power in 1951 the process was already under way. It could be slowed down, but not reversed or checked. The Commonwealth system was decided on as the best means of allowing Britain to retain economic and social ties with the colonies, while abolishing the political link. There appeared to be no possible alternative, although doubts about the ability of the Commonwealth idea to function where countries with non-European governments and populations were concerned still remained. Accordingly, when a conference of Commonwealth leaders met in London in April 1949 to discuss a future arrangement with newly independent India, a new definition of the Commonwealth emerged. By 1950 India had become a republic with its own head of state. The only link was that the British monarch was recognised as the symbolic head of the Commonwealth. The Commonwealth concept had been stretched to its limits: without any easily recognisable structure and institutions, it became little more than a cooperative association within which members could collaborate if they felt so inclined. It had evolved into a 'concept of convenience'.[1]

Unlike the British Commonwealth, France had previously arrived at a scheme of integration or assimilation. Under this plan French colonial policy had been aimed at educating and indoctrinating colonial elites, but not colonial populations, with French culture. The end product was to be the transformation of the native leaders into Frenchmen. The policy was more rigid than the British design in that it aimed only at a small group of people. It was perhaps shortsighted in that, if successful, it might have alienated the leaders completely from the population, thereby causing a breakdown in the whole plan. Where the policy did get under way this threat was ever present. The essential flaw was probably that in the last resort it relied upon the acceptance of France's civilising mission by the colonial leaders; quite often this was far from forthcoming. French aid, culture, and educational facilities might be welcomed; acceptance of assimilation was usually rejected.

Wartime events determined that any postwar attempt to re-establish assimilation would have to labour against heavy odds. As mentioned above, the French colonies had been involved in the war or otherwise according to the views of the local military commanders. De Gaulle, in an attempt to lure more colonies to

[1] J. D. B. Miller, *The Commonwealth in the World*, London, 1958, p. 275.

his Free French Movement and to commit more closely those which had already pledged their support, promised that after the war the colonial structure would be reformed along more democratic lines. He suggested that the colonies might be incorporated into a French Union which would not be assimilationist, but an association. The French Union was later introduced in theory. In practice it never worked or was not allowed to work by French authorities. Clauses were inserted in the French Constitution of 1946 guaranteeing the creation of a Union which would function through a series of consultative bodies including both French and colonial representatives. France retained control of the reins: the new structure was never permitted to develop any independent powers. Paris continued to be the only constitutional decision-making centre in the French colonial system: while decisions were denied to the natives, 'illegal' decisions by local French authorities were usually condoned:

> The history of the French Empire reflects well the paradoxes of the French political system. Justified as a source of military strength and prestige it became after World War Two one of the pervasive causes of the decline of French power; dedicated to the realisation of one of the most grandiose schemes of the French Revolution—the assimilation of the natives into French culture and law—it evolved in a manner which brought the incompatibilities between France and the native cultures into sharp relief. Patterned upon the Napoleonic institutions of centralisation, according to which all parts of the far-flung empire were to be ruled from Paris, it allowed a situation to develop in which local French civil and military authorities became autonomous centres of power that frustrated the decisions of the government; inspiring high hopes for economic advantage, capital investment, and trade, it required substantial subsidies that turned it into a financial liability.[1]

However, provisions had been made for representatives of the colonies to be elected to the French National Assembly; all post-war parliaments contained about eighty overseas deputies. In some colonies the election was rigged by the local French leaders to produce amenable deputies, but universal suffrage gradually spread to become the basis of elections at the same time as it became

[1] R. C. Macridis and B. E. Brown, *The De Gaulle Republic*, Homewood, 1960, p. 188.

more difficult for local Frenchmen to manufacture the desired result. What it meant was that these colonial deputies differed basically only in degree from those native nationalists who agitated for independence from within the colonies. They were nothing more or less than a relatively influential parliamentary interest group whose main concern was to press for colonial independence whenever opportunities presented themselves.

The Rate of Independence

The colonial empires may be classified into three broad geographical areas: Asia, Africa (including the Arab North), and the Arab Middle East. Independence in these three areas advanced at different rates. The particular rate in any one area seemed to be linked to its level of political consciousness and the extent of its cultural development. In this way independence progressed most swiftly in the Middle East, while the slowest rate was that of Africa.

The Arab world should not, perhaps, be classified as a colonial area. Nevertheless, it is legitimate to include it in any discussion on decolonialisation as before 1939 and during the war the area was closely controlled by European powers. On the whole the latter were exercising the task of taking care of mandatory territories which before 1919 had been part of Turkey's Ottoman Empire. The process of steering these mandates to independence had in fact already begun: Britain had given independence to Iraq in 1937, while France had promised the same to Syria and the Lebanon. Paradoxically, the war both interrupted and increased the tempo of this movement in the Middle East.

After 1945 the departure of European political authority was never in doubt. In fact it could be said that evacuation degenerated into an undignified scramble between Britain and France to grant independence before the other and so show which was the better friend of the Arab world. In both acquiring and disposing of colonial territory, therefore, Britain and France still seemed to regard each other with suspicion as the principal rival. In a sense, this was true: America was unwilling to play a greatly enlarged role in the area while Russia was not yet in a position to do so. After dragging its heels previously, France 'liberated' Syria and the Lebanon in 1945; Britain promptly followed by leaving Transjordan. The final act in decolonialisation of the Middle East came in 1954 when Britain signed an agreement to leave the Suez Canal zone within the next twenty months. Although there remained the problems of Cyprus and Aden, British influence in Egypt had for long been the hub of British policy in the area. The 1954 agreement formally marked the end of this influence, while the abortive British–French Suez Expedition of 1956 showed how impossible it was to regain it.

The end of empire in Asia was more complicated. In 1945 South-East Asia was largely, at least in theory, the property of three European powers: Britain, France, and the Netherlands. Yet it was in this area that the key to independence lay, rather than with the rather special case of the Arab states. If independence could be gained by nationalist movements in this area, which had been involved in the late global conflict, then a precedent would have been set for the less culturally developed colonies. Thus the granting of independence to India in 1947 and to Indonesia in 1949 can be taken as the two most significant events in the process of liberation.

India, with its teeming population of over four hundred million, was the epitome of colonial rule, for its population was equal to that of the rest of the colonial world. Moreover, the British Raj had, for several generations, been regarded as the centre of the empire. The subcontinent was fortunate in that preparations for independence had at least been under way for several years. Here the British authorities had followed a systematic policy of educating and training local administrators. By the 1940s, therefore, there was in existence a comprehensive structure of native administrators and judges. In administration it was hoped that the transition to independence would be achieved relatively painlessly. Above this, India possessed within its dominant Congress Party a number of experienced political leaders who had worked responsibly for independence for a number of years. They had rejected previous British offers that fell short of this target, and consequently had spent part of the war in prison (this seems to be an essential course in the education of a colonial nationalist leader).

With the Labour Party in power after 1945 the situation was

entirely different. Independence would come as quickly as possible. Only one obstacle, which proved to be serious, lay in the way. This was the religious question. A substantial percentage of India's population were not Hindus, but Muslims. Their dominant political movement, the Muslim League, feared submergence or even persecution if Muslims were to remain in an independent Hindu state. The League therefore demanded that they should be given a separate state. Such a policy was opposed by both Britain and the Congress Party. It was fraught with difficulty, for in most communities Muslims and Hindus lived side by side, but the potential religious conflict remained insoluble. The only way out was the creation of two separate states, and this could be achieved only by partition. Partition is an unsatisfactory and arbitrary way of settling problems of this nature, but where two sides are irreconcilable it is so far the only method which can be said to guarantee a certain measure of success: hence its application in Germany, Korea, Palestine, and Vietnam and its advocation in Cyprus. In the summer of 1947 the independent nations of India and Pakistan came into being. Both eventually decided to become republics: therefore the Commonwealth concept was widened further, not only to admit the first non-white states to its membership, but also to admit two republics into a union which had a monarch at its head.

The remaining major British possessions in Asia soon followed India and Pakistan along the road toward independence. Ceylon opted for Commonwealth membership, while Burma preferred to stay outside. Burma thus preferred to tackle by itself the problem of guerrilla warfare sparked off and aided by the Communist victory in China in 1949. Chinese Communist expansion became a very real threat throughout South-East Asia: it was the strength of Communist guerrillas which was the main drawback to the remaining British colony, Malaya, achieving independence. Britain wished to quell the Communist threat here before granting self-government, which eventually came in 1957. The policy was successful. The British campaign in Malaya marks the only successful attempt so far to stamp out Communist guerrillas.

When we turn to look at the French and Dutch colonies in Asia, a different picture presents itself. Official Dutch policy did not recognise any claims to independence by Indonesia, while many influential quarters in France were determined to retain full control over Indo-China. In these colonies independence was not won primarily by negotiation and conference, but by an insurrectionary demonstration to show that full colonial authority could never be reimposed.

To any realist in 1945 independence for Indonesia was inevitable. The Japanese armies had retained full control throughout the war: the Dutch returned by virtue of the atomic bomb. They found that nationalist organisations, which had developed during the Japanese occupation and often had been encouraged by Japanese authorities, were the sole ruling bodies during the interregnum period. The nationalists were therefore in a much stronger position than the Dutch. The only recourse seemed to be negotiations for some form of self-government: the unwillingness of the nationalists to accept anything short of independence and the reluctance of the Dutch to concede anything that implied a lessening of their control meant an inevitable breakdown in the consultations. They had to resort to military force. The battle lasted for four years, although the result was never in doubt. The Netherlands did not possess the military capacity to subdue the nationalists and the cost of retaining a foothold was soaring: moreover, no help was forthcoming from friendly nations which either saw no hope in the Indonesian imbroglio or were immersed in their own problems. In 1949, the Netherlands granted independence to Indonesia, but refused to hand over to it the underdeveloped island of New Guinea, which now was the only relic of Dutch rule in Asia. This decision, coming on top of a four-year war, destroyed any possibility of a *rapprochement* between the two countries. Dutch New Guinea, or West Irian, became a bone of contention plaguing them until the 1960s.

The French problem was Indo-China. Here the situation was more complex: the insurgent guerrillas were, after 1949, in a better position to receive aid from Communist China, while France was better able than the Netherlands to wage a long and drawnout jungle war. Indo-China had held a peculiar position during the last years of the war. It was the only major French colony that had retained an allegiance to Vichy. As a consequence, there were in 1945 two French factions in Indo-China; the original commanders being opposed by agents loyal to de Gaulle and his Free French Movement. Japan itself only formally occupied French Indo-China in the closing years of the war. Two other political forces further blurred the picture. China, which still claimed the colony to be an integral part of its own territory, was active in the northern border areas, while nationalists under the Communist, Ho Chi Minh, controlled substantial areas in the eastern region (which was to become Vietnam). In fact, the sub-merged wartime conflict and the postwar colonial struggle were largely limited to Vietnam. To the immediate west, the two French protectorates of Laos and Cambodia enjoyed relative peace.

With the end of the war the Gaullist agents became the official French representatives. The immediate problem to be faced was what to do about Ho Chi Minh's nationalist movement. Though Communist, it appeared to have avoided becoming a mere appendage of Moscow, and moreover it undisputedly claimed wide popular support. Backed by the French Government in Paris, the most satisfactory course open to the Gaullists appeared to be cooperation with the nationalists for some form of self-government. Ho Chi Minh was invited to Paris to pursue these consultations on independence. It can be argued that the Indo-China War was forced upon the two main political protagonists against their wishes. The negotiations were not popular with large sectors of French political life nor with certain quarters of the army. In Indo-China, meanwhile, an uneasy peace was maintained, but war was precipitated when a local French commander ordered a bombing raid of a nationalist stronghold.

The Paris government was unwilling and unable to reverse this subordinate decision. It allowed the action of one commander to grow into a full-scale colonial war by the end of 1946. The inability of the French Government to deal satisfactorily with its army and colonial representatives was an outstanding characteristic of the Fourth Republic. Time and time again, French governments, even if they wished to pursue liberal and 'decolonial' measures, were compelled to adopt policies determined by spontaneous actions taken by French colonial administrators and colonial army officers.

In Indo-China, in fact, the power of the local representatives was so great that they were able to censor all news sent to Paris. They held back for ten days a telegram sent by Ho Chi Minh to Paris appealing for further negotiation: by then it was too late to be effective. The action which sparked off the Indo-China War was the first in this chain of insubordination; it offered a precedent for all future decisions of this kind. By failing to act in 1946 the French Government left itself indefensible against repetitions of this type of behaviour.

In the event, nearly eight years passed before a precarious peace came to Indo-China. The war was fought in the jungle, consisting almost entirely of eroding skirmish actions by guerrillas against small units of the French Army. It was a war which France could never hope to win; the superior French military capacity could never be concentrated for an attack upon an outstanding enemy stronghold. The inability of the French to point to a conclusive win in a battle, the need to spend more and more time searching for an elusive enemy in the jungle, the knowledge that French authority could be maintained only in a decreasing area around the cities of Saigon and Hanoi—all these factors made the war ever more unpopular in France. It proved to be a constant drain on the still weak French economy and military capacity. The mortality rate was so high that French military academies could not fill the gaps. Only professional soldiers were used: the war's unpopularity meant that any government which sent conscripts to Indo-China would automatically be destroyed. Certain army officers welcomed this turn of events: only the reputation of the professional French Army would be involved, and for many the conflict represented a search by the French Army to regain the reputation it lost in 1940.

The nationalist armies were strengthened by the victory of the Communists in China in 1949. They now had a readily accessible supply base just across the border. This affected the strategy of both sides: it made Ho Chi Minh more susceptible to Chinese demands, while it made the French more sympathetic to the demands of the non-Communist nationalists. Given their need to retain as much ground control as possible, the French army leaders had to give more political control to local non-Communists. The latter, in effect, were gradually gaining the independence which the French military had originally been deployed to prevent.

A year later, the focus of world attention in South-East Asia switched from Indo-China to Korea. When the Chinese intervened in the Korean War, it seemed that France still had a chance to salvage something of their previous authority over their recalcitrant colony. It now could be argued that the two wars were primarily two different fronts of the same conflict against Communism. This was partly the view of the United States, which previously had opposed the French effort to hold Indo-China because of its anti-colonialist sympathies. American aid in the shape of supplies and money, though not troops, was sent to Indo-China; by 1954 American aid covered three-quarters of the total cost of the war. It was, however, already too late to hold the weakened French position, let alone regain lost ground. It was perhaps doubtful whether American aid from the outset would have helped France, given the pattern imposed on the war by the geographical terrain.

When the Korean War ended, the United States pulled out of Asia. American public opinion was in no mood to support an unpopular war in a French colony. The result of the Indo-China struggle thereafter became more obvious, as Chinese assistance, freed from the Korean commitment, steadily increased. The failure of France to hold Indo-China was finally symbolised by their failure to hold Dien Bien Phu. For some reason, the French command concentrated its strongest forces into the isolated fortress of Dien Bien Phu near the Chinese border. The stronghold was besieged for many months. It eventually fell in May 1954, and a substantial part of the French Army passed into captivity. The only hope of salvation would have been American intervention, but the United States had no desire to create a second Korea.

Its fall meant the fall of France in Indo-China. The war had not been forgotten in France: the end of Dien Bien Phu marked the rising protest within France against continuing to fight a lost cause. In a wider context, it was a protest against the immobility and inherent defects of the Fourth Republic. The government had to resign. The new prime minister was Pierre Mendès-France, who had promised to find a settlement for Indo-China even if it meant a total French evacuation. This he proceeded to do. In July 1955 a meeting of foreign ministers in Geneva agreed to independence for Vietnam (Cambodia and Laos had already gained their independence). Because of the opposition of Communist and non-Communist nationalists, partition was again found to be the only possible solution. The non-Communists were to rule South Vietnam, while Ho Chi Minh was to head a government in North Vietnam.

The end of the Indo-China War was unsatisfactory for both France and Asia. In Asia the area was still a battleground between Communism and anti-Communism: the demarcation line had not been tacitly accepted as it had been in Europe. Henceforth, American influence would replace French influence in South Vietnam. In France the peace highlighted the failures of the Fourth Republic, bringing the parties into further disrepute. Moreover, it fostered a new 'stab in the back' legend within the French Army. Officers, who had considered the war to be an anti-Communist crusade, felt betrayed through a continuous lack of understanding and support from the politicians and Paris. The discontent so generated did not disappear. It remained to explode past the danger point when France and its army were again involved in a losing battle in Algeria.

In Africa the pace of liberation began more slowly. But once started it snowballed so rapidly that the face of political Africa changed almost overnight. Liberation was slower in coming to Africa first because of the lower cultural level of the native populations, and second because of a more intransigent attitude adopted by the colonial powers. This intransigence was due either to the claim that their African colonies were not ready for independence or to the claim that the colonies were an integral part of the mother country, thereby making independence out of the question. But once the floodgates had been opened, because of the Asian examples and the unwillingness of the colonial powers to become snared in colonial wars unpopular with the rest of the world, independence progressed at a breathtaking speed. Paradoxically, it sometimes seemed in the late 1950s and early 1960s that the European powers were even more anxious than local nationalist leaders to grant independence with the minimum of delay. This haste caused a relatively chaotic transition period, leaving residues of rancour on both sides.

In 1950 Africa was still controlled by European powers in the same manner as fifty years earlier. Already liberation had been granted in Asia: the movement spread to Africa in 1951 when the United Nations decided to grant independence to the ex-Italian colony of Libya. From that date, independence for Africa was inevitable. Again, although more intransigence was apparent here than in their Asian policies, the European powers held different attitudes on the problem: again, Britain seemed to be more liberal than France, with Belgium and Portugal remaining adamant.

The postwar Labour Government in Britain had drawn up plans for the future of their African colonies which were subsequently reaffirmed by the Conservative governments of the 1950s without much radical alteration. The scheme was to implement long-term proposals for economic development and administrative education in the colonies: gradually local officials would be given more authority until the final step occurred when all power would be handed over to the nationalist leaders. In addition, they sought safeguards for certain British interests and attempted to rationalise the territorial legacy of nineteenth-century imperialism by introducing plans for federation of neighbouring colonies.

The first fruits of this policy were the 1954 agreement to renounce all treaty rights in Egypt and the 1956 withdrawal from the Sudan, formerly administered jointly by Britain and Egypt. The first granting of independence by Britain in 'black' Africa did not occur until 1957 when the Gold Coast became the independent state of Ghana. The biggest dilemma facing Britain in Africa was the settler problem. Since this did not exist in the West African colonies, these were a logical starting point. This was also true of the French colonies in this area. The Gold Coast, moreover, possessed a relatively stable and well developed economy. Ghana was soon joined in independence by the large state of Nigeria. The remaining British territories in West Africa were underdeveloped: movement toward liberation was therefore slower, but the end was never in doubt.

East Africa presented a very different picture. Here the climate was much more congenial to Europeans. Consequently these colonies possessed numbers of white settlers who, although small minorities, were utterly opposed to independence. South Africa, with its strict apartheid policy within the Commonwealth, was the example which many wished to follow. Naturally it followed that the two sides were driven further apart. In Kenya bitterness erupted into violence as the secret Mau Mau society waged its own war against white domination. However, in fact the conflict was primarily a tribal one: more Africans than Europeans were killed by the Mau Mau. The latter's intransigence meant a more intransigent attitude by Britain which felt that military repression was the only available course. Once the 'rebellion' had been crushed, however, British policy swung rather violently toward independence. By the 1960s not only had Kenya gained independence, but it was also being watched with interest as the first experiment in Africa of an independent multiracial society and multiracial government. This had been one ambition of British colonial policy for a number of decades. Britain's other East African colonies were also slowly progressing toward independence. The only problem lay in the British attempt to form a multiracial government in a new Central African Federation of Nyasaland and the Rhodesias: it failed because of the gap between the African leaders and the federal government led by the whites of Southern Rhodesia. Nyasaland and Northern Rhodesia went their own ways into independence, while Southern Rhodesia remained technically a colony, but under its own white government.

At the other extreme were the Portuguese and Belgian colonies. None was prepared for independence by any standards. Indeed the policy here was to integrate the colonies as closely as possible with themselves: a separate identity was firmly discouraged. This was clearly possible in the case of the two vast Portuguese territories of Angola and Mozambique, where the dictatorship at home strictly pursued the same policy of debarring political activity in both Europe and Africa. It meant an absence of racial conflict and discrimination, strengthened by the influential role of the Catholic Church. All these factors added up to a relatively mild form of paternalism. Finally, the two colonies were not as exposed as other areas to neighbouring nationalist movements in that they bordered South Africa and its apartheid policy. South Africa, therefore, served both as an inspiration and encouragement to the Portuguese in Africa.

At one time the same could have been said of the massive Belgian colony of the Congo. But by 1960 the Congo was faced in the north and north-east by independent African-ruled nations. A rash of riots urging independence broke out in 1959. The Belgian Government suddenly decided to reverse its previous policy of only gradually releasing authority to Africans and instead to grant independence immediately. Independence was set for June 1960: the Belgians more or less effected a clean break politically, militarily, and economically with their colony. The new state had hardly begun to breathe when it collapsed. The Belgians had not educated sufficient Congolese to handle administrative matters, and they had not scratched the surface of the problem of eradicating tribal differences. Conflicts between tribes was one of the more serious problems facing independent Africa: the large undeveloped area of the Congo magnified these differences a hundredfold. The army mutinied and a reign of terror began. To protect the whites who remained, Belgium sent back military units to hold key centres, while business interests encouraged the rich Katanga Province in its efforts to secede from the Congo. The riots spread into an international incident. Still largely excluded from Africa, Communists seized their opportunity and threatened intervention in order to prevent 'the re-establishment of imperialism'. The only possible mediator was the United Nations, which swiftly accepted the responsibility of bringing peace to the Congo: its police forces, with large contingents of African troops, eventually succeeded in restoring some kind of order in an impartial manner by the end of 1960.

Apart from the Congo crisis, the main troubles in Africa were between France and its North African possessions. French colonial authority had not had an auspicious postwar beginning. Still holding firm to the policy of assimilation, France sent troops to Algeria in 1945 and Madagascar in 1947 to repress nationalist revolts in a brutal manner. In Algeria France officially admitted that there were 1,500 casualties: but the nationalists claimed that there had been 45,000 victims. The severity of the French retaliation effectively discouraged armed protest in its colonies for a number of years. During the 1950s France pursued two different policies in Africa. North of the Sahara an intransigent attitude was adopted; south of the Sahara the French were less reluctant to concede to nationalist demands or to prepare these colonies for independence.

A framework law was adopted in 1956 which gave these colonies representative government under French tutelage. Two years later the upheaval which marked the end of the Fourth Republic and the beginning of the Fifth gave the African colonies a golden opportunity. De Gaulle announced the creation of a new French Community to replace the Union along lines similar to the British Commonwealth, but with French predominance. The colonies were offered the choice of enjoying an autonomous status within the Community (and consequently enjoying more French aid) or of becoming completely independent. Only Guinea opted for the latter course, and France withdrew all aid.

The Community itself proved to be an illusory conception. In the first flush of independence, African leaders were extremely reluctant to admit any limitations upon their newly won sovereignty. Consequently attempts to form some kind of African federation failed as well as the original conception of the Community. Many of the new states, too weak to control their population, were in danger of disintegrating like the Congo, particularly because of tribal differences. It seemed that 'balkanisation' was a very real threat in black Africa, particularly in the small states of the west. Certainly the French Community could not prevent this type of occurrence. If the Community was to survive, its best way out was to construct an elastic framework like the Commonwealth where all states had an equal standing and could not be dictated to on their internal or even foreign policies. This course, on the other hand, was not acceptable to de Gaulle, who wished to retain the primacy of France which had been the central idea in the original conception of the Community. However, de Gaulle did not seek to use the Community as a means of retaining French primacy once it was evident that this policy was unacceptable to the African leaders.

The gradual progress of the black African colonies of France toward independence was a sharp contrast to the political events in France's Arab colonies in North Africa. The basic problem was again that of a substantial European minority: these areas were outstripped only by South Africa in the proportion of the population who were of European descent.

Tunisia and Morocco were in a more advantageous position than Algeria to seek independence. In theory they were protectorates, not colonies. As a consequence, both possessed their own rulers and institutions around which nationalist sentiment could focus. Moreover, France itself recognised these two territories as being Muslim, not French: the numbers of French settlers were rather small, and having come later to North Africa did not have the same fierce sentiments as the Algerian settlers. The preconditions for a straightforward and peaceful transition of power were present in Tunisia and Morocco whenever France decided to yield any claims on the territories. In the early 1950s, an immediate settlement seemed remote: the French reaction to Libyan independence in 1951 had been to increase their repressive policy in North Africa. In 1952 the new resident in Tunisia even arrested and deported the constituted ministers.

The turning point was the Dien Bien Phu crisis. Mendès-France, already committed to gaining peace in Asia, conceded Tunisian demands shortly afterwards in 1954. Independence followed in 1956. The situation in Morocco was more complicated. The French resident had decided to depose the ruling Sultan, Mohammed V, in favour of his more amenable uncle. Following the pattern set in Indo-China in 1946, this decision was not opposed by the weak conservative government in Paris, which in any case contained many sympathisers of French primacy in North Africa. The manœuvre failed: the deposed Sultan became the leader of the various nationalist strands as well as being the recognised monarch and religious leader. Tension and violence steadily grew. At the same time as the Tunisian peace was being negotiated, a liberal newspaper proprietor was murdered by right-wing policemen. A new resident, sent out to rescue some authority, found his every move sabotaged by army and administrative elements. Frustrated at every turn he resigned: it became painfully obvious in Paris that peace could be gained only by allowing the Sultan to return. This put the French Government in a worse dilemma; the price was nothing less than full independence—the very thing that the local administrators in 1954 had hoped to avoid.

Tunisian and Moroccan independence had come about not simply because of a change of heart on the part of France. The French Army could not have concentrated sufficient units in these countries to maintain even an uneasy peace; the troops were required to sustain the French position in neighbouring Algeria where the most serious rebellion since Indo-China had just begun. To France, Algeria was more important than Tunisia and Morocco. Here was the largest area of European colonial settlement—over 10 per cent of the population of ten million. Many French Algerians had been born in North Africa and considered themselves as Algerian as the Arab population. This large French settlement had in the past led French governments to incorporate Algeria into metropolitan France. The Algerian nationalists were therefore regarded by many Frenchmen as being on the same level as mutineers or traitors. A French Algeria, however, had carefully preserved French primacy: over 90 per cent of economic activity was controlled by Europeans. Muslim Algerians enjoyed a lower status and fewer economic privileges than French Algerians: less than 7,000 had received more than a minimum of education.

The Algerian war started in late 1954, only four months after the weary French Army had stopped fighting in Indo-China. France was in no mood to countenance a further retreat, particularly in what they considered to be an integral part of metropolitan France: moreover, the army was eager to apply the lessons of guerrilla warfare it had painfully acquired in Asia. Thus the revolt was countered by a rigid policy of repression. As the war dragged on, governments in Paris fluctuated somewhat on their Algerian policy. Liberal attitudes, however, did not last for long, and French policy always returned to the fundamental basis of military force, refusing to negotiate except from an overwhelming position of strength. The pursuance of this policy was possible first because of the determination of several military leaders to erase the spectre of defeat which haunted the French Army, and second because of the wholehearted aid given by French Algerian extremists. Compromise was out of the question: France would settle only for unconditional surrender, the Muslims for full independence. A military victory was also impossible. France had sufficient troops never to be defeated outright, but never sufficient to gain a decisive victory; the nationalists, on the contrary, had a firm base in mountainous areas plus substantial aid and encouragement from neighbouring Arab countries.

The two sides steadily grew further apart. A military war degenerated into brutal acts of repression and torture by both sides. The conflict imposed another never-ending and more serious drain on French resources. Now even conscripts had to be sent to Algeria: French troops were steadily taken away from NATO and other commitments until by 1956 most of the French Army was serving in North Africa. Political affairs in France, which tended to stagnate at the best of times, became completely centred on the Algerian conflict. Events and policies were judged in the light of Algeria, while more and more French monetary resources were redirected to North Africa. The war imposed a tremendous burden on France; it eventually became identified with all that was wrong with France. The Algerian conflict proved to be the final crisis of the regime; in 1958 the Fourth Republic was toppled from its pedestal primarily because of its inability to find a way out of the impasse, but Algeria itself still had to wait a number of years before independence could be obtained.

The Effect on Europe

The passing of colonialism naturally left its mark on European politics—quite apart from the necessities of the colonial powers to fight wars to maintain their hold over rebellious colonies. It meant primarily a process of adjustment. In economics and industry it meant a rethinking and replanning of strategy and market outlets; in government and administration it meant the end of a lucrative profession. For colonial administrators and settlers it invoked a painful choice: to remain in the new independent nations, or to be rehabilitated in the mother country. Either choice usually meant a much reduced status and income.

The political and economic effects of this withdrawal back to Europe were rather different. Many economists argued that de-colonialisation was a blessing in disguise, giving the colonial powers greater freedom. The freedom involved was the greater capacity to develop the national economy. Oil had been perhaps the strongest economic argument for continued European control and influence in colonies and ex-colonies: it was argued that without this control national economies would fail. However, economists were gradually discarding this line of argument. Italy, without any political interest in oil-producing areas in the Middle East, was successfully undercutting those powers which attempted to retain some political influence. Furthermore, the outstanding contrast between France and West Germany suggested that colonial power tended to be a heavy drain on the European nation involved, particularly if force was required to maintain control; while any profits that were forthcoming from colonial investment did not tend to benefit the home population or the home economy, but only small groups of industrialists and investors. The economic choice was to be dragged down into the mire or to concentrate on creating prosperity at home along the lines of the West German 'miracle'. Disengagement from colonialism allowed more time to be spent on the latter course. By the late 1950s more people were accepting the fact that Europe was better off without colonies.

Ironically, the political effects of the 'liberal' process of winding up the colonial structures was to strengthen forces of nationalism and conservatism in Western Europe. It tended to introduce more strongly the issue of race into domestic politics. Many Europeans still dreamed of empire and their civilising mission. Consequently they were bitterly opposed to the course of postwar events in colonial affairs. Their cause was supported by the colonial settlers, whether these were living in the colonies or had returned to Europe. The return of many colonists from Asia and Africa naturally strengthened European conservatism. Their common aim was to demonstrate, if only once, that Western Europe could not be hounded from pillar to post by the new independent nations: the latter should be taught to respect European attitudes. The event which finally demonstrated that the colonial powers could not defy determined world opinion and resort to punitive action on their own in Asia and Africa was the Franco-British Suez Expedition of 1956.

The Conservative Government in Britain, now led by Anthony Eden, had respected the treaty to evacuate the Suez Canal zone. In 1956 Colonel Nasser, the Egyptian leader, decided to nationalise the canal itself in order to use the dues to finance public works programmes in Egypt upon which America and Britain had reversed previously favourable decisions. The imperialists within the Conservative Party urged that punitive measures be taken against Egypt, and they found a ready spokesman in Eden, who clearly saw Nasser as a potential Hitler. It was hoped that Nasser would be forced to leave the government, and so the action would check extremist Arab nationalism of which Nasser was the outstanding symbol to many Arabs. Moreover, the Middle East had always been regarded by Britain as being of paramount importance to the country's security: even Clement Attlee had admitted as much. France, the other European country with a major interest in the canal, was willing to cooperate. Egypt was already giving the Algerian nationalists much aid: French action against Egypt might deprive the Algerians of one of their most important supply bases. In addition, the French Army, which had been fighting hopeless colonial wars since 1945, epitomised the revival of European nationalism by seeing a military action against Egypt as an excellent opportunity to show the new nations that France (and Europe) refused to be humiliated any further. This was the essential issue at stake for Britain and France.

However, they delayed too long. Nasser had taken over the canal in the summer of 1956. The first Franco-British attack did not come until the end of October. By then it was doomed to failure, as world opinion was swiftly arrayed against it. A summer invasion might very well have succeeded, not in the military sense, but in a political sense. The nationalisation had aroused tempers throughout the world: by November these had subsided as the Egyptians proved that economically the administration of the canal was functioning as smoothly and successfully as before. It became obvious that the two European powers had delayed their assault because a third party, Israel, was involved. Israel saw it as an opportunity to punish Egypt for its continuous border harassments. Consequently the first invasion of Egypt was made by Israeli forces on 29 October. Britain and France then had a second string to their bow: as the Israelis made rapid progress, they could intervene to restore peace to the area.

World reaction, however, was swift and unanimous. Russia threatened to intervene actively in the area, which the West was not desirous to see. Even allied and friendly countries were at best only lukewarm sympathisers. The United States refused any support whatsoever. The Americans, who all along had disapproved of involvement, were annoyed because the attack occurred just before their presidential election: to them it appeared that the date had been deliberately fixed so that American attention would be focused exclusively on domestic matters and would not be in a position to act. Faced with a complete lack of world support and an almost unanimous hostile vote in the United Nations General Assembly and Security Council, Britain and France had no alternative but to withdraw. Britain took the lead in this withdrawal. The dramatic British reversal strained Anglo-French relations severely, for France had been more willing to defy world opinion. Their place in the canal zone was occupied by a United Nations command which proceeded to reinstate the *status quo*.

The Suez expedition was the final fling of European colonialism. It was a temporary check for decolonialisation, not a reversal for liberation—'a recrudescence of imperialism'.[1] In many ways it was an invaluable lesson in that it illustrated that in the vast majority of cases the process of liberation could not be reversed. In the wider sphere of international politics, it pointed to the numerical strength of the new Asian and African states in the United Nations. It also emphasised the inability of Western European nations to act individually in a major world crisis without effective American support: in many ways Europe still relied heavily upon the United States and was susceptible to American pressure. For Britain, it suggested the financial inability to undertake a major military assault on its own. Britain's gold and dollar reserves slumped and there were hints that the pound might have to be devalued: according to Eden this was a crucial factor in Britain's decision to accede to United Nations resolutions. The intervention had repercussions in France, for it may have strengthened the view of de Gaulle, when he came to power in 1958, that France should

[1] R. Emerson, *From Empire to Nation*, Cambridge, Mass., 1960, p. 401.

disengage itself from American involvement: it suggested to the French right that association with America meant the denial of France's basic interests. But above all, the failure of the Suez expedition was the burial ceremony of old-fashioned imperialism with its gun-boat philosophy.

12 Conservative Government and Socialist Opposition

Life's better with the Conservatives—don't let Labour ruin it.

British Conservative election slogan, 1959

No experiments—Konrad Adenauer.

West German CDU election slogan, 1957

Between 1953 and the end of the decade the same political trends were apparent within all four major powers of Western Europe: Britain, France, Italy, and West Germany. In all four the swing toward conservatism which had begun in the late 1940s continued to gain impetus. In Britain and West Germany the Conservatives and Christian Democrats respectively held satisfactory majorities while in Italy the Christian Democrats also provided the focal point and major partner of all governments. Party stability was not so apparent in France. Nevertheless, an increase in conservative strength was noticeable in the closing years of the Fourth Republic, and in 1958 the triumph of de Gaulle meant the return of France to an authoritarian conservative form of government. The mood, it appeared, was widespread. By 1960 Adenauer and de Gaulle had both emerged as patriarchs of their respective countries. In Britain the image of Harold Macmillan, the Conservative Prime Minister, also seemed to hinge upon the tendency to regard him as a kind of father-figure. Only Italy failed to produce an outstanding personality or image along these lines.

The success of traditional conservative parties during the 1950s reflected the continuation of an economic boom. With material prosperity evidently gained, people were more sympathetic toward those parties which emphasised stability and a strong reluctance to abandon the *status quo* for reform and experimentation. Material prosperity and stability formed only one side of the picture: the other side was much darker. The achievement of prosperity was accompanied by a growing complacency and a reluctance to become too involved in political activity. Party membership figures, which almost everywhere fell steadily during this period, were but one indication of the strong apolitical nature of the electorates. Although the abandonment of too close a commitment to ideology, except perhaps in France, was a good sign for the health of the democracies, a more or less complete abandonment, which the 1950s seemed to indicate, was an unhealthy tendency.

The chief losers in this process were the parties of the left, especially Socialist parties, which traditionally and almost inevitably had to base their justification for existence upon some form of ideology. Their electoral performances tended to deteriorate rather than improve, until it seemed highly probable that Socialist parties in countries without a long tradition of Socialist governments were doomed to permanent opposition short of a radical and massive realignment of political allegiance on the part of the electorate. The weakness of left-wing parties in these countries carried a basic threat to the concept of democracy itself, for democratic government implies a healthy competition between parties for public office. This competition appeared to be generally lacking, and no amount of intra-party discussion or competition within the governing party could make up the deficit.

Conservative Stability

The most stable picture was presented by West Germany. Britain had the Suez crisis which at one time threatened to engulf the Conservative Party, while Italy and France had the problems of finding an acceptable leader and a coherent government coalition. In Germany, Chancellor Adenauer led the Christian Democrats through constant electoral victories and along fairly consistent policy lines. In 1957 the Christian Democrats increased their percentage of the vote again, actually winning an absolute majority for the first time in a democratic Germany.

Adenauer chose still to rule in coalition with any willing non-Socialist partners. His basic policy was clear. His large 1957 majority was due not only to the failure of the Social Democrats (who actually increased their vote) and to the appeal of his own personality to the electorate, but also to the assimilation by his party of several small moderate and right-wing parties. By persuading the remaining conservative parties to operate in coalition with the Christian Democrats, who by now were clearly dominated by conservative leaders and groups, Adenauer hoped to increase his party's strength still further by swallowing up the small coalition partners. In the event this policy mainly succeeded. In the 1961 election only the Free Democrats succeeded in preventing the two major parties from monopolising all the parliamentary seats.

Adenauer and the CDU benefited enormously from the German 'economic miracle'. The boom was seen largely as the handiwork of Ludwig Erhard, the Minister of Economics, who had defied the Allies in launching the *laissez-faire* economic system at the height of the tensions and depression of the late 1940s. The electorate's endorsement was at this time also largely a vote of confidence in and gratitude for Dr Adenauer; the main CDU campaign slogan of 1957 was simply 'No Experiments—Konrad Adenauer'. Given the divided state of Germany, foreign policy was ever a serious political issue. Although in tying West Germany more closely to the Atlantic alliance Adenauer made the likelihood of German reunification more remote, his pro-Western policy was largely instrumental in raising West Germany's international status from that of a defeated power toward that of an accepted and equal partner.

The return of West Germany to the fold of the major powers was seen largely as Adenauer's personal triumph. Moreover, Adenauer himself refused to accept the partition of Germany as final, but regarded a solution as being out of the question in the existing cirumstances. This was a view endorsed by many Germans. It was felt that West Germany would be more capable of caring for its own interests and those of Germany as a whole when in a position of strength rather than remaining neutral and dependent upon Russian generosity, which in all probability would be given only if it were almost certain that a reunited Germany could be placed under Communist control.

This anti-Communist intransigence was carried to the extent of outlawing the West German Communist Party (KPD). The case had been laid by the government before the Constitutional Court in 1952, at the same time as the charges against the Neo-Nazi

Socialist Reich Party, but it was not until 1956 that the Court eventually delivered its verdict. The decision was perhaps an error of judgment. The KPD was a negligible political force and had been steadily declining even further throughout the 1950s. By allowing it to continue to function West Germany could have demonstrated its inability to attract voters; by being outlawed, the KPD was given an opportunity (admittedly slight at the moment) of presenting itself as a martyr should the situation ever arise.

The banning of the KPD in West Germany can be only a minor criticism of the Adenauer era. Of greater significance was the impact of the Chancellor's own personality upon the government structure. The 1949 Basic Law had provided for a number of checks and balances designed to prevent a recurrence of the chaos of the closing years of the Weimar Republic. The strongest institution in the constitutional structure was that of the Chancellery. With the Christian Democrats in such a dominant position and without any serious challengers from within the parliamentary CDU, Adenauer took the strong constitutional position of the Chancellery, and combining it with his own indomitable personality, carved a niche for himself that paralleled that of Bismarck.

Critics coined the phrase 'Chancellor Democracy'. Parliament was in many instances no more than a rubber stamp. Cabinet ministers were not permitted to develop any individuality or responsibility; it was not unusual for them to receive their first intimations of German foreign policy decisions from other sources. All the reins of power were firmly held by Adenauer or were neutralised. Only the permanent civil service and perhaps the *Bundesrat*, the upper house (representative of the *Laender* governments) retained any freedom of action and political power.

Too much reliance upon one man was bad for democracy (if not for the stripling German variety). As a manifestation of this pattern of behaviour, all issues likely to cause controversy were not allowed to become matters of public and parliamentary debate. Furthermore, the excessive identification of Adenauer with German politics had a debilitating effect on his own party. With the Social Democrats in too weak a position to challenge the government (and in any case after 1957 they were perhaps primarily concerned with reforming their own structure and public image), more importance had to be attached to the interplay of democratic forces within the CDU. Quite often these became bogged down in petty jealousies and personal recriminations, or were firmly suppressed with Adenauer acting as a dam. All the ideas and forces which were being held back were building up pressure underneath. In time they would reach the critical explosion point, and the one main target of attack would be the autocratic methods of Adenauer himself. This came about in the early 1960s when a very large part of CDU energy was devoted to the problem of how to uproot Adenauer from his entrenched position with the minimum amount of damage.

The issue of an old and tired leadership did not achieve the limelight in Britain until about 1962 or 1963. During the 1950s the country had had three different prime ministers. Churchill stayed in office until 1955, despite his slender parliamentary majority. During this period the Conservatives largely accepted the innovations of the postwar Labour Government. They contented themselves with denationalising steel and road transport and with improving the organisation and efficiency of the new social welfare system. The 1955 election, held by Churchill's successor, Anthony Eden, reflected the basic satisfaction of the electorate. The Labour Party was accused of being the party of austerity and controls. By being in office when economic improvement eventually began, the Conservatives were able to draw upon popular satisfaction and to increase their majority to a substantial margin. The election also reflected the general apathy towards politics which characterised the 1950s in Europe: the electorate was largely disinterested in the campaign, and large numbers abstained from voting.

It was during Eden's term of office that the only real major crisis of the 1950s occurred in British politics. The 1956 Suez expedition, designed to reassert respect for British authority in the Middle East, divided British public opinion completely. A bipartisan approach was out of the question; the Labour Party moved into uncompromising opposition. In addition several Conservatives were seriously perturbed about their leader's action. Faced with this internal unrest and with accusations and hostility from nearly every quarter of the globe, Eden was forced to back out of Suez. The tension of these months caused his health to fail, and shortly afterwards he had to resign as prime minister. The succession went to Harold Macmillan, who was preferred to R. A. Butler.

Macmillan's primary task in foreign policy was to restore the relations destroyed by the Suez episode, and internally he had to repair the damage it had inflicted on his own party. He was ideally suitable for this role. Probably the most shrewd politician available to the Conservatives, he allowed nothing to turn him aside; he came to symbolise the adjective 'unflappable'. Within an extremely short period of time he had unified the party behind him, assuring both the moderates that there would be no more Suez escapades, and the imperialist wing that British prestige would not be damaged further—in fact implying that it had not been damaged by Suez. The opinion polls reflected the recovery of Conservative unity and confidence. From a nadir in 1957 their rating steadily improved until in 1959 a further electoral victory was an outstanding possibility.

The 1959 election gave a Conservative victory of almost land-slide proportions. Like the West German CDU they had increased their percentage of votes in three successive elections. Once again the campaign revolved around the themes of satisfaction and material prosperity; the Conservative slogan of 'You've never had it so good' reflected the prosperous and complacent mood of Britain. By now Macmillan was emerging as the dominant personality in British politics: 'Supermac' was becoming to Britain what Adenauer was to West Germany and de Gaulle to France. He in fact seemed to dominate his cabinet to such an extent that some observers began to suggest that Britain had or was moving toward a presidential form of government.

With the Labour Party torn by internal dissension—like the German SPD, partly caused by repeated electoral failures—the Conservatives seemed set to rule Britain for an indeterminate period. But an acute ear could already hear faint rumblings of discontent underneath the calm exterior. The Labour Party was beginning to display a new militancy, which was contrasted to the over-confidence and complacency of the Conservatives. Here also economic prosperity had led conservatism, successful at the polls, into complacency, which was to hinder all efforts to move the party out of the rut into which it began to sink in the 1960s.

The Search for Conservative Stability

On the surface, Italy appeared to display the same tendencies as Britain and West Germany. The Italian Christian Democrats, whose conservatism was also becoming more pronounced, remained as the premier government party throughout the 1950s. Here, however, the similarity ended. The Christian Democrats, like the German CDU, was essentially a broad coalition embracing many diverse political groups and interests from the moderate left to the conservative right. But the Italian party lacked a dominating personality who could hold the coalition firmly in place or who could pursue a coherent policy despite an inchoate party. Whatever coherence the movement possessed was primarily due to the peculiar role of the Catholic Church and its overwhelming hold on over one-third of the Italian population. But naturally an active political Church tends to generate an active anti-Church political mood.

Consequently a basic instability was a feature of Italian Christian Democracy as well as of the political system as a whole (in 1958 over 40 per cent voted for radical right- and left-wing parties). This latter instability was reinforced by the refusal of the Christian Democrats to associate with the Communists and Socialists who maintained their extremely close alliance until the autumn of 1956, and by the reluctance of moderate Christian Democrats to rely upon any assistance from the radical Monarchists and neo-Fascists who had gained in strength in the 1958 elections.

Thus the difficulty facing Italy after the elections of 1953 and 1958 was the old one of the largest single party, the Christian Democrats, being clearly supreme but lacking a majority in the Chamber of Deputies. To gain a majority, they had to find coalition partners from the remainder of the centre, which was in any case an extremely narrow sector of the political spectrum. On occasions when a coalition agreement was not forthcoming, the

Christian Democrats, due to the absence of any alternatives, had to maintain an uneasy single-party government. On the whole the most important political battles in Italy occurred within the ranks of Christian Democracy among its three broad factions: the left, centre, and right. Because of this unceasing intra-party struggle, prime ministers could not ensure a long tenure of office for themselves unless they could control or manipulate all three factions: none after de Gasperi was able to do so. Between 1953 and 1960 six men held the office of prime minister for short periods, averaging only about one year each. Their coming and going represented temporary victories of the several Christian Democrat factions. All permutations, with or without the aid of the smaller democratic parties, were attempted. All were of no avail: no ministry could guarantee itself a lifetime of even two years.

The facts that political decision-making took place primarily within the Christian Democrat party and that there was no healthy competition between parties to force the ruling group to maintain a sense of proportion meant that the real issues and problems facing Italy were rarely broached, let alone solved. Governments could not indulge in long-term planning with any certainty of the programmes being sustained and carried through. Italy therefore was largely paralysed by the inabilities of the Christian Democrats to close their ranks and embark upon a united policy. It was far easier to allow the country to drift along without much direction. Here, too, the outcome of this situation was a mood of complacency among many politicians and a general apathy among an electorate that felt that governments were corrupt and disinterested in public problems.

In the main the advantage during the 1950s lay with the conservative and pro-clerical tendencies within the Christian Democrats. The powerful economic and clerical interests which supported the party were deeply suspicious of many of the ideas of the more moderate wing of the party: parish priests would even point out the party faction which loyal voters should support. This situation of flux and permanent instability clearly could not last indefinitely without some crisis occurring. This crisis came when the Christian Democrats seemed to be moving even further to the right. Governments turned a blind eye towards neo-Fascism, tended to favour more authoritarian solutions, and preferred to dispense with the assistance of other democratic parties and to rule as a single-party ministry relying upon Monarchist and neo-Fascist votes to give them a parliamentary majority. In return for their support these right-wing parties were promised that Christian Democrat governments would continue to refrain from drafting or implementing the social and economic reforms which the country desperately needed: at the local level, the cost of right-wing support was a share of the vast system of official patronage (*sottogoverno*). At best, a justification of this political pattern could only argue that it prevented the radical right from indulging in revolutionary tendencies—even though the extreme right failed to collect 10 per cent of the votes in 1958.

Public discontent erupted in the summer of 1960. Leftist-inspired strikes and demonstrations broke out in the northern cities, and such was the weakness of the incumbent right-wing government that it fell quickly. For the first time since the crisis-ridden months of 1947 and 1948 Italy appeared to be approaching a revolutionary situation. This threat was the stimulus required to force the Christian Democrats to close ranks. Amintore Fanfani, a leader of the moderate left-wing faction of the party, became prime minister of a government that included three former premiers and which was representative of all centrist political opinion. This could be only a short-term expedient, as French politics had so often demonstrated. As such it could do nothing to solve the basic quandaries of Italian political life; once the emergency had passed, the old factionalism would resume its sway. The theme of Italian politics was still one of 'unstabilised stability'.[1]

Despite the several factions within Italian Christian Democracy, only two fundamental courses of action were open to the party. In its hesitating drift toward the right Christian Democracy had tried one of the paths, but had found it to be unacceptable to the populace and possibly an avenue to revolution. The previous decade had demonstrated that the Catholic Church, the most powerful buttress of the right, could help preserve the *status quo* in

[1] J. P. C. Carey and A. G. Carey, 'The Italian election of 1958—unstable stability in an unstable world', *Political Science Quarterly*, December, 1958, pp. 566–89.

terms of both voters and policies, but lacked the ability or the initiative to expand in fresh directions.

Thus it could be argued that the alternative course could offer the only way out of the dilemma: this was an alliance with the Socialists. The 'opening to the left', as it was known, was supported by the Christian Democrat left-wing as the only possible means of giving Italy a stable political leadership. Fanfani had been a prominent advocate of this policy. Together the two parties could provide a majority and hence embark upon a programme of social and economic reform without running the most obvious dangers of being untimely ejected from office. The centre-left argument came into prominence after 1956 when, as a result of the Russian reprisals against the Hungarian uprising, Pietro Nenni and his Socialist Party eventually broke away from the Communists. The popular front had been a disastrous policy for the Socialists; more and more, they had found themselves being drawn into the Communist orbit. The reaction to Hungary was the catalyst around which the pro-democratic forces within the party coalesced to give it the necessary impetus to permit it to escape from the Communist sun. After Hungary, in fact, Nenni returned the Stalin Peace Prize which he had been awarded in 1953.

During the closing years of the decade, however, majority opinion within the Christian Democrats was still against such a move, and after 1958, which was hailed as the beginning of Italy's 'economic miracle', many saw even less justification in the idea. But the climax of 1960 once again placed the centre-left possibility in the limelight. The time, however, was not yet ripe; several years would elapse before the two parties would come together in a government. Nevertheless, the significant breach in the dykes of prejudice was made in 1960. The Socialists were willing to join in discussions with the Christian Democrats to find a suitable meeting place. For the moderate Christian Democrats the next few years would be spent not only in negotiating with the Socialists, but also in quelling the opposition of their more right-wing party colleagues. Only by moving back to the left, which meant some form of agreement with the Socialists, could the Christian Democrats convince outsiders that they had not lost glimpse of the original reforming goals of the party and that they had not degenerated into a mere political arm of clerical forces. In Italy, also, therefore, the opening of the 1960s hinted at the possibility of a change in the political mood of the country, embodying an ending of complacency and a return to some concern with values.

The Conservative Revolution

The troubles and problems facing Italy perhaps sink into insignificance when compared with those confronting France. France departed somewhat from the general pattern of conservatism observed above by having a Socialist-dominated government in 1956 and 1957. But this government survived only on the sufferance of conservative support and most of its policies were actually conservative-oriented. Conservatism, therefore, prevailed also in France. But whereas in Italy, Britain, and West Germany, the spread of conservatism was limited to observing the rules of the game and taking over the existing political system, the eventual victory of conservative forces in France meant the end of the Fourth Republic and its parliamentary system. In its place arose the more conservative Fifth Republic dominated by the rather authoritarian personality of Charles de Gaulle. In reality the Fourth Republic had been born badly deformed; only a minority of the electorate had actually voted for it in the 1946 referendum, while a substantial percentage of French politicians had never accepted it. Again, it had never operated in the manner originally conceived. It must therefore be given some acclaim for performing in a fairly creditable way for twelve years. Its final death throes, escaping undetected, began with the fall of Dien Bien Phu which was the last in a long line of crises caused by the colonial war in Indo-China. The final *coup de grâce* was delivered by yet another colonial crisis, in Algeria. Between 1954 and 1958 the Fourth Republic made a last vain attempt to change and strengthen its nature.

The new Indo-China crisis had swept Pierre Mendès-France into power. Within a very short time Mendès-France, one of the few democrats with an outstanding personality and the ability to direct France along democratic lines, successfully ended the war in Asia, began negotiations for liberating the North African protectorates, and succeeded in disposing of the problem of the EDC. Yet these problems were perhaps peripheral to the basic dilemma of France. This was the general dilapidation of its political and economic life. Mendès-France had scarcely started to move toward reforming French agriculture and the languishing sectors of French industry when his ministry was brought down by its various opponents who were agreed only on the question of defeating the prime minister. Even reformist Europeans opposed him for not fighting for EDC (normally they were strong allies of anyone seeking to strengthen the Republic). His government had lasted for only seven months.

Out of office, Mendès-France stood less chance of achieving his political and economic reforms. Indeed it is doubtful whether he could ever have succeeded in the existing circumstances, for the crux of his plan was to turn the loose aggregation of individuals that was the Radical Party into a disciplined mass party along the left-wing or British pattern. A Radical Party strengthened in this way was seen as the centre of pro-democratic forces and could sustain the Fourth Republic by ensuring longer terms of office for governments (quite often Radicals had helped to vote their own colleagues out of office). It was a brave attempt, but resulted only in making matters worse; the party became hopelessly divided between those for and against Mendès-France. There were virtually two Radical parties.

Once again French politics returned to the old diversion of frustrating compromise and indefinite postponement. This game was so absorbing that the rest of the world was ignored; in 1949, for example, the King of Cambodia, in France for negotiations over a treaty, had to wait for three weeks before a government was found with which he could deal. However, reformers saw an opportunity to escape from this morass in the general election scheduled for 1956: for this end the Radical followers of Mendès-France and the Socialists joined forces. For both groups it was a logical commitment. The Radical reformers were closer in spirit to the Socialists than their more conservative *confrères*, while for Guy Mollet and the Socialist leaders, as long as they refused Communist overtures and as long as the religious question prevented them from cooperating fully with the MRP, this alliance was the best possible means of recovering some of the ground lost to conservative forces in 1951.

The centre-left coalition of Radicals and Socialists was the chief victor in the election, although the Communists clearly emerged as the largest party in the National Assembly. As the largest of the democratic forces, the new coalition necessarily would have to be the nucleus of the new government. Since the Socialists were the larger partner Guy Mollet was invited to assume the premiership. But the Mollet government, which survived longer than any other Fourth Republic ministry, disappointed even its most ardent supporters. It was crippled by the system. Three separate but insistent pressures prevented it from carrying out a progressive programme. In the National Assembly, the Communists, with 25 per cent of the seats, were a persistent stumbling block. In addition, the election had returned about fifty supporters of the right-wing demagogue, Pierre Poujade, who rejected the rules of the Fourth Republic's political game. Finally, outside parliament the Algerian settlers proved to be a powerful reactionary pressure group; with a great deal of sympathy from conservatives in France, they were successful in preventing any advance being made in negotiations with the Algerian nationalists.

Blocked where domestic reform was concerned, the Mollet government became increasingly involved in foreign and colonial policy, and gradually drifted into a conservative course of action. After a visit to Algiers in February 1956, where he was confronted by hostile demonstrations, Mollet seemed to abandon any ideas of reconciliation in Algeria; he turned instead to continue the repressive policy of his predecessors. His policies pleased only the French right; his own colleagues became increasingly disenchanted and hostile. Mendès-France dissociated himself from the government in May. Several prominent Socialists resigned from the party. Those who remained to try to influence policy from within were often expelled from the party. Mollet was proving to be as conservative and authoritarian as the right. His course of action naturally delighted the conservatives. It was preferable to have a socialist pursuing the reactionary line of action that they advocated since then they would not be the target of reformist criticisms and attacks. Furthermore, if Mollet stepped out of line, the conservative forces, with the end of his coalition, could almost certainly guarantee his defeat. This in fact did bring about the fall of the Socialist Government in 1957: when Mollet turned to consider reform of the tax system, which, although favouring the lower classes, was immediately and primarily concerned with finding additional revenue to finance the accumulating costs of the Algerian war, his government was defeated by the conservatives. To foreign observers Mollet's government was memorable for its length of service and its paradoxical reactionary policy in Algeria; it was during the lifetime of this government that the Algerian imbroglio began to make a definite political and economic impact in France. And, of course, there was a similar paradoxical action in the abortive Suez expedition, where we had the amazing sight of an avowed anti-colonial Socialist premier quoting Marx to defend a neo-colonial policy.

There was no obvious successor to Mollet. The right turned down the challenge and responsibility of government. Governments were again the result of protracted negotiations, and the tenuous agreements on which they rested were likely to be broken almost immediately. Experienced politicians were extremely reluctant to accept the responsibility for the Algerian War; and most were also opposed by influential groups in the National Assembly. Consequently it was younger men who were given the job of prime minister; as yet their enemies were few and they still had to establish a reputation.

But no attempt could be made to revive the failing Fourth Republic. Governments were almost solely preoccupied with the question of their day-to-day survival. The Algerian situation deteriorated further in February 1958, when French planes bombed the Tunisian border town of Sakhiet, which the Algerian nationalists had been using as a supply base. This act, which followed the precedents of local commanders acting on their own initiative, reflected the frustrations of the French Army in its failure to make any headway against the insurgents. The result was catastrophic for France. The raid isolated France even more in international affairs, and when President Bourguiba of Tunisia declared his intention to place Sakhiet before the United Nations, it meant that France had failed in its prime motive of keeping the Algerian problem as a domestic, and not an international issue. Britain and the United States attempted to calm the troubled waters by offering to act as arbiters between France and Tunisia, but this only aggravated further the French right and pushed it further along its reactionary road. One conservative deputy even declared that America was a greater menace to France than the Soviet Union.

Two months later the French right yet again brought down the government. It proved to be the last ministry of the Fourth Republic. Pierre Pflimlin, a moderate left-wing leader of the MRP, was given the task of finding a new and, it was hoped, more stable governmental base. But at this point rumours swept through Algeria that Pflimlin, who certainly was not a favourite of the settlers, had included in his provisional governmental list a prospective minister for Algeria who was convinced that conciliation was the only way out of the impasse. The long-threatened storm eventually broke. On 13 May 1958 ultra-nationalist and neo-Fascist groups in Algeria rose up in rebellion, with the acquiescence of many local army units. Very quickly they took charge of the Algerian administration and established in Algiers and other major towns 'Committees of Public Safety' which disowned the French authorities in Paris. The Algerian uprising by both civilians and soldiers was the last desperate attempt to end French frustration and the process of decolonialisation. They regarded a firm authoritarian regime as the only way of achieving these ends.

The situation caused by the revolt was extremely confusing, with many gradations of views and opinions. Many army commanders believed that direct military rule should be imposed; the ultra-nationalists wished their proposed authoritarian structure to control the military, but had no outstanding personality around whom they could congregate; while the Gaullists, who were waiting for such an occasion and were well organised to utilise the situation for their own ends, saw the time as being ripe for the return of de Gaulle. But quite clearly the losers were the Fourth Republic and the politicians in Paris. The settlers and insurgents knew what they wanted; the politicians, on the other hand, could not agree on a policy. Moreover, almost the whole of France's military forces were stationed in Algeria, and these were sympathetic to many of the settler demands.

The situation clarified itself somewhat when General de Gaulle let it be known that he would return to political life if invited to do so. De Gaulle, in fact, was the only alternative to total breakdown. The mystique which had gathered round his name was still strong. He was still the liberator of France and he was not associated with any of the failings of the Fourth Republic. Moreover, his conservative and somewhat authoritarian inclinations were acceptable to most of the French right, while his Resistance role and his refusal to adopt unconstitutional means of gaining power gave him some support among the French left. But de Gaulle's own refusal in 1940 to accept the decision of his superiors to surrender was, paradoxically, a justification and a precedent for the present army rebellion in Algeria.

As negotiations went on, the threat of revolution spread to metropolitan France itself. The rebels had gained control of the island of Corsica; it was rumoured that the police were unreliable; while there was a threat of a parachute assault on Paris. The President of France, René Coty, who had come to accept de Gaulle's return as inevitable and desirable, threatened his resignation as head of state if the National Assembly did not invest de Gaulle as prime minister upon his own terms. This the National Assembly proceeded to do on 1 June; and as the last act of the Fourth Republic it gave de Gaulle's ministry a blank cheque to rule as it chose for a period of six months while drafting a new constitution. The investiture of de Gaulle had not been the aim of the Algerian revolutionaries nor that of the army; they had perhaps desired someone with a more reactionary philosophy, but in the absence of any such leader, they were prepared to accept de Gaulle if he in turn accepted their demands. The Fourth Republic, on the other hand, could perhaps have been able to deal with the settlers or the army without the presence of the other and of de Gaulle; for twelve years it had proved capable of resisting de Gaulle and his followers. But the juxtaposition of events and all three forces in 1958 proved too overwhelming.

De Gaulle had refused to accept governmental responsibility unless he was constitutionally accredited to act. This having been achieved, his first main task was to construct a new constitutional edifice for French government. However, his return to power was in essence the product of a revolutionary situation. Without the determined minority in Algeria and the army forcing their will upon the irresolute National Assembly, de Gaulle would probably have had to remain even longer at Colombey-les-deux-Églises. For despite the fluid nature of governments, the French bureaucracy had shown itself highly capable of handling political problems—but only as long as it had received policy guidelines from the politicians. In economic affairs, for example, the civil service had received their directions from the progressive Monnet Plan and its implications, but in foreign and colonial affairs no new policy had been forthcoming, and the civil service continued to administer the colonies in an utterly outdated manner. Without the shocks delivered from outside France, from colonial and foreign policy, it is quite conceivable that the Fourth Republic, which, considering the adverse circumstances, had developed a remarkable resilience, could have survived for an indeterminate length of time. Of its performance this sympathetic epitaph has been written:

Its twelve years were an uphill struggle to re-establish Republican parliamentary government in a country convalescent after the triple ordeal of defeat, occupation, and liberation, and scarred by the deep wounds of social schism and civil war, it proved able to draw upon hidden sources of strength. It kept at bay the power of Communism without the aid of the anti-parliamentary forces of Gaullism and Poujadism. It presided over the economic recovery of France after extreme dislocation and impoverishment. It showed a resilience that confounded its critics and surprised even its friends. It inaugurated a reshaping of relations between France and her overseas territories which made possible the New Community of 1960. It reshaped France's place in Europe and among the world's powers.[1]

The new constitution drafted by de Gaulle and his advisers was ready to be presented to the electorate by September. A popular referendum gave its approval by a massive majority, with only Communists and a few left-wing democrats in opposition. The

[1] D. Thomson, *Democracy in France*, p. 257.

popular rejection of the tired Fourth Republic was confirmed two months later. Elections to the new National Assembly produced a convincing conservative victory. The new Gaullist movement, the Union for the New Republic (UNR) emerged with over one-third of the seats, while the old Independents and their associates gained a further one-quarter. The MRP also increased its representation for the first time since 1946. Although the Socialists and Radicals suffered serious losses, the chief wounds were inflicted upon the political extremes. Most of the remaining Poujadists deserted their leader for the Gaullist cause; the others were obliterated. Communist voting strength decreased slightly, but the new electoral system, among other things aimed at reducing the number of Communist-held seats, cut their representation to less than 2 per cent. If the new conservative alliance could achieve a modicum of unity, the National Assembly would be theirs: certainly there would be no danger of Communist obstruction. Finally, de Gaulle was elected as President of the new Republic by an electoral college designed to produce a strong conservative bias. The Fifth Republic was ready to start functioning as a fully operative political entity.

In constitutional matters the Fifth Republic was also revolutionary. Traditionally the constitutional argument in France had been between left and right. The left had always argued for parliamentary supremacy, and this had been achieved in the Third and Fourth Republics. The right, on the other hand, rejected this as unfeasible; they claimed it led to weak government and the dominance of party manœuvres. Instead the right wished to see a strong executive with the power to overrule the National Assembly and the ability to offer firm leadership. De Gaulle's decision to move from the premiership to the formerly ceremonial presidency indicated the change of the power centre in the Fifth Republic. Strictly speaking, the new constitution was a compromise between the French parliamentary tradition and straightforward presidential rule. But the prestige and personality of de Gaulle made it obvious that during his reign at least effective power would lie with the government rather than the Assembly, and with the president rather than the prime minister. To emphasise this point, the National Assembly had had its sessions shortened and its freedom of action, particulary its ability to overthrow or hinder the government, drastically restricted.

The new constitution, moreover, was extremely ambiguous in its wording. Thus in some respects de Gaulle could operate it as he desired; in fact it had been specifically designed for de Gaulle in the same way as the parties had drafted the 1946 Constitution to limit de Gaulle. Although the responsibility of government belonged to the prime minister, de Gaulle assumed this responsibility from the outset. His first prime minister, Michel Debré, was largely no more than an administrator of de Gaulle's decisions. Ministries increasingly came to be headed by civil servants and technocrats instead of politicians. In those areas of policy-making described as the presidential sector, especially defence and foreign policy, de Gaulle brooked no interference. Thus the problems of decolonialisation and of Algeria became his concern alone. He did not follow the general pattern for which the settlers had supported his return. A new French Community was promised with substantial autonomy. Those colonies which did not wish to maintain this close relationship with France were promised immediate independence. In Algeria the nationalists were promised independence if a cease-fire could first be negotiated. On the other hand, he continued to conduct a severe policy of repression and reprisal in the war against the Algerian nationalists. It may well be that this was a 'cover' in an attempt to lull the still hostile suspicions of the French *colons* in the territory until he was sufficiently strong to move against them. By 1960 it was too late for the Algerian settlers to continue to dictate terms to the government in Paris. In that year a further resort to the barricades brought only adverse repercussions from Paris. De Gaulle had demonstrated that Algeria could no longer dominate Paris, but it was still too early to say that the French Government controlled Algeria. But henceforward de Gaulle could proceed with his policy toward the Algerian nationalists without being too much troubled by serious sniping and unrest in his rear.

For he was also in control of France. In the 1960 Algerian crisis France presented a united front, illustrating how far the country had come from the hesitations and disinterest in the fate of government so apparent in the previous crisis of 1958. De

Gaulle was accepted as the only person capable of giving France stability, direction, and prestige. The parties were still largely under the cloud of public disapprobation. Moreover, they had not yet recovered from their shattering defeat of 1958 and had not defined their new *modus vivendi*. The Communists were in the wilderness; the Radicals and Socialists were torn by internal debate; the MRP was fluctuating between supporting de Gaulle, thereby perhaps gaining some influence in policy-making, and complete opposition.

France still possessed a democratic appearance. The traditional democratic liberties were still observed: certainly criticisms of arbitrary government action in this sphere failed to point out that the instances involving arrest and suppression were no more numerous than during the closing years of the Fourth Republic. In many ways the Algerian situation gave the government some justification for acting in this manner. Yet the question still had to be asked: was France a democracy? The parties were politically powerless or inactive. The people, having found their saviour, were tending to withdraw even further from political interest. Parliamentary criticism of government action was prevented or ignored. De Gaulle's own strongwilled personality coupled with the ambiguities of the new constitution allowed him to interpret the latter as he saw fit. In many ways the best way of describing the actuality of the Fifth Republic was to call it a 'monarchy' following a pattern of patriarchal benevolence. De Gaulle did not believe in bothering with the details of politics; these he left to his subordinates. Instead he concerned himself with the grand design. As long ago as 1946 he had declared his belief that above political in-fighting there should be a national arbiter who would act when necessary in the best interests of the people. It was this role of national arbiter in which de Gaulle saw himself and which dominated his political actions. From this pedestal he could direct the destiny of France. These three ideas—national arbiter, national unity, national destiny—were the core of de Gaulle's political thinking. Accordingly, his foreign policy was designed to introduce an independent French course of action. Thus he sought to emphasise the role of France in the Western alliance, protesting against American dominance and the 'special' Anglo-American relationship. He turned to attempt a *rapprochement* with Chancellor Adenauer and West Germany. The two men had much in common, and the understanding reached between them will rank as one of the significant events in Europe in the twentieth century: the rivalry and suspicion between modern France and Germany had ever been a divisive force in Western Europe. Similarly, France had to have a renewed and independent military force. Early in 1960 France joined the nuclear powers by exploding a small atomic bomb in the Sahara.

In the first years under de Gaulle, therefore, France appeared to be pursuing paradoxical policies. In domestic affairs de Gaulle's government was able to grapple with the problem of economic modernisation and to develop a long-term programme. Such a policy had been needed since 1945. The Fourth Republic had begun the attempt, but its 'stop-go' nature was primarily one of very long halts and very short, relatively rare hesitating and groping jerks forward. On the other hand, de Gaulle's foreign policy decried modernity. In its emphasis upon destiny and national grandeur it was in many ways a return to a past when France had been in the first rank of world powers. For one European power to go it alone in this respect in the second half of the twentieth century appeared absurd and futile. It clashed strongly with the idea of European union whose drive had in many instances been provided by Frenchmen. It was an ever-present threat and challenge to the development of the European Economic Community. The EEC (or Common Market) treaty signed by six nations, including France, in 1957 was Western Europe's latest and most ambitious attempt to submerge national differences in a working supranational arrangement that would be, its protagonists hoped, the foundation of a new political, social, and economic unity on the continent.

The Tribulations of European Socialism

The de Gaulle revolution was the greatest single symbol of the predominance of conservatism in Europe in the late 1950s. His foreign policy was merely typical of the kind of nationalist policy conservatives had usually favoured. In contrast, the socialist parties were left out in the cold, apart from the 'neo-imperialist' French Government of Guy Mollet in 1956 and 1957. The neat pattern of conservative government and socialist opposition was most obvious in Britain's two-party system. Not so obvious, but still definite, was the similar picture in Italy and West Germany. The death knell of the Fourth Republic put France on the same level, after the pre-1958 picture had given the impression that the country was fluctuating between centre-right and centre-left coalitions.

The great paradox involved in this pattern was that those parties which symbolised change were denied office during a period when the rate of change was noticeably quicker than ever before. The conservative parties which suspected and feared change were given the task of supervising this change. What had gone wrong? European Socialist parties had, in essence, failed to adapt themselves to the changes that had actually taken place and that were still continuing. Instead of meeting the conservative challenge and analysing why conservatism was proving so successful, the Socialists too often indulged in acrimonious internal debates and disputes; for example, there was the 'Bevanite' revolt of 1954 in the British Labour Party over the question of German rearmament. While usually starting out as debates on principles, these arguments rarely failed to degenerate into bouts of personal insults.

The conservative parties, on the other hand, had learnt how to direct their appeal to the electorate. Taking advantage of the economic boom, they identified themselves with the new material prosperity, while at the same time accepting the changes already achieved. Conservatives presented themselves as better and firmer supporters of social security and welfare. In addition there was a perhaps deliberate attempt to shut out great political issues with a possibly divisive character from open debate. The conservatives benefited from prosperity, and in turn did their best to foster it since it seemed to possess an inverse relationship with political involvement and interest. There appeared to be a great deal of spontaneous improvisation about conservative actions, which in some of the more important issues, such as European union, paid rather large dividends.

In contrast, the Socialists appeared to be shackled by an archaic party organisation which suppressed all but the narrow-minded routinist. This question of party organisation did, in fact, appear to be one of the major differences between the parties. The conservatives gave the impression of being parties of leaders who controlled their organisation; the socialists appeared to be parties whose leaders were controlled by machine-like organisations with consequent stultifying effects. Conservative parties had a long tradition of accepting change and then using it to the best advantage; this they continued to do after 1945. Socialists did not have this tradition. Instead they had clung to their beliefs of a utopian future which could be achieved only if one path, and one path only, was followed, of remaining loyal to their traditional ideological position. In other words, their prime result, intentional or unintentional, was to create a ghetto for themselves and their supporters. But this path had already been proved to be only one of several alternatives. Society had not developed in the anticipated direction, and Britain under the postwar Labour Government had achieved nearly all its main Socialist proposals, yet utopia had not come any nearer. Overall we can say that party politics in Europe had cast off much of their traditional relationship with classes. Concepts such as the welfare state became gradually accepted by all social groups. On the other hand, Socialist parties, in the electorate's eyes, were clinging to the idea of a class struggle which was no longer valid. One further point is that Socialism on the continental mainland bore the accusations and weight of past failure. This was particularly true of France and Italy: here the extreme results of this awkward position were evident, because of the strength of Communism. Either one dismissed the democratic freedoms as meaningless and became a Communist, or one attempted to push through slight revisions of doctrine to overcome the existing paralysis only to see the party become greatly weakened and in no position to challenge a much stronger Communist Party. Italy and France respectively displayed these two tendencies. Consequently Socialism appeared to be completely disoriented, clinging to its old beliefs with such tenacity that it was more conservative than conservative parties.

But at the same time it was quite obvious that Socialist parties were the only possible focal point of left-wing political opinion which could offer a serious political challenge in a democracy. Left-wing non-socialist parties in Germany were virtually non-existent. The British Liberal Party and the Italian Action Party had failed to turn themselves into progressive parties with a comprehensive organisation and mass following. This was also the basic idea behind Mendès-France's attempted reform of the French Radicals: and it too had failed. So people had to return to the Socialists as the only starting point possessing the possibility of success. The problem was to discover how the continental parties could break free of the voting straitjacket imposed upon them. The parties were limited to a certain proportion of the votes (varying from 15 to 35 per cent in each country) and had never been capable of overcoming this electoral hurdle. Similarly, the British Labour Party seemed unable to attract new converts. At best this situation induced a state of apathy and an inclination to pursue internal debates; at worst it resulted in the compartmentalisation of politics whereby the party became a state within a state. It organised as much social time of its own supporters as possible; in politics, it would content itself with reassuring the faithful and would make no effort at all to persuade outsiders to vote for or even listen to the party. They tended to possess a smug satisfaction at their own purity. The promised land would be found if they waited long enough. Despite the changing nature of societies during this century, the Socialist parties had not been prepared to undertake any full reassessment of their fundamental ideological assumptions. Only after the successive electoral defeats did Socialist leaders attempt to turn their parties to this task.

Two general solutions to this ideological crisis of Socialism presented themselves. The first, more widely accepted, gained greater currency in Britain and West Germany, whose Socialist parties were perhaps more conservative than those of France and Italy—probably because there was no serious Communist alternative to draw away loyal supporters. Both parties had suffered a series of electoral reverses, seeing their principal opponents steadily attracting a greater share of the popular vote. The propositions of the party leaders, which in both cases were officially proposed in 1959, suggested nothing less than an almost complete abandonment of original Socialist goals. The German Social Democrats, never having held office in the postwar world, had seen their vote hold steady and even improve. There was, therefore, cause for optimism. The criticism focused on the party leadership of Erich Ollenhauer. Reformers argued that the party was too routine-minded, and that more personalities were needed, especially in the short term to counteract the appeal of Adenauer. But the final programme adopted at Bad Godesberg in 1959 was nothing more or less than a total rejection of Marxist dogma. Nationalisation, which in Germany had lost its urgency because of the application of the codetermination principle, was demoted; it was now accepted as only one of several alternatives for controlling and directing the economy. The class struggle, it seemed, no longer existed. The party also renounced its previous 'pacifism'; it accepted German rearmament and, if anything, became more pro-American than the ruling Christian Democrats. Even the term of address, 'brother', was retained only to soothe the feelings of the older members; in time it was expected that the term would disappear completely from the party vocabulary. The overall change was symbolised by the adoption of Willy Brandt, the young and popular mayor of West Berlin, as the party's candidate for the chancellorship for the 1961 election. In other words, the party had tried to discard its stultifying shibboleths. What it wanted to create was an ability to run a programme of member-ship and leadership recruitment and to follow an effective policy formulation process which would occur in an atmosphere of maximum efficiency and flexibility. The Social Democrats were seeking to change their image from that of a workers' party to that of a German party.

The Socialist 'revolution' in Britain was less clearcut. After the 1959 electoral defeat, the moderate policy of the party leader, Hugh Gaitskell, was criticised by the left-wing. But Gaitskell continued his attack upon the collectivisation of the means of distribution, production, and exchange—the hallowed Clause Four of the party constitution. However, the strength of the left-wing and the growing radical protest in the party—problems which the German Social Democrats did not have to face—forced Gaitskell to follow a compromise course. Gaitskell's defeat over

Clause Four illustrated that a frontal assault on the party's prime doctrines would fail and that a more devious course of moving the party toward the centre would have to be pursued.

In France Guy Mollet was torn between this policy and that of retaining a strong militancy. It meant that the Socialist policy was virtually all things to all men. The party knew well that a moderate policy might result in further defections to the more militant Communists without the compensation of new moderate supporters, but notwithstanding, Mollet accepted the greater need of sustaining the Fourth Republic. Since the party's main support came from white-collar workers, Mollet was in part justified in his overall policy of ignoring class differences and attempting to turn the Socialists into a non-dogmatic party of the left.

We can now sum up the general objects of this alternative. Basically, protagonists wished to end a static situation by instituting flexibility. Policy-making would therefore be the outcome of research on specific problems and not restrained in the strict mould of a somewhat irrelevant ideology. Practicality, not idealism, was their goal, and this was one of the principal targets of their opponents, who suggested that supporters were drawn to the party particularly because of its idealism and unified ideology. The leaders, on the other hand, countered with the charge that traditional idealism with its revolutionary connotations was somewhat misplaced in the modern world, that it was no longer a magnet sufficiently powerful to attract new converts: it was not without an element of truth that young West Germans, for example, were called the sceptical generation. To attract this new generation, the reformists argued that the answer could be found in pragmatic plans which applied to specific problems.

The second socialist solution was naturally proposed by the militants, nearly all of whom were to be found on the left flanks of the various movements. Its strongest proponents were among the Italian Socialists, dissident French Socialists, and the left-wing of the British Labour Party. The policies advocated by these groups often suffered from a great deal of woolly thinking, from a misplaced loyalty in the rationality of humanity, and from the fact that they were not constructive, but destructive. This was especially true in the field of foreign policy: primarily the Socialist left

opposed the emphasis upon armaments and the excessive involvement of the conservative governments with the United States.
But the solutions proposed were various and often ambiguous.
The clearest positions were adopted by the Italian Socialist Party,
which contented itself with arguing that no nuclear weapons
should be stationed on Italian soil, and by rebellious French Socialists who were avowed neutralists. But the groundswell of protest
was more widespread. In Britain the Campaign for Nuclear
Disarmament (CND) enjoyed much sympathy within the Labour
Party. At the 1960 party conference the CND succeeded in seeing
its claims, involving a total British renunciation of nuclear arms,
accepted by a majority. The party leadership, however, was in
opposition; Gaitskell successfully defied the conference and the
following year managed to obtain a reversal of the 1960 conference decision. Again, until 1959 the German Social Democrats had
officially advocated German neutrality, but this was only because
they conceived that the chances of German reunification were
considerably lessened by a military alliance with the West. But
overall, it was not clear what the radicals wanted: complete neutrality, a kind of neutrality within the American defensive system,
or an Atlantic alliance based only on conventional, and not nuclear,
armaments. The inability to come forward with a clear alternative
hindered the left in its search for extra support.

The same criticism applies to left-wing attitudes toward
domestic policy. They often failed to realise the changing nature
of society and the significance of Keynesian economics. Gaitskell,
Brandt, and their fellows were denounced as traitors to the cause—
but no progressive alternatives were proposed. Not having to face
the responsibilities and realities of government the left fell back
upon old time-honoured but tried and discredited slogans. Basically they wanted to return to the unsullied purity of the early
years of the Socialist movements; the demand for a more militant
approach was often nothing more than a yearning for a golden age
when the aims and the goal were undisputed and just around the
corner. The problems which such militant thinking caused in
the second half of the twentieth century are best illustrated by the
Italian Socialist Party (PSI). The PSI traditionally had been the
most left-wing European Socialist Party, and under Nenni after

R

1945 it maintained this guise. A good deal of electoral support was forthcoming because of the generally backward nature of much of Italian society. It had settled for nothing less than the maximum programme. But this policy had condemned it to a wilderness in which it was indistinguishable from the Communists; it ran the gauntlet, therefore, of being unable to attract the extremist votes, and, when attempting to gain additional moderate support, saw its efforts rejected and some of its already committed support draining away to the Communists. Unless it came out into the open as a clearly democratic party, the PSI seemed doomed to be squeezed out of existence between the pincers of the system and the Communists.

To be consistent, the picture was not as simple as this. Both arguments in several variations were present in all parties, and the situation was often in a state of flux. Even the PSI, for example, was moving steadily closer to the system; in 1949 it had utterly opposed Italian participation in NATO, but by 1957 it was prepared to accept Euratom and not to vote against Italy joining the Common Market. And, momentously, in 1958 its leader, Nenni, asserted that Italy was a loyal component of NATO and always would be.

But on the whole the general social picture of the 1950s seemed to suggest to most serious thinkers that the more moderate line was the one to adopt if their party ever wished to reverse the trend of the decade and gain power. The dominant right argued that the way to power lay through the conversion of the middle classes. This, they argued, could not be achieved unless the party convinced them that Socialist governments would not, in domestic policy, demolish private property, and in foreign policy would not relax the vigilant opposition against Communism. Thus, since the electorate have preferred the values put forward by the conservative parties, the socialists must attempt to compete with them on realistic grounds. The left, on the other hand, argued that the right was primarily looking at short-term factors, that it was willing to forget long-term social priorities and justice in order to win power and accept individual satisfaction. In opposition to the right's 'pragmatic' approach, the left offered a more ideological course of action. For this reason, nationalisation, probably the most single important item in Socialist thinking, was retained by the left, not primarily because of its economic value, but because of its function as a symbol of the moral change which Socialists desired to be wrought in society, a change from an emphasis upon individual concern to a concern for the whole community. In this way nationalisation became the focal point of arguments between the right and the left.

By 1960 the pragmatic approach was dominant:

The immediate results of the doctrinal crisis are found in an increased political opportunism, a distrust of visionaries and reformers and a desire to solidify the obvious social gains extracted in a mixed economy and a bourgeois order, events which themselves confute the Marxist heritage further.[1]

The old ideology, however, was far from being extinct. With the possible exception of West Germany, it was in fact showing signs of rejuvenation. While the dispute thereby ran the risk of being rigidly polarised between the two sides, there was always the possibility, hitherto practically ignored by most protagonists, of the realisation that the two were not mutually exclusive, but possessed a great deal of common ground. If the reawakening of political interest could be shorn of ideological conceptions that were definitely outdated, and combined with a realistic analysis of modern society's needs and aspirations, then it could be hoped that a revived Socialism would become a major political force in Western Europe.

[1] E. B. Haas, *The Uniting of Europe*, London, 1958, pp. 429–30.

13 Integration: the Great Leap Forward

> Those who drew up the Rome Treaty . . . did not think of it as essentially economic; they thought of it as a stage on the way to political union. . . . If [it is] bound to happen, so much the better; but it is wiser to work steadily and urgently to make [it] happen.

Paul-Henri Spaak, 1964[1]

By 1954 there was a mood of despondency surrounding the whole idea of European unity. Only ECSC had survived the 'holocaust' caused by the failure of EDC; and while the success of ECSC might be forecast, it could not be prophesied with any great degree of certainty. Moreover, although European trade had doubled in content by this time, it was now facing intransigent national protective barriers which OEEC had so far avoided because of the difficulties involved. While 'advanced' groups like Benelux pressed for a speedier liberalisation programme, others, including France within the 'little Europe' network, were dragging their heels. Economically as well as politically, the integrating schedule in Western Europe was losing its postwar momentum. The crucial question was whether or not the supranational urge had foundered completely beneath the weight of intergovernmental functionalism. Hope might stay alive as long as ECSC was a viable entity, but could supranationalism ever get beyond integration by sectors? The question received its answer only three years later when the Treaty of Rome was signed, thereby short-circuiting the tortuous progress of integration in much the same way as the stillborn European Political Community was designed to do.

The Road to Rome

It has already been stressed that perhaps the primary motive for accepting the principle of European unity in the first postwar

[1] Council of Europe, Consultative Assembly, 15th ordinary session, Deb. iii, p. 596 (12 January 1964).

decade had been the anxieties caused by the proximity and strength of the Soviet Union. As long as the fear of Russian expansion was dominant, national differences and prejudices were submerged under the protective covering of European unity. As soon as this outside pressure eased, as it did somewhat after the death of Stalin, these differences were forced out into the open: until they were disposed of, integration could not proceed on a satisfactory basis. The defeat of EDC coincided with the relaxation of Soviet pressure in Europe. The great leap forward of the integrationists after 1954 can be partly attributed to the fact that they were not now motivated primarily by fears of a Communist takeover, but were willing to operate on the positive and constructive basis of wanting union for its own intrinsic value.

Furthermore, the advocacy of coexistence from both sides of the Iron Curtain and the knowledge of the new strength of its own economies allowed Western Europe to examine more critically its dependence upon the United States. Suspicions had been aroused by Dulles's threat of an 'agonising reappraisal' during the EDC crisis. In 1956 they were reawakened by two interrelated factors. First, there was the American reaction to the prolonged Suez crisis and negotiations. While most countries refused to endorse the Anglo-French attitude and subsequent invasion, they certainly had cause to wonder whether the United States Government was coming under the influence of the so-called 'Fortress America' strategy, which suggested that with the development of long-range strike and retaliatory weapons, America could cut its overseas defence commitments quite severely and still wage a successful war from its own shores. This interpretation of the trend of American foreign policy and strategic thinking also caused Western Europe to consider more positive ways of cooperation without excessive reliance upon outside assistance.

So far as defence was concerned, the defeat of EDC did not mean a reversal to the traditional pattern of isolated national defensive systems linked only by a mutual aid treaty. This was emphasised by the solution found to the EDC dilemma—the adaptation of the 1948 Brussels Treaty. While WEU, which began to operate in 1955, was clearly a functional intergovernmental structure—British participation would otherwise have been impossible—it did illustrate that integration had not been denuded of all its strength. In defence terms, however, once German rearmament became a *de facto* reality, EDC was unimportant. Its importance lay in the significance of its success or failure in the mainstream of European unity. And here the main debate would inevitably be based upon political union and the more realistic economic union.

Protagonists of unity may have been despondent about the defeat of EDC, but were never routed. Realistically, they accepted that they had suffered a reverse, but refused to admit that they had lost the war. Even before the reverberations died down, the Common Assembly of ECSC announced that there should be established a committee to study means of further integration by extending the role and powers of the community system. Instead of seeking a comprehensive political community, they now desired an overall common market or economic community. Again, in May 1955 it returned to the attack with the suggestion that the foreign ministers of 'little Europe' should meet to discuss and draft a schedule for the next stage of development.

European unity thus showed a remarkable resilience in the face of adversity. Its success during this crucial period was due in no small measure to the fact that while it retained its committed supporters, it was continually finding new recruits. Whether these were persuaded by federalists or made their decision on the basis of their own analysis of the contemporary situation and current trends is unimportant; what mattered was that they joined the groundswell of opinion behind integration. In this process Jean Monnet performed a valuable role. After resigning from the presidency of the ECSC High Authority, he formed an Action Committee for the United States of Europe in October 1955. This committee, with the prestige of Monnet's name behind it, played a greater part than most people thought possible. It had members throughout the six nations of 'little Europe' and enjoyed support equally among parties of the democratic left, centre and right, as well as among businessmen and trade unions. More specifically it will be remembered for its efforts to remove the deep wedge which EDC had driven into the French Socialist Party, and the promise of support it gained from the leader of the West German Socialists, Erich Ollenhauer. The German SPD had been a bitter opponent of EDC and German rearmament, not only because of its traditional pacific sentiments, but also because it feared that they would make possibilities of German reunification even more remote. Now, however, its leaders were slowly coming round to accept Adenauer's view that West Germany could, in world circumstances, best advocate reunification from a position of strength within a Western defensive system and an integrated Western Europe.

Added to this changing mood of opinion was the assessment of economic trends. Within the healthier current situation the trade figures were no longer satisfactory. For those who wished to press for a significant economic advance to be made, the existing organisation for Europe, OEEC, was totally inadequate. Although the blame could not be attached to OEEC itself, which had quite limited functions and aims, the state of affairs did mean that no new economic proposals could be implemented without the previous consent of all member nations. Instead of openly advocating a political community, the protagonists of closer union had a legitimate economic argument with which to advance their cause through an 'intermediary' stage of a common economic market open to any willing OEEC member state.

The lines of division on the subject of political unity and economic integration versus association and cooperation had already been clarified and determined by the previous debates over the Council of Europe, ECSC, and EDC. Thus it was not surprising that the initiative was taken up only by the six countries of 'little Europe'. These states accepted the resolution of the ECSC Common Assembly to study possible future developments. In May and June 1955 the six foreign ministers met at Messina and there drafted for publication a joint proposal for the pooling of information and work concerning the uses of atomic energy and the establishment of a comprehensive customs union leading to a common market. An intergovernmental committee, headed by the tireless Paul-Henri Spaak, was established to develop these schemes further: complete approval was again given by the foreign ministers of the Six at subsequent meetings in Venice and Brussels. Finally, the Spaak blueprint was open to public debate in March 1956, in a special session of the ECSC Common Assembly.

Only one vote was registered against the proposals for a treaty establishing a customs union and preparing the groundwork for a full economic community. This vote was a striking endorsement by the Common Assembly, which was representative of all political views in the Six except the two political extremes. The last preparatory act was the approval of the governments concerned: meeting in Paris in February 1957 the six premiers reached agreement on the various points that had been raised during negotiations. On 25 March 1957 two treaties, one establishing a European Economic Community and the other a European Atomic Energy Community, were signed in Rome by the Six and referred to the national parliaments for ratification. Only three years after the reversal of EDC and EPC the movement for European unity had been stimulated to make a great leap forward into the future.

The Six had reverted to Schuman's original view that closer political and social union could be achieved in time through strenuous and sustained efforts to obtain greater economic integration. The new economic community also avoided the problems raised by the existence of OEEC. The community was to reduce tariffs and trade restrictions within its region only gradually over a lengthy period of time. This provision allowed it to come to terms with concurrence with the world agreement of GATT (General Agreement on Tariffs and Trade), to which all OEEC states belonged. Signatories of GATT could not cut tariffs if this discriminated against third parties; however, it was permitted if spread over a fairly long period of time so as to allow third parties to accommodate themselves to the new state of affairs.

The drive towards integration was caused by both political and economic factors. In the mid-1950s the impetus was derived from a temporary conjunction of political and economic forces. The road from Messina to Rome was relatively short because the Six, having agreed to press on, were anxious to take advantage of the current political constellation: the later accession to power of de Gaulle illustrates how temporary and tenuous this coalition was. This coalition fortunately coincided with a growing acceptance of the need to reform Europe's economic situation. The net result was the Common Market, with a pedigree going directly back through Messina to ECSC. While less revolutionary than EPC, it was still an ambitious scheme. Its particular form was constructed in this way first to satisfy other states because of the OEEC and GATT requirements, and second in the hope that the economic shroud over the ultimate political ambitions would permit it to be accepted by internal doubters and critics. The Common Market was designed to accommodate as many people and groups as possible. Economically, it was fulfilment, but politically only a gateway to the ultimate goal of a United States of Europe. The preamble of the treaty stresses the political goal by its desire 'to establish the foundations of an ever closer union among the European peoples'.

Towards the Common Market

After the fiasco of EDC, the French National Assembly was universally accepted as being the place where the European Economic Community treaty and its Euratom sister stood or fell. By the time they were ready for ratification there was a very real question-mark over their success here, as the weak but longlived Mollet government had departed and Fourth Republic politics were entering their final prolonged crisis. In the event, the treaties overcame this baptism of fire by a satisfying three to two margin only three months after Rome, thereby to some extent redeeming the Assembly after its EDC behaviour; it was the first parliament to approve this stage in integration. In the next few months the treaties were approved by the other parliaments. In December 1957, with the ratification of the Dutch parliament, EEC and Euratom were ready to operate. On 19 March 1958 EEC began its existence with the first session of its assembly meeting temporarily in Strasbourg. Meeting as it did in the town of the Council of Europe it brought back memories of that body's first session nearly ten years earlier. Certainly the same mood of excitement and the making of history was present. However, to emphasise the difference between its expectations and the reality of the Council of Europe, it called itself the 'European Parliamentary Assembly'. To symbolise this name, the seating organisation was arranged according to political orientation and not national delegations; hence they formalised the tendencies of political parties to coalesce across national boundaries which had already been apparent in ECSC and, to a lesser extent, in the Council of Europe. They carried this aggressive spirit one step further by refusing to accept the nominee of the six foreign ministers for the presidency of the Assembly; instead they honoured one of the pioneers of European integration by electing Robert Schuman to the post.

The provisions contained in the EEC treaty are naturally very complex, since the new organisation was to range over an extremely wide area of activities. Broadly speaking, the transformation of the member states into a common market was to be spread over a period of twelve to fifteen years. Even here there were disagreements. France, particularly under de Gaulle, tended to regard the period as being too short, while others wanted to move faster. There is nothing in the treaty to bar others from establishing a smaller customs union, and this, in fact, the Benelux states did in February 1958. Within the treaty, however, are clauses which emphasise that EEC does not intend to stop at a simple customs union; its aims include the abolition of all national barriers to the free movement of labour and capital, the destruction of all measures designed to restrict or damage trade, a common investment policy both inside and outside EEC administered by EEC agencies, and the coordination and rationalisation of social welfare policy. If EEC could fully harness these aims it would be well on the way to becoming a fully fledged supranational organisation, but as national interests could not be swamped entirely escape clauses (which did not appear in the original Spaak report) were included to allow divergences of national policy where, for example, questions of national security took priority. Such escape clauses, being of the traditional functional type, restricted EEC in its movement towards supranationalism. Furthermore, there were some thorny economic problems which could not be dealt with by the ordinary arrangements. Agriculture, for example, was designated as a special economic activity, and it was agreed that agriculture as a whole within EEC would be handled completely on a supranational level so as to produce not free trade but only a liberalisation to an extent compatible both with EEC principles and the maintenance of agriculture in all member countries.

The institutions created to administrate the work of EEC are drawn from their successful predecessors of ECSC. Since Euratom is the identical twin of EEC, except for its more limited and specialised field, it can safely be ignored here. The supranational element in EEC is again provided by a quasi-executive, here called the Commission. It has nine members appointed for renewable four-year terms by the participating governments. West Germany, France and Italy each appoint two members, while the other states each appoint one commissioner. However, because EEC is in many ways a more radical body than ECSC, the member states were not willing to concede as much sovereignty as previously. Hence the Commission enjoys considerably less freedom of action than the ECSC High Authority. It does possess the ability to decide, but more usually can only recommend. The Commission's main responsibility is the administration of the Treaty of Rome. Since 1967 it has also headed Euratom and ECSC.

Authority generally rests with the Council, the organ of the national governments, which carries the main burden of ensuring coordination of policies in the various economic spheres. Voting in the Council is complex and depends upon the nature of the issue under discussion. On Commission recommendations Benelux can be outvoted by the 'big three'; on other occasions, a 'qualified' majority of twelve votes from at least four countries is necessary.[1] Where the Council wishes to modify a Commission proposal, a unanimous verdict is required. Because of these stipulations we can see that EEC is not, overall, an improvement on ECSC. If a member state drags its heels over issues, as France and West Germany were to do in the early 1960s, the whole programme of EEC can be delayed or halted. The change in the relationship between the supranational authority and the member governments was occasioned by the ECSC experience. There it had been learnt that progress could not be made if the national governments objected to a particular part of the programme. The substitution was an attempt to ensure much closer collaboration between the Commission and Council than existed in ECSC. On the whole this design has worked well and, other things being equal, it has

[1] Qualified majorities are due to a weighted voting system. The weighted voting in the Council is as follows: France 4; Italy 4; West Germany 4; Belgium 2; The Netherlands 2; Luxembourg 1.

been a Commission–Council axis which has been the mainspring of EEC. As in ECSC, the Commission and Council have underneath them a consultative institution, the Economic and Social Committee, which contains representatives of national interest groups.

The third major institution is the Parliamentary Assembly which again enjoys the right of consultation and recommendation, but less so than in ECSC for the balance of power here rests with the Council: it possesses no legislative authority, though it was later given some marginal budgetary powers. It possesses the power to dismiss the Commission, but has no influence in the selection of a new one. A European parliament has still to come into existence. The fourth major institution of EEC is the Court of Justice, which is composed of seven justices appointed for renewable six-year terms. The Court has the responsibility of cases arising from the treaties or from disputes between members. In the last resort the implementation of its verdicts depends upon the national governments and the national court systems. It has, however, decided against all six governments and against the Commission at one time or another.

One problem which the creation of EEC raised was the proliferation of institutions within 'little Europe', let alone the institutions of a 'greater Europe' in which they were also represented. The first stage of rationalisation was carried through by making only one assembly serve ECSC, EEC, and Euratom: its powers, of course, vary according to the capacity in which it is sitting at any given moment. In 1965 a new treaty was drawn up which provided for the creation of only one Commission and Council for the three communities. The schedule called for the establishment of a single European Community by 1970. The 1965 treaty was the most significant constitutional development since the Treaty of Rome, in that it also provided for a review of the purposes and activities of the Community.

The first test of the Treaty of Rome came in January 1959, when the preliminary stage of tariff reductions was due to go into operation. Several protagonists were apprehensive not only because of the newness of EEC but also because of possible French opposition. In the event the cuts were made without any opposition from France. De Gaulle, however, was fully occupied with a war in

Algeria which was still seriously disturbing French society. It was nevertheless still apparent during this first round that he had not shed his distaste for federalism or supranationalism. During the first few years of operation progress was more than satisfactory. By 1961 the internal tariff barriers had been substantially reduced, and quota restrictions on industrial products had almost been eliminated. Trade within the EEC had increased at a rate double that of trade with non-member countries. In effect, it seemed that notice had been served that EEC was a fully functioning entity. Certainly other countries were regarding it as such: for example, as early as mid-1959 two members of OEEC, Greece and Turkey, had drawn this conclusion and had applied for some form of association with the Common Market.

In any event EEC would not have been a viable proposition if it had run into serious trouble less than one year after it began to operate. A hint as to its future development could be gleaned from Benelux. EEC was attempting to do in twelve to fifteen years what Benelux did in three; and yet it was only at the end of this transitional period that serious difficulties began to afflict Benelux. The much wider scope of EEC and its larger membership would undoubtedly cause grave strains long before the end of its transitional period. Yet paradoxically this very scope demanded that such stresses should be resolved as soon as possible, for the significant point about the new community, and one which became apparent during its initial years, was 'the scope of the tasks assigned to the central institutions, and the extent to which these tasks appear to be inherently expansive; that is, the extent to which integrative steps in one functional context spill over into another'.[1] But amid the initial enthusiasm over the breakthrough of EEC in the integrative field, by the close of the decade it could be seen that a much greater momentum than that supplied solely by the Treaty of Rome would be required to push the Six firmly into full economic union and political unity. EEC could achieve a customs union and perhaps go beyond this, but before the ultimate goal could come into view a vast amount of political education would have to be done.

[1] L. N. Lindberg, *The Political Dynamics of European Economic Integration*, London, 1963, p. 293.

Britain in the Wings

The great advance took place without British participation, since British acceptance of the fundamental supranational element could not be given. In fact, in many ways Britain disapproved of the whole idea, while lending vocal encouragement to the idea of unity. The drive toward integration upset British conceptions about the relationship with Europe, no matter how outmoded the old balance of power concept was. For those countries outside the 'little Europe' club, Britain was the natural leader: many, indeed, would be willing to join the Six in their ventures if Britain also joined. After the defeat of EDC, which heartened many in Britain, the British approach to Europe during the 1950s can be seen to consist of three general stages: Western European Union, the 'Grand Design', and the Free Trade Association.

The establishment of WEU has already been discussed in some detail. In many ways it placed on Britain as great a burden as EDC membership would have done, with the pledge to maintain troops on the continent at all times. In 1957, for example, when the British Government decided to switch the basis of their defensive commitments from conventional to nuclear arms, negotiations with WEU had to take place before the number of British troops on the continent could be reduced. In many ways WEU was an anomaly. It was a defensive organisation designed to permit German rearmament, yet West Germany soon became a member of NATO, a much more comprehensive defensive system. Once West Germany was a *de facto* member of NATO, it would be virtually impossible to remove the Federal Republic against its will without disrupting or destroying the whole alliance. Once the original justification sank from the realm of public concern, WEU seemed to many to be a useless appendage. Even Britain, who had taken the initiative in founding WEU out of the wreckage of EDC, was not prepared to allow it to intrude upon Anglo-American relations, and placed it a clear second to NATO.

The only values it possesses are that its executive body, the Council, which meets only sporadically, has the authority to formulate decisions that are binding on the member governments, thus placing it between the Council of Europe–OEEC arrangements and those of the 'little Europe' institutions. But since the Council consists of the foreign ministers, or in their absence the London ambassadors and since decisions are gained only after a unanimous vote, this is perhaps meaningless. Its other value lies with its Assembly (comprising the relevant delegates to the Council of Europe) which is the only parliamentary body which is entitled to discuss matters of European defence. Otherwise it exists amid confusion, its commitments overlapping with those of NATO, the Council of Europe, and OEEC (or OECD), with 'little Europe' going its own way in the field of integration. Critics argued that its functions could be performed equally well by NATO, and queried its efficacy as a European defensive arrangement. They ask what value is gained by not incorporating Scandinavia or the other European countries that constitute NATO. For the other side, it is argued that it is the closest link between Britain and the Six; its value in this role is debatable. Although after its application to join EEC had been turned down in 1963 Britain suggested that closer cooperation could best take place within the confines of WEU, it is still quite legitimate to consider WEU as a complicating and superfluous organisation.

The gulf which separated Britain and the Six, apparent long before WEU was created, was too wide to be bridged by such a tenuous organisation. In terms of close relationship and integrative effort WEU was a very inferior substitute for EDC and its ultimate aim of political union. But for Britain WEU was no doubt satisfactory: it did allow British association with the continental leaders of integration, and probably permitted some form of British influence. This state of affairs changed rather abruptly with the Treaty of Rome and its implications. If Britain wished to deter European integration or even to maintain what was considered to be a special position for itself as the link between the United States and Europe, some new system would have to be found: WEU was now clearly insufficient.

The first clear sign of Britain's attitude toward the changing situation came at a NATO council meeting in December 1956, when Foreign Minister Selwyn Lloyd introduced proposals for what became known as the 'Grand Design'. These were further elaborated by Britain in the Consultative Assembly of the Council of Europe in May of the following year. The essence of the British suggestion where European union was concerned was that the time had come to rationalise the proliferation of European institutions that had sprung up in the past decade. This was to be done by introducing a single European assembly which, unrelated to any organisation, would serve them all. The proposal immediately aroused the suspicions of the pro-Europeans within the Six, for it was typical of previous British offers: it was so vague as to be virtually meaningless or free to be interpreted in any way whatsoever.

Suspicions were easily aroused, for almost simultaneously Britain had announced a desire to reduce the number of troops maintained in West Germany under the WEU arrangement in order to reform its defence organisation under the guiding light of nuclear armaments. Nevertheless, discussions took place on the basis of the British proposals. All Western Europe was involved, as the negotiations ranged not only over defence but also over economics. The second part of the British scheme was a comprehensive free trade area covering the whole of Western Europe: this was Britain's counter-effort to the projected Common Market.

In both defence and economics countries adopted their traditional postwar stances: the debate was on an Atlantic or a European community. On the political and defensive issue the main argument actually took place over a more limited and realistic Italian amendment that a single assembly should cover only WEU, EEC, and the Council of Europe: to its supporters the reconciliation of NATO and the rest seemed to be impossible. The Italian scheme was preferred for discussion because the British design offered startling changes for the existing structures without any concrete improvements. Furthermore, for federalists the British proposal once again seemed to seek to destroy everything that had been created since 1949 and freeze European organisations in the 'primitive' intergovernmental mould of the Council of Europe and OEEC. It ran into further objections from neutrals who wanted to avoid close integration. It was suggested that the new free trade area would not cover agriculture; for all other economic spheres it was proposed that no common external tariff should be applied, but that members should negotiate separate tariffs with non-members.

It was obvious to the Europeans that Britain was seeking to obtain the best of two worlds: to take advantage of the market opportunities in Europe through a steadily decreasing tariff while still retaining the special economic arrangements with the Commonwealth. If adopted, the clash of Europe and Commonwealth—for example over farm produce—could have had serious implications. Overall, therefore, it seemed to the defenders of union that Britain's entire policy was devoted to destroying everything that had been achieved by diluting it beyond recognition, of trying to 'drown Europe in the Atlantic'.[1]

One major stumbling block was the problem of giving the military bodies of NATO and WEU and the economic organisations the same parliamentary assembly. Fundamentally, the gap between the two sides that could not be bridged was caused by the simple fact that Britain was not proposing a customs union for a greater Europe, but a free trade area. Considering that this concept was retrograde so far as a common market is concerned, it is extremely surprising that the Six were willing to negotiate in the first place, and that the meetings nearly achieved a solution to satisfy everyone in part. The Six, however, naturally had a strong disincentive to pursue the free trade area discussions simply because they had already completed their plans for a common market, and thus tended to present a united front on the complex of issues involved.

The opposition within the Six was derived from two different sources. First, there was the clear economic argument of certain protectionist groups which felt that countries outside the Common Market, particularly Britain with its preferential Commonwealth arrangements, would be in too advantageous a position. The second type of opposition gradually grew stronger as the negotiations dragged on. No matter how much its supporters desired British association with their ambitions, they feared the adverse effect of a free trade area on the ultimate goal of political union. These protagonists knew that several economic groups within the Six had supported the foundation of EEC primarily because of the advantages accruable in a larger market. If these advantages could be obtained without the closely knit EEC

[1] U. W. Kitzinger, *The Challenge of the Common Market*, Oxford, 1961, p. 86.

structure, then the whole drive towards economic and political integration might well falter or be destroyed. Hence the pro-Europeans, still not in a position to guarantee success within the Six, were hostile to the British proposals. Only in the future would they be willing to accept such negotiations when EEC was better organised and in a powerful position to resist attempts to submerge it in a large, amorphous 'pseudo-European' body.

The key lay with France and, to a lesser extent, West Germany. If these two countries had agreed to the Grand Design then it almost certainly would have succeeded. In December 1958 the negotiations were abruptly broken off by France, which meant that the remaining five countries of EEC had to follow the French lead or wreck the Common Market. Since de Gaulle had met Dr Adenauer at Bad Kreuznach only the previous month, it appears likely that the West German Chancellor knew of and perhaps endorsed the French action. The latest effort to prevent too wide a wedge being driven through the concept of Europe had failed.

The net result of the abortive free trade area negotiations was a sharp deterioration in European relations. They had done nothing to diminish the rather hostile isolationist attitude of Britain, and simultaneously had confirmed the belief of pro-Europeans that any British proposal was a wolf in sheep's clothing. Moreover Britain had failed to convince de Gaulle that it could be nothing but a rival to France for European leadership. De Gaulle's known views on reforming NATO, his desires for a grand reawakening of French prestige, his ambition to effect a lasting reconciliation between France and Germany—all influenced his final decision on the negotiations and were still partly the basis for his rejection of the British application to enter EEC a few years later.

Britain's next act was to go ahead with the formation of a European Free Trade Association, which Austria, Denmark, Norway, Portugal, Sweden, and Switzerland agreed to join. Negotiations proceeded very quickly and by July 1959 the relevant ministers had approved of the plan. In November the Stockholm Convention was signed by the 'Outer Seven', and shortly afterwards EFTA was ratified and began to operate. The economic aim of EFTA was to work for tariff reductions among the members. By 1970 it was hoped that tariffs would be completely abolished. But there EFTA's work would be ended; it was not intended to continue to seek economic unification or integration. It is perhaps arguable whether this was Britain's real motive for founding EFTA. Economically, the six smaller nations received far greater benefits from the organisation than did Britain. It is quite possible that the ulterior motive was to impress the Common Market nations, which could not enjoy EFTA's low tariffs, that they were excluded from a valuable organisation, with the end purpose of persuading EEC to come again to the conference table to consider schemes of association (but not unity) for the whole of Western Europe.

This was the interpretation prevalent within the EEC. It was strengthened by the debate in the House of Commons upon the Stockholm Convention, in which the speakers concentrated far more upon the relationship with the Common Market than the organisation and aims of EFTA. The popular attitude towards Britain's role in these proceedings was admirably summed up by Roy Jenkins, a Labour spokesman, who said: 'I have a feeling that in negotiating the EFTA we have been too much concerned with showing the Six that what they rejected is a perfectly workable arrangement. I think that the EFTA will be perfectly workable, but I do not believe that in the last resort the Six rejected the Free Trade Area because they thought it would not work. They rejected it because, whether it worked or not, it was not what they wanted.'[1] Soon after EFTA started to operate, it was clear that the 'lesson' had not been assimilated. EFTA only served to alienate France even further, while failing to gain any sympathy from West Germany, Britain's only possible major ally within the Six. As the 1950s came to a close, Western Europe was truly at sixes and sevens. In the long term, however, Britain's role in the establishment of EFTA might be considered as an important step in the country's movement towards a greater involvement in Europe.

It had taken ten years for the nations of Europe to decide definitely where they stood on the questions of integration and association. The pattern which had emerged by 1960 seemed likely to remain for some time, with the countries of the EEC preferring to attempt a maximum degree of integration and supranationalism,

[1] 615 H.C. Deb. 1076 (14 December 1959).

and the remainder opting for a minimal level of intergovernmental association. This arrangement would perhaps have
been satisfactory but for the rancour aroused in previous years.
With the breakdown of the free trade area negotiations, EEC and
EFTA went their separate ways and more and more began to
regard each other as a rival, not a partner. Since most of the
nations involved were members of the Western alliance, this
deep rift in Western Europe was a matter of grave concern to the
United States. American policy disliked EFTA as an unnecessary
complication, not for what it was, but because it was inferior to
the EEC which the United States supported wholeheartedly
because of its goal of political union. America therefore decided
to step in to preserve some semblance of close unity. Since the
immediate problem was an economic one the United States proposed that the OEEC be reconstituted to allow non-European
membership and to concentrate on international problems of
economic development. OEEC was therefore reconstituted as the
Organisation for Economic Cooperation and Development,
although obviously wider economic arguments also made such a
reorganisation advisable. It was a less satisfactory organisation
than OEEC, but it did have one significant implication. The
establishment of OECD merely reinforced the lessons of the free
trade area negotiations that Britain was not something special;
through OECD the supranational organisations of EEC were
offered a more direct link with Washington, with Britain in the
wings.

14 Cold War and Thaw: Outlook Variable

When internal and external forces that are hostile to socialism try to turn the development of some socialist country towards the restoration of a capitalist regime, where socialism in that country and the socialist community as a whole are threatened, it becomes . . . a common problem and concern of all socialist countries . . . Military assistance to a fraternal country designed to arrest the threat to the social system is an extraordinary step, dictated by necessity.

Leonard Brezhnev, 1968[1]

This war (the Vietnam one) is ending. In fact, I seriously doubt if we will ever have another war. This is probably the very last one.

President Richard Nixon, 1971[2]

The opening of the 1960s did not seem auspicious for the Western alliance. Very rarely, if ever, had the West appeared to seize the initiative in the silent struggle for world leadership. While not as serious as the situation in 1947 or 1948, there was still grave cause for concern. The United States had drifted towards stagnation and non-involvement during the closing years of President Eisenhower's administration: the aura of goodwill that had cloaked an earlier summit meeting had been dispersed in 1960 after the U-2 incident in which an American reconnaissance plane had been shot down over Soviet territory. In Europe, Britain and France were becoming more suspicious of each other. Despite its role in EEC and NATO, West Germany was still torn between its commitment to the Western alliance and its dream of German reunification, yet the necessity for clarifying its attitudes towards the East was becoming more apparent. Overall, Russia and its leader, Nikita Khrushchev, were the stars of the world stage, their brilliance symbolised by the lead Soviet Russia had displayed in space exploits.

[1] Quoted in *The Times*, 13 November 1968.
[2] Quoted in the *Economist*, vol. 238, no. 6655 (13 March 1971).

During the following decade world attention tended to be focused outside Europe, on such widely separated areas as Cuba, South-East Asia, the Middle East, Nigeria, and the Indian sub-continent. The spotlight moved to Europe only on a few occasions—sporadically on Berlin, and on Czechoslovakia in 1968. By the middle of the decade it seemed as if the détente of the 1950s had become even more consolidated. The invasion of Czechoslovakia in 1968 by the Warsaw Pact countries under Russian leadership did not, in a sense, change this. For it characterised a prominent feature of international relations: both the United States and the Soviet Union were undergoing a period of introspection and concern about the solidarity of their own defensive alliances, while participating at the same time in an on-going series of bilateral and multilateral consultations designed both to accommodate each other's interests and to ease the pressure on each within the existing *status quo*. Within this bipolar relationship, two themes are of particular importance for Western Europe: the failure to arrive at any solution to the German question and, more specifically, the problem of Berlin; and the debate over the nature and role of a Western defensive alliance.

America and Russia: an Accommodation of Interests

One of the more significant episodes in the relationship between the two super-powers was the Cuban crisis of 1961 and 1962. The attempt by American-backed forces to regain control of Cuba (the Bay of Pigs fiasco) from Fidel Castro and his left-wing government served to discredit American foreign policy even further. This, however, was later redeemed to some extent by President Kennedy's prompt ultimatum to Russia either to withdraw missile bases secretly established on the island or to risk a direct military confrontation. The ensuing dialogue between Kennedy and Khrushchev, which attempted to preserve both the interests and the prestige of the two powers, illustrated the true nature of their relationship. Castro and Cuba were not consulted. Bipolarity meant that in essence problems could be solved only by bilateral American–Russian negotiations and agreements. In the last resort smaller countries were quite irrelevant to this dialogue, although in times of 'normalcy' it was becoming evident that both super-powers were finding it more difficult to keep their erstwhile allies or client-states under firm control. In a sense the confrontation of the two states over Cuba marked the end of a phase of their relationship which had begun with the Cold War. While it is true that Cuba emphasised that a satisfactory solution to many world problems arising from the spheres of interest of the two military giants could in the last resort be resolved only by direct consultation, it is also true that the 1960s illustrated the obverse. Neither the United States nor the Soviet Union could completely control world politics. For example, the unresolved nature of the conflict in the Middle East between the Arab states and Israel backed respectively by Russia and America, and the determination of both super-powers not to be outflanked in a region which they regard as strategically important, resulted, especially after the latest episode of the six-day war of 1967, in an arms race between their clients which both seemed forced to encourage against their wishes.

The fear of being pushed into a military conflict against their own will is one reason why America and Russia have found a certain communion of interest. Both have found that extrication can be much more difficult—at times perhaps impossible—than involvement. The construction of a direct telephone link, the so-called 'hot line', between the White House and the Kremlin indicated that both sides have a common concern in reducing the possibility of military confrontation, particularly where there is no apparent direct clash of interests, or where it seems that such a possibility may occur because of the force of circumstances.

Until the invocation by Leonard Brezhnev, the new leader of the Russian Communist Party, of his eponymous doctrine—that Russia had a right to intervene in Czechoslovakia or in any other socialist country to preserve socialism against both internal and external threats—it had seemed that Europe, apart from the almost intractable German problem, was not a major concern of the two super-powers. The decreasing concern with security meant that countries within both blocs were more and more emphasising their individuality. In the West France under President de Gaulle pursued an increasingly independent foreign policy; in the East Rumania, which refused to participate in the pacification of Czechoslovakia, also pursued a distinctive foreign policy, while by the end of the decade Hungary was moving very cautiously and quietly towards some kind of political reform. However, the apparent disinterest of the two giants with Europe was due to a considerable extent to their view that here the demarcation lines were strictly drawn. Both still expressed concern when it appeared that policies of individual European countries threatened to modify or destroy the existing *status quo*: this is the reason why the Russian and other Eastern Communist leaders found it necessary to intervene in Czechoslovakia.

The increased freedom of movement by European countries was due also to the involvement of America and Russia elsewhere. The United States was bogged down in the mire of the war in South-East Asia, which had spread from Laos to Vietnam, and eventually in 1970 to Cambodia as well. Beginning with President Kennedy's decision to send 'advisers' to Vietnam, American participation in that partitioned country escalated sharply under his successor, Lyndon Johnson. The Vietnam war had two important consequences for America. First, the preoccupation of American government and military circles with the war meant that their attention elsewhere was distracted. Second, the war more and more proved to be domestically unpopular. Domestic opposition to involvement in Vietnam expressed itself in widespread popular demonstrations and disorders, and even in Congress where opponents eventually forced upon the administration a policy of disinvolvement. Vietnam had two consequences for Europe. First, unlike the earlier conflict in Korea, very few comparisons were drawn with Europe. The war was very unpopular in Europe, and NATO countries made it very clear to the United States that neither material nor moral support could be expected. It also meant that the Western European countries began to question more and more the proposition that American and European defence interests were similar. Second, the cost of running the war and the groundswell of opinion within America against the military establishment and its political influence led to a questioning both in American military circles and at the popular level of the necessity to retain a high troop concentration in Europe, particularly as few of the NATO countries seemed in-clined to honour fully their obligations in this respect. Both President Johnson and President Nixon came under strong pres-sure to reduce the level of American military manpower in Europe. This too has encouraged Western European countries to search for a more distinctive foreign and defence policy.

The most outstanding development in the Communist world was the dramatic rift between Russia and China, which turned into a contest both for influence in Asia and Africa and for leader-ship of the Communist countries. Russian worries over China increased significantly in the 1960s. The continued nuclear de-velopment of China, their common long and sparsely populated border, and the fact that several of these border regions had his-torically been and still were disputed by the two countries, the Chinese ideological rejection of Russian supremacy in Commun-ism—all helped to turn Russian attention away from Europe to its eastern border. It meant that Russia also had an interest in keeping tension in Europe at a very low level or in attempting to settle those problems still outstanding on the continent. Russian interests in this respect were aided by the perhaps not surprising adherence of the East European states to the Russian position in the Sino-Soviet dispute: only tiny Albania, separated from the Russian bloc by Yugoslavia, opted to support China. In these circumstances, the invasion of Czechoslovakia was, as Brezhnev said, an extraordinary step.

It is factors such as these which have forced America and Russia into a more or less perpetual series of bilateral and multilateral conversations, all designed to accommodate and protect their interests and to help reduce the financial burden which defence requirements place upon them in preparing for both aggressive and defensive moves in a possible nuclear conflict. Thus the two states signed a nuclear test ban treaty in 1963 and have shown a concern that neither outer space nor the lunar surface should be used for military, especially nuclear, purposes. They have also been concerned to limit the dispersal of nuclear arsenals to other coun-tries for the same reasons as cited earlier: in 1968 they accepted a Nuclear Non-Proliferation Treaty, although the success of this depends on other countries also signing the agreement.

The latest stage in this long conversation are the Strategic Arms Limitation Talks, which began in November 1969, and which still show no signs of nearing completion or basic agreement: nevertheless, both sides seem to want the talks to succeed, or at least to continue. Since 1966 the Soviet Union and its allies have been suggesting that the best way to resolve Europe's remaining problems is through a general European security conference, which would involve a series of guarantees around a peace treaty based upon the present territorial arrangements. This proposal, however, has been regarded with suspicion by the West, being seen by some as an attempt to remove American nuclear weapons and troop contingents from Europe, thus leaving the continent more open to Russian influence through the overwhelming strength of its conventional forces. In recent years, however, the Western countries have shown more interest in this idea. The outstanding example was de Gaulle's conception of a Europe stretching from the Atlantic to the Urals, which was reminiscent of what some East European leaders suggested would be the rewards of a successful security conference. While the Western allies do not now appear to be averse to the idea, they tend to make their acceptance in principle contingent upon the Russians making some positive proposals or moves on the problem of Germany, especially upon the future status of West Berlin.

Germany and Berlin: Problems of Recognition and Access

The Cuban solution could quite clearly not be applied to a similar crisis in Europe: it was inconceivable that the Russian leaders would withdraw so gracefully on their home ground. An undeclared struggle could perhaps take place in Africa and limited wars could go on in South-East Asia—in Korea and Indo-China—for here the situation was fluid. These areas were, in a sense, a no man's land where both the rules and the game were quite different. In Europe, however, the 'iron curtain' was still rigid, if not as impenetrable as previously. Its invasion of Czechoslovakia in 1968 emphasised that while the Soviet Union was willing to pursue the question of a European détente, this was acceptable only within the existing pattern of military blocs and what it conceived its established strategic interests to be.

The outstanding problem in Europe is Germany. For the West, this has several important aspects. There is the question of the recognition of the Western boundaries of Poland at the Oder–Neisse line; there is the question of pursuing reunification or of accepting the *de jure* recognition of the East German state; and there is the problem of Berlin. Present Western attitudes over the first two questions have changed considerably since the 1950s; in a sense the changes can be partly attributed to developments in Berlin in the 1960s.

Perhaps the two Germanies might more readily have been able to resolve their differences without the anomalous position of West Berlin as an enclave deep within the East German state. As it is, the situation of West Berlin is unsatisfactory to both sides, and the city has always been the flashpoint of East–West tension in Europe, although both sides still respect the unwritten rules they accepted in 1948. In 1961, after repeated alarums and excursions by Khrushchev and his hints about a separate Russian peace treaty with East Germany, the constant Berlin problem became yet another Berlin crisis. This time, in August, a wall was erected completely dividing the two halves of the city. Henceforth the flow of refugees from the East became only a sporadic trickle, and East and West Berliners found it almost impossible to cross the border points even on a legitimate basis. The United States immediately retaliated with a token reinforcement of its West Berlin garrison. However, the important point is that the damage had already been committed. Short of openly challenging Russia to dismantle the wall and thus run the risk of inaugurating a world war, the American Government had no alternative but to accept the new *status quo*. The Soviet Union itself seemed to be reluctant to push much harder; a steady undermining of the Western position in the city by relatively slight actions would more easily obtain gains without risks.

The sealing of the frontier probably gave the East German regime a much needed boost of confidence. It has been able to concentrate on economic development without its programmes and policies being undermined by a constant drain of manpower.

The increasing economic strength of East Germany, the durability of the regime, and the transformation of East German society which it is supervising all contributed to a reassessment by the Western countries, particularly by the Federal Republic, of its relationship with East Germany. Previously, the West German position had been one of no compromise on the Oder–Neisse question and non-recognition of East Germany, as if the refusal to recognise the existence of the latter would somehow cause the regime to disappear. In the 1960s the Federal Republic gradually came to accept the need for closer and less tense relationships with Eastern Europe: this meant a change of policy on East Germany. Gradually economic and even diplomatic relationships have been established with countries in Eastern Europe and both major West German parties are interested in securing more formal relationships with the East. In the last few years the Social Democrats under Willy Brandt have been particularly forceful in seeking some kind of *rapprochement* with both Poland and the German Democratic Republic. In 1970 Brandt, who had become West German Chancellor in the previous year, negotiated draft treaties with both Russia and Poland. These have yet to be ratified by the West German *Bundestag*, but it is important to note that the latter treaty involves the recognition of the Oder–Neisse line and also Polish agreement for the repatriation of its German community to West Germany. Similarly, West and East Germany have, in the last few years, also begun to speak directly to each other.

However, the success of Brandt's *Ostpolitik*, which is not without its domestic critics, is dependent on some reciprocity over Berlin. In many ways a Berlin settlement is a *sine qua non* for the ratification of these treaties. West Berliners have always been worried that they may be abandoned by the West, even by West Germany, because no solution to their situation appears to be possible. Thus in its search for some kind of answer for Berlin, the West has always found it advisable to bolster the morale of the West Berliners. Two points desired by the West are important for West Berlin. One is the restoration of movement between the two parts of the city. Since 1961 there have been very few occasions when the East German authorities have established a pass system by which West Berliners can visit East Berlin (though

West Germans are allowed to do so): except for matters of life or death, the wall has been impenetrable since Whitsun 1966. The other important point is a guarantee of unrestricted land access to the city from West Germany: road and rail links are at the moment subject to periodic harassment and obstruction by the East German authorities. It seems very clear that unless Berlin is connected to West Germany by a land corridor controlled by the West, any agreement or guarantee on surface entry to the city can be infringed quite easily. It is equally clear that such a solution would not be acceptable to East Germany, since it would involve the renunciation of some of its territory. Nevertheless, the search for a workable solution continues. Yet another series of four-power talks on Berlin began in 1970, though nothing substantive has emerged from them. In particular, the Soviet Union's favoured project of a European security conference has been made contingent upon some progress over Berlin. What is perhaps different about the present situation is that paralleling the discussions among the four occupation authorities, there is also some communication between West and East Germany, and even between East and West Berlin.

Problems of Defence

The Berlin crisis of 1961 shook West German faith in the American protective umbrella. A series of such moves by the Russians could quite possibly mean the ejection of the Western powers from the city, since open war would be the only alternative. The young Federal Republic was already experiencing a period of growing pains and a reassessment of its position in the international system, and the Berlin crisis was not calculated to ease the tension. Berlin was only partly responsible for West German unrest. The main cause was perhaps the debatable position of West Germany within the Atlantic alliance, for however much the shadow of President de Gaulle seemed to envelop European defence and political arguments in the 1960s, it was West Germany which held the key to Western European harmony.

Superficially the main anxieties facing the Western alliance appeared to be de Gaulle's well-publicised criticisms of European and Atlantic defence, which culminated in March 1966 in his decision to take France out of NATO. De Gaulle's decision was the logical conclusion of his pronouncements and policies since his accession to the French Presidency in 1958. His unilateral withdrawal was the result of a conviction that European defensive arrangements were unduly dominated by the United States and his fears that this domination was also occurring in the political and economic fields. Thus his criticisms of defence arrangements and his motives for leaving NATO were primarily political. Two aims seem to have been paramount in de Gaulle's mind. He saw his action as furthering the chances of a European settlement, and also as enabling France to establish an independent base for French leadership and influence in Europe. His view of Europe suggested that the United States was not part of Europe, whereas the Soviet Union was: thus it was sensible for other European countries to come to terms with Russia. The defensive connection with the United States was regarded as an obstacle to this accommodation. In order to pursue this policy and to establish French influence, he clearly felt obliged to free France from American domination, and NATO was seen as the clearest symbol of American supremacy. His action also emphasised the corollary view that France was the equal of the United States and Britain, and that it should be treated as such. His resentment at a special Anglo-American relationship had been growing since 1958 when, shortly after his accession to power, he had suggested privately to Eisenhower and Macmillan that future military and defence strategy in Europe should be formulated and directed by a 'troika' of the three countries: this suggestion had been rejected by the United States and ignored by Britain. His interpretation of the relationship between Britain and America seemed to be confirmed by events in 1962. In that year the United States abandoned work on the Skybolt air-ground missile. Skybolt, however, had already been promised to Britain, which was struggling to remain a nuclear power. As a replacement for Skybolt, the American Government offered the Polaris missile to Britain under special circumstances. Polaris was also offered to France, but this de Gaulle refused, preferring to continue to attempt to build up an independent French nuclear arsenal.

Quite clearly NATO was weakened by the French withdrawal. In addition several other factors affected the functioning and efficiency of the organisation: American attention was being diverted to Vietnam; Britain's economic position hindered it from playing a more positive part; several members wanted to reduce their troop commitments; while West Germany was becoming more restive under existing restrictions on its role. While adjustments were carried out quite rapidly through a series of multilateral and bilateral negotiations, the viability of NATO was still in dispute. The main significance of de Gaulle's action was that it went beyond the mere military confines of NATO and was indicative of an attitude that was by no means confined to France. The major problem was the great debate over the distribution and control of nuclear weapons within NATO, and more specifically the role and powers of West Germany. American governments, under strong pressure from domestic political forces and their own analyses of the bases of world peace, have been very reluctant to share nuclear control with any partner. Washington conceived of its alliance network as a circle, with all power resting firmly at the centre in the person of the American President and Congress. It has been feared that if other countries had an independent nuclear capacity or participated in nuclear decision-making, the American–Russian dialogue would be hindered and the possibility of an escalation into a world war would be that much greater. This was the reasoning which also led to the Non-Proliferation Treaty.

On the other hand, Western Europe has argued that its risks in the event of a nuclear war are just as great and that therefore it should have a commensurate share of the responsibility. Because of the American attitude there has been a great deal of anti-American feeling on the continent. Just as nationalism in the underdeveloped countries of Asia and Africa is an expression of independence against colonialism and resentment against the parcelling-out of the globe between America and Russia, so European resentment has been directed against the two superpowers for the same reasons. De Gaulle's break from NATO was only a symbol of this resentment: it is certain that many European politicians, while perhaps not supporting de Gaulle's decision, nevertheless approved of his proposals for a 'third force', which argued for an American–European partnership in which they would be co-equal, but which also seemed to imply a return to the prewar polycentric structure of independent national armies. However, it is quite clear that for de Gaulle a European nuclear capacity meant no more than France's *force de frappe*, and that control of this would be solely the prerogative of France; in other words, his views were very similar to those of America.

Criticisms of the existing defensive structure and its aims became more common after the French withdrawal. Views which were dismissed as both nonsensical and heretical when first expounded by de Gaulle were heard with increasing frequency. The growing unrest was, in a sense, inevitable, for it arose out of the international détente and the seeming desire of the United States and the Soviet Union to establish a working arrangement in Europe based on the existing *status quo*. With fears of a European war lessening, a direct result of the détente, the Western European nations were no longer prepared to be simply pawns in a power game played by the two giants. Thus it was inevitable that Western Europe would become involved in a reassessment of its relationship with the United States, particularly as the latter was enmeshed in a war far removed from Europe, a war, moreover, about which most Europeans were disinterested or disapproving. While the invasion of Czechoslovakia in 1968 led to an increased concern about the military viability of NATO, it did not seem to produce any greater cohesion. While the Organisation continues to be accepted as necessary, most European members appear to do so only reluctantly and have tended to adopt a minimal interpretation of their role in terms of both commitments and responsibilities. From 1969, only one year's notice is required to withdraw from the Organisation.

The American fear of escalation has been one reason why the United States has pressed so forcefully for European unification: the number of variables would be greatly reduced. It has often been hinted that nuclear responsibility would be Western Europe's reward for getting itself organised. The real problem has been the fear of the United States and of many other countries, especially Russia, that West Germany might flex its renovated muscles by demanding to be a nuclear power, a position from which it might attempt to cut through the Gordian knot of the reunification issue by force. Hence American interest in Germany has been very great since 1949, while West German governments have been among America's staunchest allies in Western Europe, seeing the American association as the best way of achieving equality for the Federal Republic. West German resentment grew in the 1960s, not so much against the denial of nuclear weapons, as against the latent refusal of other nations to treat West Germany as an equal, particularly as it was felt that the country bore an unfair share of NATO's conventional armaments. In addition, West Germany has always been concerned in case the United States arrives at a European settlement with the Soviet Union over its head, while West German governments have continually been worried by a belief that Britain does not place a high priority on a Berlin settlement. After the erection of the Berlin wall relations between the United States and West Germany became extremely strained. Adenauer once again faithfully affirmed that his nation would not recognise the East and would remain in the Western camp: at the same time he turned towards France and de Gaulle for reassurance. Later West German governments, while seeking some reconciliation with Eastern Europe, have continued to stress their allegiance to the Western alliance.

A united Europe or a Franco-German *rapprochement* would perhaps have offered a way out of the problem: in fact, tacit German support for France's independent views on defence and European union seems to have been the French price for their recognition of West Germany's then intransigent attitude toward the East. As early as 1963 either alternative was becoming less likely. De Gaulle's policies were becoming less acceptable to West Germany, while Adenauer's pro-French position was under fire from domestic critics who were slowly undermining his position of authority. By 1965 a change of German government and a shift in the balance of power within the ruling CDU, the French attempt to negotiate directly with the Soviet Union, and de Gaulle's apparent rejection of all forms of integration, pushed the two countries further apart than they had been for many years.

Short of national agreements or union, America has sought an alternative which might satisfy West Germany and other nations with nuclear yearnings, appease European resentment at American predominance within the Western military alliance, and might also contain the French urge to be an independent nuclear power. These considerations were the factors which led the United States in the early 1960s to put forward the proposal of a multilateral force. This proposal was, very briefly, that servicemen of various nationalities should be brought together in nuclear units to prevent this feeling of alienation from developing further: it was also hoped that the scheme would provide a further stimulus for European integration. The multilateral force (MLF) was perhaps a good idea. If it had been put into practice, it would have linked the two sides of the Atlantic more closely, and it would also have provided Britain with an extra link with the countries of EEC. However, it was too similar in its conception to the ideals of EDC for it to be hailed on the continent as a panacea. The similarities between MLF and EDC are in fact quite striking. Both were plans which utilised defensive and military arrangements for political purposes, and consequently the projected military efficiency of both was rather doubtful. In addition, it proved easier to mobilise forces opposed to the schemes for diverse reasons, than a coherent force in favour. While it is true that some Europeans regarded the MLF as a way of developing a real partnership with the United States, it was not popular with European governments, with the exception of the Federal Republic. British acceptance was doubtful since it emphasised the reduced or 'ordinary' status of Britain. In particular it failed to satisfy France. But even when de Gaulle predictably attacked the scheme, the tendency of some anti-Gaullists to regard support for the MLF as a necessary symbol of their repudiation of political and military autarkism was insufficient to generate enthusiasm even among their own ranks. Consequently the United States quietly dropped the plan in December 1964, without, however, formally abandoning it.

Thus the failure of the MLF proposal and France's withdrawal from NATO threw European defence arrangements into disarray. A discerning observer could see at the time that even during the discussions the United States remained adamant in its opposition to the dispensing at will of nuclear knowledge and capacity to its allies. On the other hand, it was apparent from 1964 onwards that France was having little success in persuading West Germany to loosen its close ties to the United States, and that consequently President de Gaulle's conception of European defence was also doomed to failure. The problem is that while the original justification for NATO has diminished or disappeared, it possesses no unambiguous goal. At times its purpose seems to be a protective alliance against Russia; at other times its main function seems to be the containment of a possible German resurgence. However, despite the unwillingness of the United States to continue to expend so much money and so many troops on European defence, without increased expenditure by their European allies, and despite the minimalist interpretation of NATO by the Western European countries, there seems to be little justification for scrapping NATO and little possibility of finding an adequate alternative. Moreover, American participation in it is still vital. Without the United States, NATO is nothing: without NATO the United States could not play so important a role in Europe and could not prevent a strategic vacuum from developing on the continent. What seems to be necessary is a more flexible arrangement reflecting the changing circumstances of the contemporary world. In particular it seems important that a distinctive European contribution to the organisation be encouraged, with more consultation and a considerable diminution of the role of the United States in its decision-making process.

There is perhaps little that Europe can do by itself in intervening between the two major powers. A diminishing of world tension, at least where Europe is concerned, depends first and foremost on the continuation of a harmonious dialogue between the United States and the Soviet Union. However, it has been, in fact, the very success of this dialogue in continuing that has brought Western Europe to its present position. Relations between Russia and America, especially since Cuba, have succeeded because the stress has been laid on preserving the *status quo*. Thus the détente has in fact prevented any significant changes being made in Europe, especially on the Berlin question. The détente has meant that there is a dispute over whether the Cold War phase has ended, and European unrest has been caused by the feeling that this has produced a negative attitude towards the resolution of problems. As we have pointed out, the so-called iron curtain may no longer be impenetrable, but it nevertheless divides Europe into two very distinctive and antagonistic forms of society. Within Western Europe the two major preoccupations are a continued search for an answer to the problems of Germany and Berlin and an effort to define its own position in Western and world politics. The nature of the détente, by confirming the *status quo*, has avoided the first of these preoccupations. Along with the American involvement in the war in Vietnam, the nature of the détente has also meant that the Western European nations are no longer content to wait upon an American lead: they are actively seeking some accommodation with the Soviet Union and Eastern Europe upon their own initiative. It is also the nature of the détente which has sapped confidence in NATO. Overall, what Western Europe seems to want is a reorientation of the détente along positive rather than negative lines.

15 Politics in the 1960s: Problems of Affluence, Alienation and Stability

Among the possible sources of alienation in Western democracies . . . is the new democratic Leviathan itself . . . a produce of long evolution and hard struggle, welfare-oriented, centralized, bureaucratic, tamed and controlled by competition among highly organized elites, and, in the perspectives of the ordinary citizen, somewhat remote, distant, and impersonal.

R. A. Dahl[1]

During the 1950s we generalised the situation somewhat by suggesting that a relatively neat pattern of conservative government and socialist opposition existed in the four major European democracies. During the next few years this pattern was, on the surface, to change only slightly, although strong currents of change were detectable below. Apart from Britain with its centuries of tradition and experience, government in the other three countries had been a search for stability. This search would continue, although different patterns were to emerge in each country. France appeared to be in strongest position with the personality of President de Gaulle seemingly welding the nation into a coherent whole. Italy was conditioning itself to attempt the most stable arrangement possible under the existing circumstances. Britain and West Germany presented a different picture: here the dominant conservative parties, racked by dissension, were waning in inner strength and popularity.

After 1945 the extent of wartime damage and dislocation, the dearth of economic resources, and the advent of the Cold War had posed to parliamentary democracy in Western Europe a challenge as grave in its implications as the Nazi threat. To a large extent this threat had been countered, especially in France and Italy with their large Communist parties, by the massive influx

[1] *Political Opposition in Western Democracies*, New Haven, 1966, p. 399.

of American financial aid and by the development of the plans for European and Atlantic communities. Now such measures were no longer sufficient or appropriate. The inexorable pressure of the technological age was forcing parliamentary democracy to re-examine once again some of its hallowed concepts. It was in many ways a more dangerous threat than Nazism or Communism because of its more insidious nature. The pace of scientific development had tended to outstrip the construction of adequate social and political mechanisms for administering the benefits of technology and curbing its adverse effects.

European societies were becoming increasingly complex. The effects of this development were felt at all levels of the political systems. Governments were forced to try and cope with the new technological demands and to keep abreast of developments in multitudinous yet interrelated fields of social activity. One technique was characteristic of the Fifth French Republic: the attempt to introduce non-political specialists from the bureaucracy or industry into government posts. In 1964 Adenauer also followed this example. The technique does not seem to have been very successful. It was not popular with politicians, especially in West Germany, nor, it seems, did many of the French technocrats who followed this course find it particularly profitable or successful. A second course was favoured by the West German parties, which sought to recruit specialists in particular fields of activity into parliament by offering them a safe electoral seat: this also enabled those parties which were not in the government to possess legislators who were capable and qualified to examine the technicalities of proposed government bills. But perhaps the most outstanding development in the past two decades in this respect has been the rapid growth of both interest groups and their involvement, on both formal and informal levels, with governments. In every Western European nation there is today a vast array of consultative bodies, and numerous interconnections between governments and groups: the government can, in the form of legislation and administration, give groups what they want; reciprocally the groups can provide governments with necessary specialised information and data which otherwise might be more difficult to obtain. An outstanding example of this form of collaboration is provided by the Dutch Social and Economic Council, which consists of government appointees and representatives of the various employers' and trade union federations. The government must by law consult the Council on all proposed social and economic legislation; conversely the Council can put forward suggestions to the government. Because the Council is representative of the most important economic groups and political forces in the country, these suggestions usually amount to government policy.

This kind of practice, along with the pace of scientific and technological developments, also meant that parliaments could no longer fulfil their reputed functions as satisfactorily as previously as guardians of the public interest or watchdogs of the executive: they found it exceptionally difficult to provide the necessary expertise. Increasingly, therefore, parliaments have felt themselves bypassed as governments sought out new channels to aid them in the task of formulating policy and administering legislation. The creation of administrative boards with quasi-legislative powers and the extension of bureaucratic authority is a widespread phenomenon. The accusations of 'Chancellor Democracy' in West Germany, the emphasis on the prime minister in Britain to the detriment of other office-holders, the quasipresidential regime of the Fifth Republic—all indicated the changing and perhaps weakening nature of what people believed classic parliamentary democracy to be.

The unease generated by the feeling that decision-making was becoming even more remote has certainly not been confined only to the parliamentary level: it also made itself felt with increasing force at the popular level. Popular discontent manifested itself for several reasons. In certain instances it was caused by the feeling that governments were either failing to resolve economic problems, such as unemployment and the rising cost of living, or that they were taking decisions without any regard to public opinion. Such views were particularly strong in regions which were geographically removed from the decision-making centres, as, for example, in southern Italy where this was a phenomenon of long standing, or in Scotland and Wales which in the late 1960s experienced a temporary upsurge in separatist sentiment

WESTERN EUROPE SINCE 1945

expressed in byelections and local elections in increased voting for nationalist parties. While such fears of remoteness were widespread, they received additional force where they could focus around some distinctively cultural quality in a region, such as language or ethnicism. Perhaps the most serious problem in this respect has been in Belgium, where the cleavage between Walloons and Flemings flared up in the 1960s with such force that it incapacitated governments and divided the national parties into distinctive and hostile Flemish and French-speaking factions.

Popular discontent was not merely expressed in electoral terms, either by the switching of support to other, perhaps non-establishment parties, or by violent fluctuations in party preferences (usually against the government of the day), but also in terms of direct action. In several parts of Western Europe, and perhaps most noticeably in France and Italy, this form of political activity has a long tradition. In these two countries the strike has often been utilised as a political weapon, as we have already seen in the events of 1947 and 1948. This practice continued, though perhaps with added force, especially in Italy, as the rival trade union federations were beginning to cooperate with each other for the first time since the 1940s. In Britain too, the traditionally moderate trade unions were in 1970 and 1971 involved in one-day political strikes against proposed legislation which would bring them more firmly inside the framework of law. It also cannot be said that direct action by French farmers and peasants, in the form of demonstrations, road barricades and the ceremonial destruction of produce, decreased during the decade. In 1970 and 1971 a further example was provided by the South Italian town of Reggio di Calabria which was for seven months in a state of revolt against the government and administration in Rome over their decision not to make it, the largest town in the area, the seat of a newly created regional government. In Britain the province of Ulster entered a period of turmoil in 1968, as long-smouldering Catholic grievances over partition and the refusal by the Protestant majority to grant civil rights burst out into widespread riots and street-fighting.

Direct action also characterised the behaviour of other groups, which were motivated not just by a vague feeling of unrest or by specific economic grievances, but also by an adherence to general principles which they felt that governments had abandoned. In general, these groups were left-wing in orientation, protesting that societies had become too obsessed with the materialistic aspects of life and that governments and parties had pandered to this obsession by attempting to secure or retain power by out-bidding each other in their offers of material benefits to the electorate. Such groups often felt that in this auction sale the more egalitarian aspects of social justice had disappeared. The most interesting aspect of this political activity was the mobilisation of the young, particularly students. A wave of student involvement swept over Western Europe, reaching its peak in 1968. Amsterdam, Berlin and Paris were notable centres of left-wing student activities, and in 1968 a student demonstration in May was the starting point for widespread social disorders which at one time seemed likely to topple the Gaullist regime. This kind of leftist activity suffered perhaps from two major defects in its attempt to become a powerful political force: it was badly fragmented into several groups based on mutually hostile left-wing ideologies, and its strong point was ideological dissent and protest rather than coherent organisation and positive action. The only durable political organisation based upon generational differences proved to be a party known as D66 in Holland.

Right-wing protest also made itself heard in the 1960s. It occupied very similar ground to left-wing dissenters. Again, it was very often the materialism of modern European society, particularly those aspects of it deriving from America, which came under fire. Here, however, the desire was not to create a brave new world but to enforce the restoration of what were conceived of as traditional national values. The tensions caused by the presence of coloured Commonwealth immigrants in Britain, the creation of numerous paramilitary groups devoted to law and order in Italy, and, above all, the emergence of the right-wing National Democrat Party in Germany all fed on these sentiments. Right-wing unrest was also fostered in part by the effect inflation and other economic problems had on elements within the middle classes; it was also due in several instances to a reaction against the activities of left-wing groups.

What both left- and right-wing dissent had in common was a feeling that countries and governments had gone adrift, that the established political parties had abandoned whatever principles they had once adhered to in order to find a common denominator that would enable them to attract as much electoral support as possible. In other words, the criticism was that parties were more interested in gathering votes, in order to participate in government, than in espousing principles, and that once in government the fear of losing electoral support kept parties firmly in the centre in a do-nothing attitude, or at least hindered them from formulating policies based on the principles which it was believed the parties had been formed to represent. The feeling of remoteness and the belief that parties occupied the middle ground were reinforced in many countries by the tendency for government coalitions to be larger than necessary, as for example in Holland and in the West German grand coalition. Thus we find that such groups, for example the German students and the Italian trade unions, claimed the role of extra-parliamentary opposition because they felt that they represented the only genuine political alternative in the country.

The accusation of preferring electoral expediency over principles is a criticism which has been more frequently levelled against Socialist parties, and, as we have seen, there is more than a grain of truth in the charge. The Bad Godesberg programme of 1959 of the German Social Democrats, and the decision of the Italian Socialists to enter a centre–left coalition with the Christian Democrats are but two examples of the way Socialist parties have been moving. Overall, the problem for Socialist parties has been to reconcile their ideology with the pragmatic needs of politics. It is not insignificant that in the Scandinavian countries whose postwar governments have been dominated to a greater or lesser extent by Socialist parties, there have been left-wing splinters breaking away and forming a distinctive radical party. Sweden is the one exception, but here a 'nationalist' orientation by the Communist party may have prevented a similar cleavage. Similar left-wing splinters have appeared in the Netherlands, Italy and France. On the other hand, where the Socialist party has attempted to recoup its losses by veering back towards the left, it runs the risk of losing fragments on the right. This, as we have seen, was the case in Italy in 1948, and occurred again in Italy to the reunited Socialist party just over the two years after the PSI and the Social Democrats had agreed to reunite. The increasingly left-wing stance of the Dutch Labour Party in the late 1960s led before the 1971 election to a right-wing group breaking away to establish itself as a distinct party. Even the Communist parties seem to have been attracted by the lure of government: at least they have been similarly criticised for abandoning the working class and the tenets of Marx and Lenin. To some extent this is true. In recent years the large Finnish party has participated in coalition governments, while in France and especially Italy the Communists have become more interested in collaborating with other groups and with conveying an aura of respectability. This is perhaps one reason why these parties did not benefit overly from the political unrest in the late 1960s on the left, especially among the young. Certainly the new extreme left Socialist groups in Italy and France have attacked the Communists for moving to the right, and claim for themselves the pole position on the ideological spectrum.

Britain: Economic Malaise and Political Volatility

The most noticeable feature of British domestic politics in the early 1960s was the rapid slide from popular approbation of the Conservative Party after its massive electoral victory in 1959. Issues and conflicts of personalities stretched its inner harmony to a tenuous thread: Macmillan began to lose his aura of infallibility. On the other hand, the Labour Party under Gaitskell and, after his death in 1963, Harold Wilson, had climbed out of the slough of despond and was showing a vitality and a challenge that had been lacking for some time. Perhaps the most important issue during this period was the Conservative decision in 1961 to abandon Britain's traditional isolation and seek entry into EEC.

The bid for European membership was undoubtedly seen by Premier Macmillan as the culminating achievement of his ministry: it had the tang of historical greatness. In fact there had been in recent years an increasing examination in British government and administrative circles of the possibility and desirability of entering the Common Market. Two additional factors pushed the Conservative Government in this direction. The members of EEC had begun to discuss the possibility of political union. If this succeeded, the British government feared that its influence in world and European politics would be lessened. These fears were underlined by the continuing American commitment to the idea of European unity, which had been increased by the election of John Kennedy to the presidency in 1960.

The application had the effect of driving the two major parties further apart. Under Gaitskell's leadership, the ever-present chauvinistic undertones within the Labour Party came to the surface. Under five conditions for British entry put forward by Hugh Gaitskell, the party surprisingly adopted the stance of guardian of Britain's cultural and Commonwealth heritage, and went into more or less uncompromising opposition to European membership except on Britain's own terms. A substantial minority of Conservatives were also opposed to Macmillan's move. In the event the efforts came to nought in 1963 when President de Gaulle vetoed the British application. In the months following the veto, the public pronouncements of Harold Wilson and other Labour spokesmen gave the impression of thankful deliverance from a dreadful fate: it seems certain that this attitude militated against them when, four years later, a Labour government in turn sought entry to EEC.

The crisis of the Conservative Party leadership probably began with the Profumo affair, which, with the apparent association of a government minister with people implicated in a spy and prostitution scandal, shook the party's imperturbability to its foundations. The Conservative malaise was heightened by its inability or unwillingness to handle the worsening economic situation. Economic planning was now a key concept with both parties, yet despite Conservative measures the situation continued to deteriorate. The final blow was the question of the succession to Macmillan, who in 1963 decided to retire from active politics on medical advice. There was no ready-made successor: several candidates presented themselves, but no consensus was forthcoming. Eventually Macmillan nominated the one with the least number of vocal opponents, Lord Home. The Foreign Secretary had to renounce his peerage and revert to the name of Sir Alec Douglas-Home in order to qualify to stand for election to the House of Commons.

One year later he led the still sick Conservative Party into a general election. The Conservatives concentrated on defence and foreign policy, though the electorate was clearly more interested in and concerned with domestic economic problems. The issue of entry into the Common Market was played down by both parties. The result of the 1964 general election gave the Labour Party a paper-thin majority, but it was at last offered another opportunity of showing its paces. Perhaps the most surprising point about the 1964 election was that despite their recent poor performance in government and byelections, the Conservatives were very nearly returned to office. Eighteen months later the Labour Party won a decisive electoral victory over the still dispirited Conservatives, now led by Edward Heath, to assure a firm parliamentary majority for its programme.

Prime Minister Wilson had two immediate crucial issues to face. One was the problem of the colony of Rhodesia and its white minority which defied the British Government and declared its independence in 1965. Despite the application of voluntary, and later, United Nations-backed sanctions, a rather hesitant British Government failed in its attempts to force the Rhodesians from their adamant position. By the end of the decade Rhodesia was *de facto* independent and moving towards a coherent system of apartheid modelled after South Africa.

The main problem was Britain's economic situation. The boom of the 1950s was backfiring. The pound was over-valued, and the shortage of world money meant that Britain, as an international financial centre, faced yet another drain on the pound and the possible threat of devaluation. In the event the pound was devalued in 1967, although only after prolonged hesitation on the part of the government—which did not assist in easing matters. A serious situation called for harsh measures. The Labour Government, which had previously introduced a national economic plan, had in 1966 to abandon this dream and to apply for legislation for a rigid 'freeze' on prices and incomes as the first step in its plans for reviving the British economy. By the end of the decade Britain was enjoying a healthy balance of payments, but in domestic terms the rigid measures had not been altogether successful. Because they involved a check on personal affluence, they probably were a major source of the discontent which characterised British society, particularly as the freeze was thought to affect prices much less than incomes. In addition, the freeze produced a bottleneck of wage demands which burst forth, backed by strikes, once the ban had been lifted. To most European observers of the British scene, its proneness to strikes was an outstanding feature, so much so that it was disparagingly referred to as 'the English sickness'. Moreover, it seemed that many of these strikes were 'unofficial', that is they were not endorsed, or were endorsed only belatedly, by the trade union executives: in a sense the trade unions, like their confrères in Italy and France, were suffering from the same criticisms of remoteness from their 'electorates' as had been levelled against governments and political parties. It was these factors which helped to persuade the Labour Government, and its Conservative successor in 1970, that legislation regulating industrial relations was necessary. The Labour Party, financially dependent on the unions, dropped their proposals after massive trade union pressure. The Conservatives, not being trammelled by such considerations, entered the 1970 general election with the promise to introduce a similar Bill if elected. In the event, after they were returned to power with a small majority, an Industrial Relations Bill was one of the first pieces of legislation placed before the new House of Commons.

The apparent chronic inability of governments and parties to set Britain's economy in order, coupled with the feeling that governments were becoming far removed from the world of the individual, contributed to the most prominent feature of British politics in the late 1960s—a high level of electoral fluctuation unprecedented in post-1945 British history. Particularly in 1968 and 1969 there were massive defections from the Labour Party in both byelections and local government elections, so much so that by 1970 the councils of nearly every major city were controlled by the Conservatives. In Scotland and Wales there was an upsurge in support for the nationalist parties. These high levels of fluctuation remained after the 1970 general election, as a new Conservative Government in its turn grappled with and seemingly failed to resolve unemployment and inflation: less than one year after Edward Heath became prime minister, the electorate had swung violently against his party.

Two further issues were important in British politics in the late 1960s: the problem of Ulster and the question of Britain's entry into the Common Market. The six counties of Northern Ireland, which remained part of Britain after Ireland won its independence in the 1920s, have been the scene of sporadic violence ever since, mainly along the border and in Belfast. The Unionist Party, the political arm of the Protestant majority, has always dominated Ulster politics and has ruled continuously since 1922. This has given rise to bitter criticisms by the Catholic minority of discrimination in such fields as housing and job opportunities. In October 1968 a fresh series of riots began in the predominantly Catholic city of Londonderry (which nevertheless had a Protestant council). These riots marked the beginning of the most serious crisis the province has known since partition. While riots have been mainly confined to Belfast, the troubles have shaken the roots of the Unionist Party, causing the downfall of two successive leaders and a deep division between moderates and extremists; they have involved a substantial part of the British Army who have been called in to keep the peace; and they have forced successive British governments, who probably are extremely loth to become directly involved in such an intransigent problem, to demand that full civil rights for all sections of the community are established, under the threat of direct rule from London. In many ways the problem is insoluble: it is difficult to see, for example, what direct London rule could do that has not been tried already. The basic point at issue is whether the province ultimately remains part of Britain, which all Protestants desire, or becomes part of the Irish Republic, which is the aim of the Catholics. Both religious communities have militant extremists who are prepared to resort to warfare to attain their ends. The cleavage is emphasised, especially in the larger towns, by segregated housing patterns, and by the socialisation process of individuals in the churches, the family, and a *de facto* segregated educational system. The tragedy has been that the province has been shaken out of its traditional parochialism, that a large body of opinion acknowledges the need for reconciliation, yet nobody has been able to offer a way out of the labyrinth.

While public opinion in Britain remained largely unconcerned over the problem of Ulster, except for strong indignation at armed attacks on British troops, by 1971 the issue of the EEC dominated discussions in the mass media. The population at large may have been unaware of the fine points for and against entry, but many were nevertheless prepared to deliver their own verdict. Britain's relationship with Europe was probably the most important question that British governments had to face in the 1960s, especially as ties with the Commonwealth were becoming more tenuous and as the non-existence of any special relationship with the United States became more apparent—trends that are perhaps best summed up by Dean Acheson's comment that Britain had lost an empire but had yet to find a new role. The interaction between Britain and Europe will be discussed more fully later. Here it will be sufficient to note that the Labour Government slowly abandoned its former uncompromising position to consider ways of moving closer to Europe. The process was in many ways similar to that of the Conservatives before 1961, as the Government became more aware of the limitations of EFTA, the Commonwealth, and relations with America, and the possible deleterious effect isolation might have on the British economy. In May 1967 the government submitted the second application for EEC membership. In turn this was again vetoed by de Gaulle in the following October. The application, however, remained 'on the books', to be taken up in 1970. After the election of that year, it was the new Conservative Government under Edward Heath (who had led the first EEC negotiations nearly ten years earlier), which represented Britain in the fresh round of negotiations. De Gaulle, who resigned from office in 1969, had recently died, and Britain felt some confidence that the new Gaullist government under President Pompidou would be more favourably disposed towards British membership. By June 1971 terms had been thrashed out which were acceptable both to the

British Government and those of EEC. Public opinion, however, seemed at this time to have moved strongly against entry, although it was difficult to determine whether this was in fact the case or simply a reaction against the Conservative failure to ameliorate the economic situation. Nevertheless, the choice of whether to become a fully committed European nation, a role which before 1961 it had turned down on frequent occasions, was again laid squarely on Britain's doorstep.

West Germany: The Socialists Come of Age

Dr Adenauer was still the dominating figure in West German politics in 1960, although discontent at his rather autocratic methods had increased considerably. The results of the 1961 election were disappointing for the predominant CDU. They could continue in office only with the support of the small Free Democrat Party (FDP): the alternative was to form a coalition with the Socialists. The FDP, after much haggling, insisted that a condition of its participation in government had to be Adenauer's resignation before the next election. In the event this was achieved, although Der Alte took a great deal of persuading. His successor, whom he had long denigrated and sought to destroy as his heir apparent, was Ludwig Erhard, the 'father' of the 'economic miracle'. Erhard, who did not have the authoritative personality of Adenauer and who seemed to have a deep distaste for politics, was soon deeply involved in a struggle to make all sections of the loosely constituted CDU respect his authority: strangely enough, he refused to become the official chairman of the party, thereby weakening his hold over the organisation.

It has often been said that democracy in the Bonn Republic will not have been tested until it survives a major crisis. The Der Spiegel affair of 1962 threw serious doubts upon the stability and democratic nature of the West German Republic. Franz-Josef Strauss, the Minister of Defence, took the lead in seizing an edition of the magazine, Der Spiegel, and arresting its editor for publishing what were claimed to be military secrets. He did not resort to the usual legal channels: the Minister of Justice, who was a member of the FDP, was not informed of Strauss's proposed action. The upshot was the resignation of Strauss from the cabinet, a price demanded by the FDP, and a further weakening of the influence and prestige of Adenauer. The reverberations of the affair have not yet died down. The problem partly arises from Strauss's influential position as undisputed leader of the Bavarian wing of the CDU, the Christian Social Union. His action was seen as part of his ambitious bid for the party leadership after Erhard's retirement, if not Adenauer's. While he has perhaps too many opponents within the CDU to make this a serious possibility, his influential position has made it certain that he could play the role of an extremely powerful king-maker in any succession to the party leadership. One immediate consequence of the crisis was to strain the cohesiveness of the CDU even further, particularly its relationship with the Bavarian organisation. After Erhard's election as Chancellor and a consequent change in emphasis in German foreign policy, Strauss joined forces with the still active Adenauer to form a Gaullist pressure group within the party.

West Germany went to the polls again in 1965 with a very muted campaign. Although opinion polls suggested that the race was neck-and-neck, the CDU recouped the losses it had sustained four years earlier: in this sense its selection of Erhard on the supposition that he would be an electoral asset was justified. However, the party was still short of the majority point and had to renegotiate another coalition with the FDP. Owing to the wide range of interests contained within the elastic CDU and the SPD reforms of 1959, there was very little apparent difference between the two major parties during the campaign. In fact, the main electoral debate and the main argument in West German politics was between Erhard and his supporters and the Gaullist faction. Despite all the problems of internal democratic adjustment foreign policy still dominated the German scene—not unnaturally since the divided nature of Germany is simply a microcosm of the bipolarity that has conditioned so much of contemporary European politics. The debate was, in simplified terms, between the supporters of an Atlantic alliance and those of the European path advocated by de Gaulle: the country and the party were being asked to choose between a primary association with the United States or with France. It should, however, be noted that the Gaullist faction did not support all de Gaulle's policies: they strenuously opposed his approaches to the Soviet Union and East Europe. In the sense that West Germany is, despite its economic strength, still dependent on the American presence on the continent, particularly in Berlin, the debate was perhaps rather specious: this became increasingly evident after 1964 as West German governments decided that they could not accept the ramifications implicit in further developments of de Gaulle's foreign policy. Nevertheless the debate did serve to emphasise the feelings aroused in the country over the question of the exact relationships desired with Eastern Europe and the issue of nuclear armament (Strauss, for example, had already been agitating for several years, with the support of several generals, for a nuclear German army).

By 1966 the young West German democracy was running into difficulties which had previously been obscured by the urge to regain international status as soon as possible and by the continuation of an economic boom. By the 1960s success for the former had not yet been achieved, and economically the country was at last experiencing problems that were confronting most other European democracies. Within these two broad spheres the Federal Republic was afflicted by much discontent. It was continually beset by the spectre of the Nazi past. Revelations appeared periodically about high-ranking Nazi officials enjoying posts of responsibility and prestige within government and politics. Short of forgetting the past completely or employing a rigid denazification policy—the one internationally unpopular, the other electoral suicide—there is nothing much that can be done except to treat each case that comes along on its own merits. More serious was the emergence in 1964 of the first major neo-Nazi movement since the SRP was outlawed in 1952. The National Democrat Party (NPD) was much more careful in its pronouncements not to overstep the bounds of legality. Between 1966 and 1968 it enjoyed a modest but significant success in regional and local elections. This was sufficient to arouse foreign alarm and to compel the government to watch the activities of the NPD more closely.

It was, however, the economic depression and the feeling that the country's foreign policy was stagnating which helped to spark the second major governmental crisis of the decade. The feeling had been growing within the CDU that Erhard was unable to tackle these problems, that he was overall proving to be a weak Chancellor: the party began to fear that he might prove an electoral liability. In addition, the FDP was unhappy in its role of junior coalition partner, and in October 1966 withdrew from the government over the issue of tax increases. The CDU had to face two problems. First, it had to decide whether to attempt to renegotiate with the FDP or to heed the growing number of suggestsions from its own ranks and from the Socialists that the best solution for tackling the country's economic problems and for initiating a positive foreign policy, especially with regard to the East, would be a 'grand coalition' of the CDU and SPD. The second problem was to find a successor to Erhard who, relying on the technique of the constructive vote of no-confidence to sustain him, refused to resign voluntarily. The difficulty was that there was no clear-cut successor who could reunite the party. The 'crisis' was the most protracted in the republic's history. Eventually, two months after the departure of the FDP from the government, Kurt Georg Kiesinger, the CDU minister-president of the state of Baden-Württemberg, was elected as Chancellor, and the two major parties agreed to form the grand coalition.

The significance of the grand coalition was twofold. It brought to an end a style of politics which Adenauer had imposed upon the country's political institutions and political forces, and it meant the coming of age of the SPD after thirty-six years out of office. Throughout the decade surveys showed that progressively fewer people were adamantly opposed to voting for the SPD. These views were reflected in the growing electoral support for the party. In 1965 it gained 29 per cent of the votes, its highest ever total in any national German election since unification in 1870; four years later it won nearly 43 per cent.

The grand coalition proved to be a successful combination, at least in that the economic situation rapidly improved to the extent that the country was soon experiencing a labour shortage that could be overcome only by encouraging the immigration of large numbers of foreign workers. More important, however, was the reorientation of West German foreign policy that occurred after 1966. The international détente and the arguments raging within the Western alliance contributed towards this, but equally important factors were the country's geographical situation on the continent, its need to find new export outlets, and the fact that historically Germany's trade with Eastern Europe had been very widespread. While there were powerful forces within the CDU which had been arguing for a new approach to be made to Eastern Europe, a greater stimulus probably came from the SPD, especially since its leader, Willy Brandt, became Foreign Minister: the party had already adopted the view that more positive attempts should be made to come to terms with the political realities surrounding the likelihood of reunification. Thus the late 1960s saw West Germany moving towards reconciliation and formal diplomatic relations with its Eastern neighbours through bilateral negotiations.

The grand coalition survived until the next parliamentary election in 1969. The result of this election was important in that it was possible for the CDU to be excluded from government by a coalition of the SPD and FDP. This coalition was duly constructed, not least because of the unhappiness of the FDP over its past experiences in CDU governments, and a new leftward orientation within the party leadership. Probably the most important aspect of the new government under Willy Brandt has been the continuing search for a *rapprochement* with Eastern Europe. Previously West Germany had been faced with a seeming choice between reunification or integration within the Western alliance. Adenauer had chosen the latter course, and for a number of years it had meant that West Germany's attitude to the East was viewed from the Western defensive posture: in particular, East Germany was considered not to exist. Under Brandt, conversations, admittedly without any concrete results, have been held with East Germany. The Chancellor has also made a symbolic pilgrimage to Poland, and in 1970 draft treaties with both Poland and the Soviet Union were signed. While Brandt has consistently argued that East Germany cannot be simply ignored by the Federal Republic's foreign policy, and that an accommodation with Poland is morally as well as politically essential, he has also strongly affirmed his country's adherence to EEC and the Western alliance, and that no real progress towards reconciliation can be made without some reciprocal accommodation over the question of Berlin.

Whether or not the results of the 1969 election marked a real change in power or the inauguration of a period of alternation in government is a question still under dispute. Nevertheless, the possibility of two-party competition has become more likely. The road for the SPD has been very long and at times very painful. Two factors help to explain the growth of the party. First, the radical change in the West German party system after 1949 has been due to the swallowing up by the CDU of many of the smaller parties: the tactics of Adenauer in this process have been already discussed. Only the FDP has managed to prevent the two major parties from acquiring a monopoly of parliamentary representation, and at times it too has come perilously close to the 5 per cent barrier in the electoral law. In a sense, therefore, the CDU has been instrumental in SPD success. With the successive elimination of other parties as electoral forces, the only alternatives for voters were to establish new political parties—a notoriously difficult procedure—or to turn to the SPD or the weak FDP. A second factor was probably the SPD's participation in the grand coalition, which demonstrated that the party was able to govern capably and responsibly—a point of view which had been put forward before 1966 by several SPD strategists.

While the Federal Republic appears to have reached a degree of stability as high as that of any other Western European nation, there is still perhaps some room for doubts: certainly there are many sceptics both inside and outside the country. The *Der Spiegel* affair, for example, was particularly worrisome. It is also true that the country has still to experience and weather severe economic shocks. In this respect critics point to the rise and fall of the NPD between 1966 and 1969, which corresponded fairly closely to the economic climate of those years. In particular, some commentators were worried by the alacrity with which the two major parties agreed to come together in a grand coalition. It offended their interpretation of parliamentary government in that there was no effective parliamentary opposition: certainly the small FDP, with only ten per cent of the Bundestag seats, could not fulfil this function. On the other hand, the country did weather with ease in the 1960s challenges from the left and the right. Leftist discontent made itself felt through several diverse organisations, which faced the usual problem of an inability to coordinate. Most important was the unrest of university students who resorted to direct action and, because of the grand coalition, also claimed to be an extra-parliamentary opposition—indeed, the only effective opposition in the country. However, the students failed to survive as a coherent, forceful organisation: moreover, their political pretensions tended to be more or less ignored by government circles. In 1969, even though several disparate groups banded together in an electoral alliance, the left-wing forces failed to garner even one per cent of the vote.

Left-wing agitation was also in some respects a reaction to the rise of the NDP. In turn, demonstrations and other forms of direct action by the left lent credence to the NPD's claim that it was the force best equipped to arrest the decline of traditional moral values and to reimpose law and order. The challenge of the NPD, since it does seem to have been related to the country's economic performance and because of its pedigree and claims which strike a responsive chord in many Germans, was a more serious problem. Both major parties considered the possibility of requesting the Federal Constitutional Court to rule on its constitutionality. This course of action was not favoured because the NPD had been much more cautious in this respect than its short-lived predecessor, the SRP. In addition, the parties were afraid that if the Court ruled in the NPD's favour, which was a strong possibility, then it would acquire in the public's eyes a cloak of respectability which it perhaps did not already possess. The other alternative, which was a reaction to the fear that the NPD might gain sufficient parliamentary representation in 1969 to make the system unworkable, was to change the electoral law. Neither party was willing to form a coalition with the NPD, and if the Free Democrats were eliminated from the Bundestag, also seen as a strong possibility, then the continuation of the grand coalition was the only alternative, but this would mean that the NPD would become the only opposition group. Hence both major parties in the late 1960s considered following the example set by France in 1951 and Italy in 1953 of changing the electoral system so that it discriminated against the NPD: the change proposed was to the British system of simple majorities in single-member constituencies. The parties, however, seemed rather reluctant to turn the proposal into actuality. It was eventually shelved, primarily because the SPD lost interest, fearing that the proposed system would mean CDU majorities for the foreseeable future. In 1969 the Free Democrats just survived above the barrier level, while the NPD failed by a narrow margin to reach it.

Thus challenges from both left and right failed to shake the stability of the Bonn Republic. Whether or not these challenges petered out because of their own inability to make further progress and because the somewhat 'do-nothing' attitude of the government parties reflected a conviction of their own strength and that of the country is open to dispute. It is possible that the NPD caused more concern abroad than it did in West Germany: a similar party reaching the same level of support elsewhere would not have made so many headlines. But this is, of course, an understandable reaction. While it probably underestimates the stability of West German politics, the Nazi experience was so unique that there will always be room for genuine doubt and concern, at least for several generations to come.

Italy: the Centre-Left and the Problem of Stability

The principal dilemma facing Italian politics was still that of resolving the question of stability. We have seen that during the 1950s the ruling Christian Democrats had increasingly relied on right-wing support. The tension and unrest of 1960, however, made it quite clear that substantial sections of the population would not tolerate an open condonance of Neo-Fascist and Monarchist influence in government circles. With the Communist Party still frozen out of the system, the only alternative was to search for a *rapprochement* between the Christian Democrats and the Socialists.

The 'opening to the left' had first been suggested by Pietro Nenni shortly after the 1953 elections, as the PSI began its slow drift away from close collaboration with the Communists. From this date, the scheme became a possibility and not just a theoretical speculation. Despite its domination by conservative interests after the departure of de Gasperi, the Christian Democrats still contained a substantial and vocal left-wing. The party began to prepare the ground for a left-wing alliance at its 1954 conference in Naples: the orientation itself had to wait for the tortuous evolution of opinion within both parties. By 1959 the Christian Democrats were officially ready to accept the principle of the opening to the left. The idea was given its first experimental airing in 1961 when, despite official disapproval and opposition from the Church, Christian Democrats and Socialists formed coalitions in several local governments. Two years later the two parties found their way clear towards accepting the opening to the left and came together on the national level for the first time since 1947. It was the first realistic attempt to solve the problem of political and governmental stability since the tripartite alliance crumbled: given Italy's multiparty system with its existing distribution of support among the parties, and the size of the Communist Party, a coalition of Christian Democracy and Socialism was virtually the only means by which a stable government might be achieved.

Italian Socialism has a long tradition of internecine warfare and splintering. Its move towards collaboration with the Christian Democrats in the 1960s was made at the cost of a small left-wing group who seceded to form their own party, which in many ways proved to be more uncompromising in its attitude towards the Italian political system than the Communists. Many Socialists who desired a return to collaboration with the Communists preferred to remain within the PSI and attempt to change its direction from within. It was also hoped that the loss of the left-wing would be compensated by a reunion of the PSI and the Social Democrats. This merger was in fact effected in 1966, but proved to be of an extremely short duration: in 1969 the two again parted company, causing yet another government crisis in the process. It should be noted that the new split did not exactly mirror the old division between the two parties. The new Social Democrats are much more conservative than their predecessors.

The true significance of the Socialist willingness to participate in decision-making with a non-Socialist partner depends upon the influence it has in initiating political and social reform. Since 1945 governments, and hence important decisions, have been determined not so much by elections or by parliament, but by manoeuvres and negotiations among the various factions of the Christian Democrat Party. If the influence of this behind-the-scenes bargaining, in which the extraparliamentary party apparatus occupied a key position, could be diminished, then the opening to the left would perform an invaluable service in helping Italy to lay down a solid basis for democratic parliamentarianism. Again, however, political stability cannot be achieved when there is social instability, unless it is imposed from above by a strong personality of the calibre of de Gaulle, and this usually implies a depoliticising process and severe restrictions upon parliamentary government. Thus it was essential that the new centre–left coalition should tackle the ever present dilemmas of Italian society. While willing to cooperate in such a coalition, the PSI naturally desired a price for its participation. The political programme announced by the first centre–left government showed a marked Socialist influence in its proposals for economic planning, education, agriculture and regional development.

The centre–left commitment has fluctuated in its intensity since 1963: the PSI, for example, has not been prepared to serve continuously in the government. On the other hand, the absence of a clear-cut alternative means that the reconstruction of the alliance is a top priority in negotiations about the formation of a new government. While it is true that the domestic policies all involve long-term planning, the record of centre–left governments is much more disappointing. Between 1948 and 1970 Italy has had thirty-three governments, and the present incumbents are still fundamentally attempting to put into force reforms which were first proposed in 1963—or even earlier. For example, regions which were first established by the postwar constitution were, with very few exceptions, actually created only in 1970. The most outstanding characteristic of Italian politics is still the conflict both between parties and within parties, a constant jockeying for position in order to win some quite often minor political

argument. It is this characteristic, plus the fact that this pointless
manoeuvring is particularly prominent within the Christian
Democrats, which makes every government uncertain of its
nominal majority. One example will suffice: early in 1971 the
small Republican Party left the government as a protest against
its continuing inability to inaugurate social reforms. This immediately threw a great strain on cooperation between Christian
Democrats and Socialists. The latter viewed it suspiciously as an
effort to turn the government in a rightward direction, and to
ignore the Communists and the trade unions. This immediately
provoked a reaction from the Social Democrats who continued
to insist that they would not tolerate any move further to the
left, especially one which involved cooperation with the Communists. In fact the two Socialist partners are in violent disagreement over nearly every issue. Factions within the Christian
Democrats also continued to seek to increase their influence
within the party.

While governments continue to limp along, and reforms come
only haltingly and partially, discontent has continued to grow.
In the more industrialised north, there has always been a tradition
of direct action. In the more backward south, which has 35 per
cent of the population, but where the average income of workers
is still less than half that of their northern compatriots, there has
been a growing protest against the remoteness of Rome, the
failure of governments to induce economic development, and the
vast system of patronage which typifies Italian administration.
The large sums of money channelled into the region through the
Southern Development Fund have not altered its basic situation:
in fact the economic gap between north and south has tended to
increase. The steady, even though slight, increase in electoral
support for the Communists at every election since the war,
especially in the South, is eloquent testimony of popular dissatisfaction. The tendency for this exasperation to spill over into
direct action and conflict with the authorities has been counterbalanced by a similar demand for a return to law and order, a
battlecry which tends to benefit the extreme right. After the
massive waves of strikes which began in 1969, numerous quasimilitary groups, modelled on the Fascisti, have appeared, and the

Neo-Fascist Party (the Social Movement) also seems to be more attractive to voters.

The quandary of the centre parties is that their ability to act is seriously hampered by their own factionalism, by the powerful inertia of the administrative machinery, and by the fearful attitude they have towards the extremes, especially the Communists. On the other hand, the strength of the Catholic Church in the country is still a powerful prop on which the Christian Democrats can rely: the relative coherence of the party on the 1970 bill legalising divorce is proof of its religious basis. However, Christian Democrat governments have always tended to avoid the fundamental political question raised by the strong position of the Communists. Prime ministers have continually emphasised that no compromise is possible, yet at the same time all have been fully aware that tacit Communist support is necessary for certain pieces of legislation to succeed. The Communists themselves have moved a long way from their position in 1948. The party has sought to portray a more democratic appearance and to seek for ways to move further into the mainstream of Italian politics. It has increasingly tended to adopt an individual position on issues that is quite often independent of and indeed hostile to the view of the Soviet Union, as, for example, over the invasion of Czechoslovakia which it immediately condemned. There are divisions within the party, but so far it has managed to maintain its coherence with the loss of only a few splinters. Even the threatened dichotomy between Russian and Chinese factions in 1966 failed to materialise. Party leaders appear confident that in the long run they can win power by constitutional means, and that this process can be expedited by their appearing willing to cooperate with other parties and by giving out an aura of respectability. Certainly, for example, those local and regional governments which are headed by the party are quite often among the most efficient in the country.

One further factor has perhaps helped to persuade the Communists to consider such a path. This is the behaviour of the three-party-related trade union federations in recent years. Since 1969 the unions have been prepared to use the weapon of the strike not only for immediate economic gains such as higher wages, but also to press the Government to implement social reforms. For the first time since the split in the 1940s, the rival federations have co-operated closely and have become a significant political force. Claiming that governments have been out of touch with popular sentiment, and that parliament has not provided any effective check or stimulus on government activity, the unions have tended to claim for themselves the role of an extra-parliamentary opposition.

It is interesting to note that the Communist and Catholic unions have both become increasingly restive under the tutelage of their respective parties. Both share in the credit for the union movement becoming a more cohesive political force. In turn, their activity has had consequences for the two largest parties. If the Communist Party refused to support this movement, it would retain its core support, but it might also lose some of its more moderate members who want the party to be at least effective in its protest: more important, it might damage its political image. On the other hand, if it continues its present development, there might be serious unrest and splinters on the left. The critical stance which Catholic trade unionists have adopted towards the Christian Democrats may strengthen the resolve of the party's left wing, but it may also force the conservatives into a more uncompromising stance. The social reformers within the party had already received a stimulus from the election of John XXIII to the Papacy in 1958. The impact of his more liberal views, which showed a greater awareness of the actuality of Italian politics and society, has not been eradicated entirely, even though after his demise the orientation of the Vatican returned to a more orthodox position. Certainly, many Christian Democrats not only urge closer cooperation with the Socialists, but also accept the need for some kind of *modus vivendi* with the Communists in order to win social reforms in such crucial areas as education and housing. In 1970, for example, a Bill which proposed a reform of the pattern of agricultural tenancy was sponsored jointly by a Christian Democrat and a Communist deputy, and eventually became law.

The knowledge that such a faction exists within the ruling Christian Democrats puts a greater strain on party cohesion, for it has enabled the Socialists to be more resolute in their demands. With the progressive removal of specifically religious issues from the political arena, the future continuation of the centre–left coalition may be made easier, for on such issues, the Christian Democrats, while often being opposed by almost every other party, find a coherence which is usually noticeable by its absence. The crucial points about Italian politics seem to be that the Communists cannot be simply ignored, and that, no matter how parties attempt to manoeuvre, the opening to the left seems to be the only viable political formula for the country, although many politicians are apparently very reluctant to admit it.

France: de Gaulle and Gaullism

In one sense there were no politics in France during de Gaulle's presidency. The constitution of the Fifth Republic severely limited the parliamentary activities of the political parties, while the prestige, personality and actions of de Gaulle restricted them further. The ambiguity of the new constitution has meant that the previous relationship between the National Assembly and the government-cum-president has not been reversed completely. But the rather surprising success of the Gaullist party, the Union for the Democratic Republic or UDR (originally called the Union for the New Republic) in every election since 1958 meant that de Gaulle could safely ignore the Assembly, since it was controlled by a brute mass of Gaullist votes. Two further points should be mentioned. First, the Gaullist interpretation of a 'presidential sector' has meant that no one else has been allowed to interfere in these fields of activity. Second, de Gaulle's contempt for party and parliamentary politics as played in France and his willingness to bring civil servants into the government weakened the National Assembly even further.

The overall pattern of politics under de Gaulle has been termed a process of depoliticisation. The Gaullist revolution set out in 1958 to reform the French political system to give it both stability and momentum. Arguing that traditional republicanism had given France instability, the conservatives turned to impose stability from above by neutralising or destroying as many political elements as possible. Constitutionally, it is doubtful whether these two aims have been achieved. The desired inner momentum has, in a way, been sacrificed to the need for stability, since in this respect the regime is founded on rural and conservative France: paradoxically, however, the Gaullists' primary electoral support has come from those areas which are economically advanced. Greater opposition has come from the more rural, backward areas—that part of the country which has been termed 'static France'. Constitutional stability also does not seem to have been assured. The executive power is divided between the president and the prime minister, who are elected in different ways, and the two chambers, the Assembly and the Senate, are given equal status and authority in what legislative powers remain to parliament. Thus there are ample constitutional opportunities for deadlock of the traditional nature to appear. Only the presence of de Gaulle and the size and nature of the UDR have so far prevented such stalemates from occurring.

However, the basic instability of France under the Fourth Republic—and even before 1945—was caused by social cleavages, unresolved problems, and 'ideological' hostility of which the multi-party system was the political expression. Instability was compounded either by the fact that parties were unable to expand past certain electoral limits, or because they were prone to disintegration or proved to be transitory phenomena. It is difficult to say that any positive change has occurred here. It cannot yet be said that the UDR has become a proper party in that its ability to set down enduring local roots is as yet unproven. Indeed, being formed from above primarily to contest parliamentary elections, its organisation has tended to parallel the division of the country into constituencies rather than attempting to embed itself in the local communes which are at the heart of French society. It is also largely untrue to say that the other parties have undergone reforms. On the contrary, since they were denied any right to participate in public policy-making, it might be true to say that the parties have been offered no incentive to reform. Until the late 1960s, most seemed intent on passively sitting out the de Gaulle era. Local elections, when de Gaulle did not appeal for a display of national solidarity under the Gaullist banner, showed both the weakness of the UDR and that the other parties could quite easily retain their traditional bases of support: it should, however, be pointed out that French local elections are a bad guide for an understanding of national politics.

Until 1968 France was dominated by de Gaulle. His foreign policy, especially his antagonism towards Britain and America, seemed to meet with popular acceptance, even though he alienated some people by his withdrawal from NATO. In domestic politics, he had found a way out of the Algerian impasse, he had successfully dispersed the terrorist movement which in an attempt to retain a French Algeria resorted to acts of terror within metropolitan France itself, and his economic policies seemed to bring material satisfaction to a large proportion of the population. However, there were already in the mid-1960s political signs that de Gaulle was by no means synonymous with France. In the 1965 presidential election, de Gaulle failed to win an absolute majority on the first ballot, and was forced therefore into a run-off election with the nearest contender. In 1967 the unity of the UDR was strained by electoral losses. But, despite the fact that the 1967 election marked the first serious attempt by other parties to come to terms with each other and cooperate (or even amalgamate) in order to provide an effective challenge to the UDR, the campaign was fairly muted. De Gaulle's foreign policy seemed to be acceptable, the country appeared to be relatively prosperous, and the franc gave the impression of being one of the world's strongest currencies. Yet within one year, the situation changed radically. What began as a small, almost insignificant and routine demonstration, threatened the existence of the regime itself.

In May 1968 the Gaullists were due to celebrate the tenth anniversary of the Fifth Republic. In their turn, the opposition forces were preparing to counteract the Gaullist claims for the regime. Thus the political atmosphere was perhaps more tense than usual. But the crisis began innocuously enough when a number of left-wing students were arrested for demonstrating on behalf of reforms in higher education: such protests had been going on sporadically for nearly a year. But whole districts of Paris rapidly became a battle-ground between police and students. The contagion spread to other parts of the country and other sections of the population. What began as a demand for educational reform grew into wide-reaching demands for social reforms. The students had urged the workers to rise and occupy the factories. Workers eventually did embark upon a series of strikes, without union leadership, which crippled the nation's economy, though it is dubious whether they shared the same revolutionary vision as the students, with whom they clashed in several instances. Even sections of the middle classes joined in the general unrest. It seemed as if all the dissatisfaction held back by the dam of de Gaulle had finally spilled over.

Both the government and the parties faltered in their response to what amounted to national paralysis. It had taken everyone unawares: de Gaulle himself was abroad on a state visit to Rumania. The president did possess under the constitution the necessary emergency powers to restore law and order. But in the face of such a massive wave of unrest, the invocation of emergency powers was hardly appropriate. Two contrasting methods appeared to be available to de Gaulle. One was to appeal to the country, preferably through a further election or referendum, to demonstrate its allegiance: it is important to remember that a considerable section of the society were equally distressed by the riots and strikes and would rally to any such call for law and order. The second policy was to use the army in an attempt to suppress the troubles by direct action. In the event, both policies worked in de Gaulle's favour. It seems that he did indeed obtain a pledge of the army's allegiance. In addition, the election he called the following month turned into a landslide for the Gaullist party: while falling just short of an electoral majority, the UDR won no less than 358 of the 476 seats in the National Assembly. While de Gaulle's victory starkly revealed the limitations of the demonstrators, it seems true to say that it was also due to the party's propaganda theme that if not quenched the troubles would lead to 'red totalitarianism'—and probably also to the attractive electoral package the party offered: educational reform, substantial pay increases, and industrial reform.

May 1968 damaged French prestige abroad and also seriously reduced confidence in the franc. By the end of the year, the country experienced another currency crisis: the following summer the franc was devalued by a reluctant government. Above all, however, the events of May had consequences both for de Gaulle and his party. It was clear that de Gaulle could no longer ignore popular feeling as he had done in the past; that he could not treat people as schoolchildren who needed to be lectured and chastised at frequent intervals. The question was whether or not de Gaulle, who before 1968 had often trimmed his sails to meet the exigencies of the moment, could adapt his policies and his personality to conform with the changed situation. The UDR, although it now had a huge parliamentary majority, was also reminded more forcefully of the mortality of man and that its long term prospects depended on popular support and not on a gift from Mount Olympus. Whether or not de Gaulle had become disillusioned with the electorate, his role after 1968 was more muted. In April 1969 he staked his continuation in office on a referendum in which electors were asked to vote on three issues which, if not minor, were certainly not issues on which most politicians would feel obliged to resign if their proposals were rejected by the electorate. Nevertheless, de Gaulle persisted in his customary practice of regarding a positive vote as a personal vote of confidence and an indication that the country wanted him to continue in office. After the turmoil of the previous year, it is very probable that a great number of politicians and electors also placed this interpretation on the referendum. At any rate, de Gaulle's proposals were defeated, and he promptly resigned, ostentatiously removing himself abroad on holiday until the election for his successor was held. The de Gaulle era may have ended, but this was not true of that of the Gaullists, secure behind their massive parliamentary majority. But they had to enter a new period of challenge, and a new opportunity was available to the opposition parties to recoup some of the losses they had sustained under de Gaulle.

The other parties were also taken by surprise in 1968. But in a sense this was consistent with their inability after 1958 to come to terms with each other and to appreciate the political actualities of the 1960s. While it is true that parliament had been weakened by the new constitution, a non-Gaullist majority could have seriously embarrassed de Gaulle. Their opposition to de Gaulle and the consistently proven electoral ability of the UDR to garner

votes did not persuade them to cooperate with each other. The
UDR had become the first genuine and major conservative party
in France. In the process it had eliminated most of the earlier
conservative groups and had absorbed significant sections of some
of the centre parties such as the Radicals and the MRP. By 1967,
in fact, the rump of the MRP, which had been weakened so much
by defections to the Gaullists and the more leftward tendencies
of some of its leaders, formally dissolved itself. It had been caught
between the powerful force of Gaullism on one side, and the
coming together on the other of left-wing groups: there was no
room in the centre, especially as Gaullist legislation on religious
matters had favoured the Church, thereby making the UDR very
attractive to MRP voters. Nevertheless the demise of the MRP
was a sad occasion. It had participated in all twenty governments
of the Fourth Republic, providing that regime with five prime
ministers and two foreign ministers: above all, its more or less
permanent occupancy of the foreign ministry during the first
postwar decade had enabled it to play a leading role in the search
for forms of Western European reconciliation and integration.
The other dominant party of the Fourth Republic, the Radicals,
also suffered from disintegration and found that probably for the
first time since the 1870s their political influence was commensurate with their small numerical size.

It took the parties nearly ten years to agree that cooperation
and even amalgamation was perhaps the most effective way of
challenging the Gaullist regime, particularly as it seemed that the
UDR would be capable of surviving as a major political force after
the departure of de Gaulle. A major stimulus was provided by
the introduction of the popular election of the president. For the
1965 presidential elections, after much bargaining and heart-
searching, two challenging groups emerged, one a left-wing
coalition, the other a centre grouping. Negotiations continued
after the election to form more permanent coalitions. The experience of 1965 contained the genesis of the Federation of the
Left and the Democratic Centre. The latter group hoped to
become a powerful balancing force between left and right. Its
electoral performance in 1967, however, did not give rise to
much optimism, and a disastrous showing in 1968 hinted at a

very limited potential. Greater hopes were possessed by the Federation of the Left, which included the Socialists and the bulk of the remaining Radicals. The Federation had two major problems: the first was that the old party organisations retained their identity and independence, the other was its relationship with the Communist Party, which was still deeply suspicious of any kind of association. The new Federation lasted, in fact, only until 1968. Its members were still antagonistic to each other, personal rivalries were pronounced, and the left suffered from its traditional affliction of organisational disintegration. It too had been deeply affected by the events of 1968, its members being torn in different directions, but like the Democratic Centre it went down to defeat in the subsequent election. It was not until 1971 that attempts to revive a left-wing federation were success-ful: past experience throws considerable doubts on its prospects.

There remains the Communist Party. The Gaullists have often said that France will eventually have only two significant parties, themselves and the Communists. The Communist vote has been able to withstand the Gaullist onslaught much better than the other parties. Its problem has been how to turn that support into influence. It has probably been much less influential than its Italian counterpart, and this is due to some extent to its greater unwillingness to move towards the system. It did agree to support the left-wing candidate in the 1965 presidential election, and entered into agreements with the Federation of the Left for the 1967 election, but that is the sum total of its efforts. Its fear has been that if it moves too far towards accommodation it will lose its present cohesion: on the other hand, because it is profoundly unwilling to move, its influence outside the organisation is extremely limited. May 1968 not only took the party by surprise, but also harshly revealed its limitations. The student riots and strikes threatened the existence of the party no less than the government. Since the students were equally critical of the bureaucratic nature of the party and its unions, the Communists found themselves on the same side as the Gaullists in attacking the students. The party had more success in trying to channel the workers' strikes through its own unions, but here also the 'uprising' had been spontaneous, without any involvement by the party or its union leaders, and it is questionable whether the Communists emerged with their credit intact. The imprisonment of the party within non-revolutionary confines was re-emphasised.

De Gaulle had been the dominating figure not just in French politics, but also in European politics for a decade. He will undoubtedly go down in history as one of the world's outstanding statesmen and politicians. It is certain that France cannot, at least in the foreseeable future, be quite what it was before 1958. On the other hand, the nature of the constitution and the debates over it, the nature of the political parties, the emphasis in French politics on both strong authority and an individualism hostile to that authority (two characteristics which were again emphasised in 1968)—all make forecasts about future developments difficult. At least in the short run Gaullism will survive. De Gaulle left behind him a parliament dominated by the UDR, although, of course, it is extremely unlikely that in the future the UDR majority will be so great. The party itself has shown signs of tension between those who are committed to 'pure Gaullism' and those who wish to pursue a more liberal policy, although until recently the need for an outward show of unity was buttressed by de Gaulle's resignation and his death one year later.

The presidential election of 1969 confirmed the Gaullist strength by the election of Georges Pompidou, prime minister between 1962 and 1968, with about the same level of support as de Gaulle had won four years earlier. If the UDR can survive as a strong moderate conservative force, it will perhaps strengthen the party system by filling the vacuum which has tended to exist there, and also by encouraging other parties to merge with each other. While it is probable that no one man can dominate French politics as de Gaulle did, and that both parliament and the parties will be more important than in the past decade, perhaps the major need is for a viable opposition to come forward. The most probable source for this is the left, but it is precisely this area of French politics which has been prone to internecine strife and fragmentation. Nevertheless, the non-Communist parties, in order to survive as a significant force, may find it imperative to make a real effort to gain cohesion, and to re-examine their relationship with the Communists. In turn, the Communists might find it profitable to study closely the activities of their more successful Italian confrères. One factor that, as in Italy, may help to push them further in this direction is that both Communist and non-Communist unions have been showing in recent years greater dissatisfaction with 'their' political parties and a greater tendency towards cooperation. A major characteristic of French politics has been the tendency of political elites to elevate their differences to ideological levels: this has been a root cause of instability. French electorates may in the past have expressed preferences for weak governments, but they have also made it clear that they want stable government. De Gaulle's government was both strong and stable. The riots and the election of 1968 may have demonstrated a resentment against the style of government, but they also reaffirmed a desire for stability. In this, therefore, there may be a clue to the future. There may be a 'Sixth Republic', but it is perhaps improbable that France will tolerate the return of all the faults of the Fourth Republic.

16 Integration: Attainable Goal or Holy Grail?

To yesteryear belongs the political concept of national sovereignty, the idea that the national unit, relying on itself, its own strength and skills, should be the final and the only yardstick of the historical process.

Walter Hallstein, 1964

However big the glass which is proffered from outside, we prefer to drink from our own glass, while at the same time clinking glasses with those around us.

President de Gaulle, 1965

Western Europe still remained divided between EEC and EFTA, although the tensions which surrounded the inception of the Free Trade Association had been greatly eased. As early as 1962 it seemed in fact that not only was some form of accommodation possible, but also that the avenue to a wider, more closely integrated Europe was direct and without any concealed obstacles. Applications for membership of EEC had been received from Britain and other EFTA nations, and the negotiations appeared to be progressing satisfactorily. The EEC was also considering how to accommodate countries like Sweden and Austria, whose self-avowed or imposed neutral status would prevent them from opting for full membership of the Common Market and its implications of political union. Within EEC itself, the goals of the first transition stage had been achieved, and its protagonists were looking forward with confidence to shortening the duration of the second transition phase. Prospects were optimistic because the negotiations about establishing a customs union were ahead of schedule: the Commission was forecasting that the union would come into effect by 1967, three years earlier than had been originally planned. Moreover, under persistent French pressure, EEC had also taken the basic decisions about the founding of a common agricultural policy. The Commission itself was recommending that attention now be turned to the much more

313

complicated task of establishing a genuine economic union. The Commission was attempting to utilise the changing economic circumstances within the Six to advance this policy. While until 1962 all the member states had experienced economic expansion, this was not true later. By 1963 and 1964 France and Italy had a large trade deficit, while West Germany was beginning to be embarrassed by a large trade surplus. Thus while previously there had been little need to encourage a common economic union with coordinated monetary and budgeting policies, the changed economic climate meant that governments were now becoming interested in such a proposal. Yet within the space of only a few years the optimism of the federalists and supranationalists, not for the first time, had been dispelled. De Gaulle's veto on British membership had effectively limited further progress in European union to the Six, while internal dissension within EEC threatened to destroy the whole experiment in integration. We must therefore examine these two main themes of the 1960s: the attempt to widen EEC and the debates over the exact path the development of the Community should take.

EEC and Britain: a Decade of Perseverance

In 1961 the Macmillan government had destroyed traditional British policy in one blow when it announced its intention of applying for admission into the EEC. Three general factors had contributed towards the revision of Conservative thinking. First, while EFTA had fulfilled its limited expectations, it had done nothing to counteract the growing importance of EEC. The doubts which surrounded its inception had not been cleared up. While it was becoming a full free trade area, it had always been envisaged as a temporary organisation. In addition, the EFTA nations were divided in their attitude towards EEC. Denmark, for example, was very enthusiastic in the early 1960s about coming to terms with the Common Market, or even joining it, while other members such as Switzerland seemed to be basically disinterested in such notions. The economic weaknesses of EFTA were emphasised a few years later when the British Labour Government, shortly after its accession to office, imposed a 15 per cent surcharge on EFTA imports: the surcharge meant that EFTA nations enjoyed no preferences in the British market and were in fact worse off in certain respects—for example in terms of prior notice—than the United States.

The second factor was the continuing reassessment by the British government of its role and influence in world politics, in particular its relationship with the United States. Since the Suez episode it had been painfully obvious that America either interpreted the 'special relationship' very differently or refused to admit its existence. The reorganisation of OEEC in 1960 emphasised this point, as did the election of John Kennedy to the American presidency in the same year. Kennedy's vision of the relationship between the United States and Western Europe emphasised interdependency expressed in terms of political, economic and military partnership. The basis of European participation in this partnership, however, was contingent upon both the success of the Community and its enlargement: Britain was to have no special favours. The team of advisers and administrators which surrounded Kennedy also expressed a greater enthusiasm for European unity and continually emphasised its urgency.

The third factor was the development of EEC itself. In March 1960, the Six declared their intention to speed up the programme of development in order to shorten the transitional period and introduce a common market earlier than had been thought possible. This decision made it obvious to Britain that EEC was proving to be a viable unit, unlike EDC. A few months later de Gaulle declared that the Six should now be considering ways of introducing political union. In 1961 the EEC set up a committee to consider this possibility and to draft a political treaty which would embody more concretely the ideas expressed in the earlier treaties. While disagreements among the Six prevented this committee from arriving at a definite programme, it did serve notice to Britain that EEC was viable; that if its future plans were successful, Britain's influence both in world and European political developments would decrease unless it became a member of EEC; and also that the later Britain reached a decision about wishing to join, the more difficult it would be to obtain satisfactory terms and the harder the problems of adjustment would be.

Shortly after Britain announced its intention to seek EEC membership, Denmark, Ireland and Norway declared that they would follow the British lead. Thus it appeared that the federalist dream of a comprehensive European community in both size and function had received its greatest impetus since the Treaty of Rome. The major drawback was the suspicion that British policy concerning the desirability of European union had not fundamentally changed: this attitude was to be expressed admirably by de Gaulle. Doubts as to Britain's real intentions were probably not lessened by the fact that the British application gave the impression of coming from a potential benefactor rather than a supplicant. The outline presented by Britain's chief negotiator in 1961, Edward Heath, involved a radical change in the operation of EEC, and to some extent implied its submergence in a greater Atlantic-cum-Commonwealth system. The main theme of the negotiations between Britain and the Six was a gradual but steady retreat by Britain from its original position: towards the end of 1962 progress had been considerable. However, the negotiations came to an abrupt end when President de Gaulle, in a press conference on 14 January 1963, announced what amounted to a veto on British entry. De Gaulle's statement is worth quoting at some length: he said:

England is, in effect, insular, maritime, linked through its trade, markets and food supply to very diverse and often very distant countries. . . . The nature, structure and economic context of England differ profoundly from those of the other States of the Continent. . . . The question is to know if Great Britain can at present place itself with the Continent and like it, within a tariff that is truly common, give up all preference with regard to the Commonwealth, cease to claim that its agriculture be privileged and even more, consider as null and void the commitments it has made with the countries that are part of its free trade area. That question is the one at issue. One cannot say that it has now been resolved. Will it be so one day? Obviously Britain alone can answer that.

Thus the French argument was based on its interpretation of the Treaty of Rome and on doubts about the sincerity of Britain's intentions. However, two further factors were probably more important in influencing de Gaulle's decision. The first was that British participation in Europe would have meant a challenge to the strength of French influence inside EEC and to de Gaulle's bid for European leadership, which was seen as depending primarily on a Franco-German axis. The second and perhaps more important factor was de Gaulle's interpretation of America's role in Europe. He was opposed strenuously to the concept of Atlantic partnership outlined by Kennedy, and saw Britain's entry as that of an American Trojan horse. His resentment at the nuclear exclusiveness of the two countries had been growing since their dismissal of his 'troika' proposal in 1958. Moreover, the agreement in Nassau the previous month between Kennedy and Macmillan, which provided Britain with a quasi-independent deterrent in the form of the Polaris missile, served him as both a pretext and further confirmation of his views. One further point should be borne in mind. De Gaulle's proposal of 1960 that the Six should consider ways of reaching political union had been taken up by the other members. De Gaulle regarded his own proposal as being more important than that of Britain's entry, but while the Six discussed the question during the next two years, he saw the other members, especially Belgium and the Netherlands, becoming more and more reluctant to accept any progress in this field until the matter of Britain's application had been resolved. De Gaulle's views on European union and on American influence were expressed in the same press conference of January 1963 when he went on to state:

It must be agreed that the entry first of Great Britain and then that of those other States will completely change the series of adjustments, agreements, compensations and regulations already established between the Six. . . . We would then have to envisage the construction of another Common Market which would, without any doubt, hardly resemble the one the Six have built. Moreover, the Community, growing in that way, would be confronted with all the problems of its economic relations with a crowd of other States, and first of all with the United States. It is foreseeable that the cohesion of all its members, who would be very numerous and very diverse, would not hold for long and that in the end there would appear a colossal Atlantic Community under American dependence and leadership which would soon swallow up the European Community. This is an assumption that can be perfectly justified in the eyes of some, but it is not at all what France wanted to do and what France is doing, which is a strictly European construction.

Despite protestations from the other five, the French veto had to hold. It seemed that for several years at least a united Europe would be limited to the Six, a view that appeared to be confirmed by the creation of a Labour Government in Britain in 1964. One heartening feature about the veto of the British application was that although it helped to plunge the Six into a crisis which lasted for several years, it did not tear EEC apart. Despite the discontent generated, the community held together. If it could come through such a major test, it seemed unlikely that it would be destroyed by less critical situations.

Later relationships between Britain and the Six can be dealt with more summarily because they were basically determined by the situation and opinions established in the early 1960s. The most significant feature about Britain's return to Europe was that the second application was lodged by the Labour Government in May 1967. While it is probably true that a majority of the party's rank and file were hostile to the idea, the party's leaders seem to have been converted, like the Conservatives before them, by the actualities and problems of government. More Commonwealth states were actively seeking new trading patterns. Britain's trade with the Commonwealth was consequently declining, while after 1964 its trade with the EEC had stagnated. The political limitations of the Commonwealth had also been stressed by Rhodesia's unilateral declaration of independence and Biafra's attempt at secession from Nigeria. The American attempt to introduce the MLF had emphasised anew Britain's relative loss of power: traditional Labour suspicions of the American relationship were in any case reinforced by America's increasing involvement in Vietnam, a war which the party found repugnant. In the economic field, Britain's EFTA partners were disillusioned and bitter about the imposition of a surcharge, while the internal economic situation, emphasised by a large balance of payments deficit and the need to borrow vast sums of money in 1964, contrasted strongly with the healthier economies of the Six, especially West Germany. Between 1965 and 1967 pronouncements by Labour spokesmen on the need to come to some kind of arrangement with EEC were strongly similar to those issued by the Conservatives between the failure of their free trade area proposals at the end of 1958 and their decision in 1961 to seek entry into EEC. Pointing to American predominance in such fields as space research and computers, Harold Wilson backed his application by stressing the need for Western Europe to cooperate in technological development and that Britain could enhance the EEC in this field (it should, however, be noted that this theme had been raised a decade earlier in the Spaak Report of 1956).

Despite radical changes in the conception and operation of the Common Market since Britain's first application, nothing had changed to persuade the French government to revise its opinion. Five members of EEC supported the application: de Gaulle remained opposed. This time the negotiations had hardly got off the ground when five months later de Gaulle, in another press conference, explicitly confirmed 'the impossibility of bringing the Great Britain of today into the Common Market as it stands'. While the British application remained deposited, so to speak, at the door of the Six, the second veto confirmed the view that as long as de Gaulle remained at the helm of French politics, British entry was impossible. Nevertheless, pro-British advocates within both European government circles and private associations such as Jean Monnet's Action Committee worked hard to keep open the channels of communication between the two sides. Immediately after de Gaulle's resignation in 1969, Monnet's Action Committee, which now included representatives from all three British parties, met again to plan a new campaign for British entry. In the event it was not until after de Gaulle's death one year later and the formation of a new Conservative Government that the third British application entered the stage of negotiations. France still had to be satisfied, and it was indicative of the actual power relationships between the supranational and national organs of EEC that the way towards establishing terms of entry was opened only after a personal meeting in Paris between Prime

Minister Heath and President Pompidou in May 1971. The terms agreed on between the seven governments had still to be ratified by the British Parliament, but as stated earlier, it was the first time that the choice belonged to Britain. Given the past record of failure, and the fact that British public opinion had seemingly turned against membership, it was perhaps correct to believe that if this application had also been turned down, it would have been the last application. It might also be true to say that if Britain rejects the terms, it might tempt the Six to draw the final curtain on the long drawn-out search for ways to make Britain part of Europe politically and economically, as well as geographically.

Crisis in the EEC

The tendency in the 1950s to regard the European debate as being simply between Britain and the continent had blurred several divergencies of opinion about the nature of integration and the way it should develop which already existed within the Six. There had been, for example, a certain lessening of enthusiasm for closer unity among economic interests in West Germany, which can be partly attributed to the fact that by 1958 the Federal Republic had become the leading creditor of Western Europe: in such a position, the necessity of economic integration did not possess the same compulsion as previously. The coming of de Gaulle did not cause these divergencies: it merely served to crystallise them.

The crisis which racked EEC in the 1960s for several years began with de Gaulle's veto in 1963. One immediate consequence was that it shook the confidence of the smaller countries, as it occurred in the same month that a Franco-German Treaty of Friendship was announced. The relative passivity with which West Germany accepted the veto seemed to indicate that Adenauer's silent endorsement was part of the bargain. However, it was not the veto which caused the crisis of confidence: every member had a right to blackball an applicant. Rather, it was the manner in which de Gaulle declared his opposition, without informing or discussing it with the other EEC members.

The crisis hardened two years later in clashes over the question of a common agricultural policy, which led to a French boycott of meetings of the Council of Ministers. It was in many ways a logical consequence of de Gaulle's seeking to put into practice his vision of the future Europe, which contrasted strongly to that of the committed integrationists of the school of Schumann and Monnet. It is perhaps ironical that while the British applications implied a tacit acceptance of the ultimate inevitability of the supranational principle, the Gaullist design for Europe, generally known as the *Europe des Patries*, was similar to the traditional scheme, so popular with British politicians, of an alliance sustained primarily by frequent conversations between national governments. Such a blueprint could not help but leave to an indefinite future important issues (such as the exact role of a European parliament) facing the integrative bodies already in existence. In its wider aspects it was an indication that nationalism was far from dead in Western Europe. It was, in any case, to be expected that a serious move to diminish national sovereignty would help to generate a stronger nationalist opposition. As has already been stated, pro-Europeans in 1958 had feared that, given the well-known views of the French President, France would opt out of EEC. However, France honoured the first statutory obligations of the Community, and until 1965 continued to accept without much argument the principles of the Treaty of Rome. While 1963 gave a strong indication that de Gaulle's interpretation of the Treaty might be very different, the Six on the whole tended to work in harmony. The understanding reached between de Gaulle and Adenauer undoubtedly helped to facilitate this mood of cooperation.

The internal crisis that hit EEC in the mid-1960s was a complex nexus of proposed policies affecting Commission and national governments alike. Three separate questions were involved. The European Parliament, supported by the Netherlands, wished to acquire more substantial powers for itself. Second, there was a proposal that EEC should have an independent source of revenue out of which it could finance its own activities: this proposal, naturally, was supported by the Commission. Both these proposals would have increased the supranational characteristics of

EEC: in particular, the power of the Commission would have been enhanced. It is for these reasons that France was hostile to both: de Gaulle had already suggested that the Commission already had too much power. On the other hand, there was a third proposal before EEC: the finalisation of the financial regulations concerning the adjustment of the various national agricultural industries. France was the most strenuous protagonist of a common agricultural policy, whose fundamental aim was to reduce the number of very small inefficient farmers and to create large mechanised farms within a framework of compensations that would cushion shocks of hardship and dispossession of the kind caused in Britain by the enclosure movement of the eighteenth century.

Until this point EEC had worked fairly smoothly because all, or most, major social and economic groups had believed that its advantages for their own interests outweighed its disadvantages. Agriculture was one field in which there would obviously be a marked clash of interest between supranationalism and nationalism, especially as it was the first serious attempt by EEC to inaugurate a common policy. Here it was West Germany which dragged its heels since West German agriculture would be seriously hurt by a common policy, and the ruling CDU certainly did not want to alienate one of its basic voting props, especially just before the 1965 election.

The Commission sought a way out of the conflicting demands by attempting to bring all three proposals into one package deal. In other words, if France wanted an agricultural settlement, it would have to accept an increase in the supranational characteristics of EEC. This the French government was certainly not prepared to accept. When it became clear in June 1965 that EEC would not be able to concur on the financial regulations of the common agricultural policy by the stipulated deadline of the end of the month, the French simply refused to attend further meetings of the Council of Ministers. The point was that France was not basically protesting about incorporating the agricultural policy into a package deal, but about the political or supranational elements of the package. This was not surprising in view of the well-known French attitude that the Commission was already too powerful. The French view was made clear in a press conference which de Gaulle gave in September when he stated:

But we know—and heaven knows how well we know it—that there is a different conception of a European federation in which, according to the dreams of those who have conceived it, the member countries would lose their national identities, and which ... would be ruled by some sort of technocratic body of elders, stateless and irresponsible.

De Gaulle's statement was a direct attack on the Community's methods of operation, and it stressed that France was not willing to resume participation until fundamental features of the Treaty of Rome were modified or dropped. It brought into the open the argument about what kind of Europe the Community ought to be building, which had simmered beneath the surface since 1958, but which until now had been successfully avoided.

The other five members, however, also refused to change their fundamental position. Adenauer was no longer in charge of the West German government, and his successors were noticeably cooler in their attitudes towards France. Apart from the resentment felt by the other five members about what they regarded as a French violation of EEC rules, the West Germans undoubtedly also were reacting against the pressure to accept the common agricultural policy that France had brought to bear upon them in the previous year. Although the French boycott lasted for seven months, EEC did not disintegrate under the conflicting pressures. In fact the French withdrawal had not perhaps been a serious danger to the working of EEC. The summer months have always been quiet periods in the daily management of affairs. However, by the end of the year, the stalemate could not be permitted to continue without endangering the existing form of EEC. New decisions and directives were needed. Either the five had to be willing to take these alone, or they had to yield somewhat to encourage France to return. Similarly France had to relax its position or risk seeing the five go ahead by themselves. The result was a compromise settlement, under which the warfare continued in a more disguised form. The French Government continued their efforts to reduce the power of the Commission and to prevent the adoption in the Council of Ministers of a system of majority voting on a wide number of issues. The five, on the other hand, continued to cooperate in their opposition to France's efforts.

The crises of 1963 and 1965 were basically about the same theme—the nature of the Europe that the Six were trying to construct. In both instances France conceived that its basic national interests were being threatened, in 1963 from Britain and the United States, and in 1965 from EEC itself. The effects of the crisis were far-reaching, and have still not disappeared. Several points should be stressed. The first is that France, because of the two crises, very largely lost its undisputed leadership of the European movement which it had held since the war. On the other hand, French influence remains exceptionally strong. No successor has come forward to occupy the throne: West Germany, the only possible contender, has, understandably, shown a marked reluctance to assume the responsibility. While it is true that de Gaulle failed to bring the five to their knees, his aim of reducing the supranational element in EEC and of eliminating majority voting very largely succeeded. The basic choice facing France was either to return to the Council of Ministers or to risk the five continuing by themselves, in which case the likelihood of them soliciting British membership was great. Thus France returned to the conference table. While the five may have remained united, the 'victory' largely went to France, for the door remained closed to Britain and, more important, because the crisis was resolved by negotiations and discussions between national governments. The powers of the latter increased considerably *vis-à-vis* the authority of the Commission. The Community and its methods of operation after 1965 were rather different from the picture contained in the Treaty of Rome.

Two Possible Patterns for the Future

Generally speaking, two avenues of development seem to be open to the federalists. On the one hand there is the path created by the deliberate engineering of constitutions and institutions to force countries into a tight and unbreakable mould; on the other, there is the less formal approach generated by mutual trust and cooperation. Very loosely, these two alternatives approximate the ideas of integration and association. Generally, the two approaches have already been put to a more critical test than any yet offered in the wider field of European union. The first method of approach, which has been followed by EEC, has already advanced much further in the more limited areal experiment of Benelux, while the Scandinavian countries have attempted to maximise a variant of the second approach under the guiding hand of the Nordic Council.

The beginnings of Benelux have already been discussed. When it was seen that the economic agreement of 1946 was working satisfactorily, the three states pressed on further in the 1950s. In November 1955 they drew up a convention establishing an Interparliamentary Consultative Council. Although without any legislative powers, the Council was given the authority to discuss and recommend further ways of achieving closer union; of particular interest is its ability to search for ways of presenting a common foreign policy and of achieving a 'national' unification of the legislation of the three states. This is one step which EEC clearly will have to consider more fully before moving on to a more ambitious political union. In the economic field Benelux reformed the existing customs union to coordinate financial policy as well as the deployment of capital and labour. The Benelux Economic Union was signed at The Hague in February 1958. Although a miniature EEC, the supranational powers established were more restricted than in the Common Market: given the stronger acceptance of closer cooperation, they have more than fulfilled their purpose. And in 1960 the Economic Union was further strengthened when national trade agreements were replaced by common Benelux agreements.

The Benelux countries have always been in the forefront of European integration: their spokesmen have never tired of arguing for a federal Europe, pointing to their own success in the economic field and the ability of their parties to cooperate with each other to a far greater extent than those of their larger neighbours. The economic drive of Benelux was made possible by two factors: its industrialised base and its abandonment of all pretence of world, European and colonial influence. Quite incapable of defending themselves militarily, they settled down to the task of bettering their economies. In this way they are a pilot for future European developments with their closely interlocking economies.

What lessons, therefore, can EEC and Europe derive from the Benelux experience? Benelux set out to do in three years what EEC proposed to achieve over a much longer period. Yet it was only after this transitional period that Benelux came up against the hard core of problems which still have not been wholly resolved. The currency crisis of 1971 in which Belgium and the Netherlands adopted different policies illustrates the strength of national interest. More important for the dream of political unity is the reality that national boundaries have not become less obvious. The sense of national consciousness was not caused by trade barriers, and hence it is unreasonable to expect a Benelux national consciousness to emerge just because trade discrimination has been abolished. Even within national boundaries, Belgium and the Netherlands have not successfully resolved the deep cleavages of religion and language which exist within their societies: in fact, their established parties have in recent years been strained further than those of most European countries. A great deal of political education still remains. Benelux has had a merited success, but its unity is primarily an elitist concept, with little popular support. The advance of Benelux illustrates how hard it is to transform the argument for European political unity into one with massive popular support.

Scandinavia, on the other hand, presents a unique approach, and one that is probably impossible for most countries. With a common ethnic root and a common language structure (apart from Iceland and Finland) Scandinavia has a long history of cooperative efforts. But no formalisation was attempted until after 1945. Then the proximity of Soviet Russia and the events in East Germany and Czechoslovakia caused a defensive system to be imperative. However, a Scandinavian defensive alliance would, for Sweden, have had to be separate from any other. Unfortunately, Scandinavia could not defend itself without American assistance, and the United States would not aid any system that was not integrated with its own alliances. In 1949 the proposal fell through, with Norway and Denmark joining NATO and Sweden retaining its neutral status. A close defensive alliance was perhaps unrealistic for, as EDC illustrated later, defence is a last sector for integrative purposes.

In the event defence was the only Scandinavian failure, although later developments have not perhaps attained the original expectations. The major step forward was taken in 1952 when the Nordic Council was established. It is essentially a functional intergovernmental and interparliamentary body, but because of the countries involved it has been a more effective body than, for example, the Council of Europe. It is a consultative organ: no government is forced to bring anything before it or to act on any of its recommendations. Yet the interesting fact is that Nordic Council recommendations are nearly always accepted without reserve by every member and introduced as national legislation. Under the auspices of the Nordic Council Scandinavia has achieved such goals as a common body of law including international judicial precedent, a common social benefit system for any individual residing in a 'foreign' Scandinavian state, common legislation, and a common labour market. Despite the presence of two neutral countries, a coherent foreign policy has been obtained: defence presents no problems simply because it is never broached. In addition there has been an effective division of labour for international organisations whereby the delegate from one country will represent the interests of all.

The emphasis within the Nordic Council is on flexibility. Governments and states are free to do as they like while still retaining membership: Sweden and Denmark, for example, have played a more prominent role in cooperative endeavours than their neighbours. Nevertheless, it is obvious from the brief resumé of achievements that a common purpose has largely been obtained. The Nordic Council is rather a unique arrangement whereby mutual trust seems to be enough to win the day. It is similar to Benelux in many ways, not least in the fact that a close group of neighbouring countries may achieve what a larger unit cannot.

In this sense Scandinavian cooperation as experienced after 1945 offers some valuable hints for pro-Europeans. It offers an illustration of the opposite approach at work. The Nordic Council, though an institution itself, seems to scorn the creation of institutions through which political elites can attempt to impose a common purpose upon their nations. Undoubtedly Scandinavian institutions would have provided a focus for such a purpose and for elite leadership—if this had in fact existed. Scandinavia has not deliberately sought integration and unity, yet unconsciously has moved in this direction: there is much more of a 'Scandinavian consciousness' than a 'Benelux consciousness' or an 'EEC consciousness'. The Nordic Council is one example of how political and social unity could be achieved for, although integration may not have been the original intention or the ultimate goal, 'when countries adopt the habit that they should consult each other before making decisions and when they regard the agreements reached in these consultations as binding, let alone only morally and not legally, the idea of sovereignty is already in a process of dissolution'.[1] The major lesson for the protagonists of a United States of Europe is a realisation of the difficulties ahead in achieving a popular basis of support: this is something which cannot be obtained simply by founding a mass of supranational institutions and closely integrated economies.

EEC after the Crisis

In many ways EEC would be very difficult to destroy. There is a widespread acceptance of its aims, far wider than in the previous decade, and leading national groups have increasingly tended to define their own interests and values and to plot their actions upon the supposition that EEC is a permanent organisation. The economies have become more interlocked and would be difficult to prise apart. Trade in Europe has been freed from high levels of national control, as the British Labour Government discovered when they imposed a surcharge on EFTA imports: during their last spell in office, such unilateral controls were accepted, but by the 1960s they were frowned upon by convention. Despite the climacterics of 1963 and 1965 the Six governments illustrated

[1] N. Andren, *Government and Politics in the Nordic Countries*, Stockholm, n.d., pp. 218–19.

through their actions their acceptance of the value of EEC. In the face of French opposition, the other five realised that the alternative of destroying EEC over the question of British membership was more unacceptable to them than it was for France. On the other hand, the French Government accepted the need to pursue at least some parts of the EEC timetable. Despite its boycott, France did cut internal tariffs at the end of 1965 along with the other member states, although it was questionable until the event whether France would obey this provision of the Treaty. These facts alone indicate a realisation of the fundamental importance and vitality of EEC. Integration has perhaps become a positive political concept like democracy: and like democracy, it has many differing interpretations, each of which claims to be pro-integration. In addition, the world influence of the organisation has also increased. For example, the fact that the EEC countries act as a bloc in trade negotiations, despite the seemingly insurmountable obstacles that are raised internally in arriving at such a common position, gives them considerable influence and bargaining power, as for instance in the Kennedy round of tariff cuts in 1967.[1] In addition, their trade tentacles have spread to give preferential agreements to all France's ex-colonies in Africa and to most of the Mediterranean states, and also to make them the first to offer preferences to all developing countries on most industrial goods.

The defects which have already been mentioned still remain. The 'new start' in integration after 1966 has run into problems. Progress towards economic unification has been slow and limited, while political union exists only on paper. The basic feature is that economic decision-making still remains firmly in the hands of national governments, although an industrial customs union has been established and the free movement of labour introduced in 1968. The two major problems of recent years have been the

1 The Kennedy round related to multilateral negotiations to cut tariff barriers within GATT. It was named after Kennedy because the project was proposed by his administration as part of his scheme for American-European partnership. Its political aims were destroyed by the French veto on Britain, as its immediate object was to limit the injurious effects on world trade that might be caused by an enlarged European customs union.

working of the common agricultural policy and the desire to introduce monetary integration. The common agricultural policy has proved to be rather a frail offspring. Its method is basically protectionist: this is achieved by maintaining high, uniform prices and by the Commission playing off the diverse interests of the different members against each other. It is a policy which has not been popular, not least among the farmers themselves, because it has meant that in inflationary periods, such as the late 1960s, the real incomes of farmers have fallen. Moreover the policy, ever since its inception, has been put under tremendous strain by frequent crop surpluses or because of currency fluctuations like that of 1971, which led to changes of parity within the Community. The latter problem contributed towards the urgency to establish a common monetary policy. At a meeting in The Hague in December 1969 the six government leaders and their foreign ministers agreed to inaugurate an economic and monetary union, and also to consider yet again means of creating a political union. A few months later financial agreements for the common agricultural policy were made: these also gave some limited budgetary powers to the European Parliament. However, the only real decision taken on a monetary policy was to reduce, but only on an experimental basis, the margins between their countries against the dollar. The devaluation of the franc in 1969 and the subsequent revaluation of the mark emphasised both the dangers and difficulties that currency coordination entailed. The struggle to get the monetary policy working went on throughout 1970, but with very little success. The weakness of such a policy and the strength of national governments within the Six were both re-emphasised in 1971 when after a prolonged currency crisis, West Germany allowed the mark to float to find its true value against the dollar. France had been strongly opposed to such an action, but the German government went ahead with the policy. Several other countries, including the Netherlands from the EEC, followed the German example. It seemed debatable, therefore, whether the policies introduced within the EEC in the 1960s to lead members towards economic and political union have been very successful.

In another sphere EEC displays the problems of positive actions and control which have confronted national governments. It is still an elite-based organisation in which progress is maintained and quickened primarily by the bureaucracy, but such progress is only possible where the Commission and its administrative departments have the cooperation and strength of the national governments behind them. The relatively weak parliamentary body, despite having some budgetary power, has little direct influence in this respect. It has been suggested that the great variety of reasons for supporting integration actually makes the process easier to direct.[1] It might equally be said that the great number of reasons makes coordination more difficult. Certainly, one of the great virtues of the Commission is the ability it has consistently shown in exploiting these different reasons and coordinating them in some coherent policy. Success, however, depends upon two conditions: the willingness of political elements, especially parties, to cooperate fully across national boundaries, and supranational institutions with the power to focus these motives in the correct direction. Both conditions were present to some extent in ECSC, but have not had much success in EEC. Underneath the supranational structure there is still an absence of a popularly accepted European attitude or community spirit which alone could provide a stable basis for a political community, although there are indications that such a spirit has been slowly increasing in strength. The Commission itself has been well aware of this problem, which was a primary reason why it undertook to issue considerable amounts of information advertising the work of EEC. Of this activity one commentator has written:

Largely as a result of these activities the Community has been an alive and interesting organization in a way no other international body has yet become. The hold that the Common Market now has on the popular mind throughout the Community owes a great deal to the energy and sophistication of the information services. Perhaps, at times, the information services have come a little too close to providing 'European' propaganda rather than simple information; perhaps at times individual commissioners have gone rather too far in criticizing governments. But the fact that information has been provided so efficiently and so liberally and that the commissioners speak freely and

[1] E. B. Haas, *The Uniting of Europe*, pp. 155-9.

can and do criticize the member governments has helped make the Community a living organization and one that arouses intense interest and support.[1]

However, the most outstanding institutional feature of the contemporary Community emphasises more than anything else the limited unification of EEC. This is the relative weakness of the Commission *vis-à-vis* the Council of Ministers. While this was apparent in the Treaty of Rome, the aftermath of the 1965 crisis increased the importance of the Council of Ministers even further. It has already been stated that a settlement of the crisis was achieved not by the Commission but by consultations between the national governments. In particular, a major condition of France's return to the conference table seems to have been that all major questions must be resolved by a unanimous verdict in the Council, or be shelved indefinitely. Thus the Treaty of Rome, which laid down that majority voting would apply on a greater range of topics after 1966, has been radically modified. In theory decision-making takes place in Brussels, with the Commission's authority resting on its power of policy initiation and its ability to put proposals before the Council of Ministers. In practice nearly all major proposals and initiatives emanate from the national governments: in particular, negotiations between France and West Germany have been of decisive importance. It means that the Commission rarely makes a decisive move without the groundwork already having been prepared in one or more of the six national governments. The Commission's role is therefore not as a policy formulator, but as a broker whose primary task is to find compromises between national viewpoints and packages which are acceptable to the six capitals. It must be said, however, that the Commission has proved to be very efficient in this trying task. Two recent examples will suffice to emphasise this point. In January 1971 the West German Chancellor, Willy Brandt paid a routine visit to Paris under the terms of the Franco-German Treaty, but the meeting was the decisive factor enabling France and the Federal Republic to agree on a common view about EEC's plans for monetary union. Second, West Germany took unilateral action in 1971 by floating the

[1] M. Camps, *European Unification in the Sixties*, London, 1967, pp. 107-8.

mark against the wishes of some of its Community partners. All this means that if Europe should achieve a federal or supranational structure, the major role will be played by the national governments.

The years since 1945, taken together, have not been particularly bad for Western Europe. Within a generation, its wealth has tripled. On the other hand, compared with 1939 its political influence has declined: Germany has been divided, and the influence of the two wartime victors, Britain and France, has diminished in almost every way. Technological advance has made Western Europe both smaller and more dependent upon both internal cooperation and external factors. While Western Europe's wealth may have increased, this represents in global terms a relative decrease: its increase in industrial production, for example, is just over one-half that of the United States in the same period. Greater dependence, therefore, has gone hand in hand with greater prosperity. It is factors such as these which have persuaded some people that cooperation is both valuable and necessary. The countries are entangled in a web of organisations, whose filaments seem to be forever spreading: in 1971 for example, the other three applicants to EEC—Ireland, Denmark and Norway —were invited to become members of WEU. Within this web EEC remains the most ambitious attempt at economic and political union. This is why every other organisation and every non-member has had to acknowledge its importance and even to seek some accommodation or membership from it. And within EEC, the most outstanding feature has been, notwithstanding the magnetic personality of de Gaulle, the growing economic strength of West Germany, which has caused concern not just to other countries but also to the West Germans themselves. West Germany's strength endangers the balance within the Community, and also the influence which France has wielded over EEC. Within the foreseeable future it is unlikely that any French government will be able to emulate de Gaulle: it is equally unlikely that a West German government would be prepared to accede to French obstruction to the same extent in order to preserve European harmony. In fact, the critics who have accused de Gaulle and France for placing national interests over integration would do well to consider the case of West Germany. While it is true that since 1958 the Federal Republic has opposed French views on EEC development in order to increase the supranational element of the Community, it is equally true that in a more quiet manner it has placed national concerns before conformity. In several instances it has been West Germany which has opposed supranationalism, as for example over the agricultural policy in 1964 and 1965. Again in 1971, West Germany was a leading protagonist of monetary union, but only a few months later the whole project had to be shelved because of the Federal Republic's action in floating the mark.

The embarrassing economic strength of West Germany would remain even if the Community expanded. Nevertheless, it seems that France now welcomes British membership in order to introduce a further balance to German power. On the other hand, West Germany regards its role within an enlarged Community as an important factor in its changing foreign and economic policy. While the realities of post-1945 politics and its defence and economic commitments have tied West Germany firmly to the United States and Western Europe, its geographical location, historical factors and its commercial strength have been turning it towards its traditional markets in Eastern Europe. The search for a new relationship with East Germany and its other Eastern neighbours has been balanced by Brandt's continual emphasis that the success of his *Ostpolitik* can only be achieved within a European Community. It is these considerations which make West Germany the key to so much of European politics. Western European integration and the problem of Germany, especially Berlin, are the two major challenges of the future: it is in the Federal Republic that they meet.

Postscript

The revisions to this book were done in the summer of 1971 against a background of an at times heated debate within Britain on the principle of joining EEC. The bipartisan attitude towards European integration, which had been a feature of British politics in the past few years, gradually eroded during the summer as the Labour Party turned away from Europe, eventually to oppose entry to the Common Market on the terms agreed between the EEC members and the Conservative Government. A substantial minority of Labour members continued to emphasise their adherence to the principle of membership in defiance of the official party policy, while a small group of Conservatives persisted in their vigorous opposition to British membership. The new Labour policy, and the apathy and opposition of public opinion to EEC membership, as indicated by opinion polls, were two factors which led people to believe that the Conservative Government's proposal might well be defeated. The vote in Parliament took place in October 1971, and proved to be something of an anticlimax. The Government obtained a comfortable majority in favour of membership, despite the fears to the contrary. While several differences between the Six and Britain still remained, notably on the question of fishing rights, and while the enabling legislation still had to be passed by the British Parliament, it is perhaps fair to suggest that this vote marked the most progressive development in European integration since the Treaty of Rome.

Bibliography

The following bibliography is merely selective and is intended to offer the reader a fairly extensive guide to further reading. Books published in foreign languages and shorter articles in academic journals etc., have been excluded. However, the books mentioned below will provide references to these and many other sources, including official papers and documents.

ALBRECHT-CARRÉ, R. *The Unity of Europe*, London, 1966
ALLEN, J. J. *The European Common Market and G.A.T.T.*, Washington, 1960
ALMOND, G. A., ed. *The Struggle for Democracy in Germany*, Chapel Hill, 1949
ALMOND, G. A. and VERBA, S. *The Civic Culture*, Princeton, 1963
AMBLER, J. S. *The French Army in Politics*, Columbus, 1966
ANDREN, N. *Government and Politics in the Nordic Countries*, Stockholm, n.d.
ARNDT, H.-J. *West Germany: Politics of Non-Planning*, Syracuse, 1967
ARON, R. *France: Steadfast and Changing*, London, 1960
ARON, R. and LERNER, D. *France Defeats EDC*, London, 1957
AVRIL, P. *Politics in France*, London, 1969

BALL, G. W. *The Discipline of Power*, Boston, 1968
BALL, M. M. *NATO and the European Union Movement*, New York, 1959
BANFIELD, E. C. *The Moral Basis of a Backward Society*, New York, 1958
BARRACLOUGH, G. *European Unity in Thought and Action*, Oxford, 1963
BEEVER, R. C. *European Unity and the Trade Union Movements*, Leiden, 1961
BEHR, E. *The Algerian Problem*, London, 1961
BELOFF, M. *The United States and the Unity of Europe*, London, 1963
BELOFF, M. *Europe and the Europeans*, London, 1957
BELOFF, N. *The General Says No*, London, 1963
BENOIT, E. *Europe at Sixes and Sevens*, New York, 1961
BERGER, C. *The Korean Knot: A Military–Political History*, Philadelphia, 1957
BODENHEIMER, S. J. *Political Union: A Microcosm of European Politics 1960–1966*, Leiden, 1967
BÖLLING, K. *Republic in Suspense*, London, 1964
BOSWORTH, W. *Catholicism and Crisis in Modern France*, Princeton, 1962
BOWETT, D. W. *The Law of International Relations*, London, 1963
BOYD, A. *United Nations: Piety, Myth and Truth*, London, 1962
BOYD, F. *British Politics in Transition 1945–1963*, London, 1964
BRANDT, W. *A Peace Policy for Europe*, London, 1969
BRINTON, C. *The Americans and the French*, Cambridge, Mass., 1968
BUCHAN, A., ed. *Europe's Future, Europe's Choices*, London, 1969
BUTLER, E. *City Divided: Berlin 1955*, New York, 1955

CALMANN, J., ed. *Western Europe: A Handbook*, London, 1967
CAMPS, M. *European Unification in the Sixties*, London, 1967
CAMPS, M. *What Kind of Europe?*, London, 1965
CAMPS, M. *Britain and the European Community 1955–1963*, London, 1964
CAPELLE, R. *The MRP and French Foreign Policy*, New York, 1963
CARRINGTON, C. E. *The Liquidation of the British Empire*, London, 1961
CARTER, G. *Independence for Africa*, New York, 1960
CATLIN, G. E. G. *The Atlantic Commonwealth*, London, 1969
CHALMERS, D. A. *The Social Democratic Party of Germany*, New Haven, 1964
CHARLOT, J. *The Gaullist Phenomenon*, London, 1971
CHILDERS, E. B. *The Road to Suez*, London, 1962
CLAY, L. D. *Decision in Germany*, New York, 1950
COLE, A. B. *Conflict in Indochina and its International Consequences*, Ithaca, 1956
CONLAND, W. H. *Berlin: Beset and Bedevilled*, New York, 1963
CONNELL-SMITH, G. *Pattern of the Post-War World*, London, 1957
COOMBES, D. *Politics and Bureaucracy in the European Community*, London, 1970
COOMBES, D. *Towards a European Civil Service*, London, 1968
CRAWLEY, A. *De Gaulle*, London, 1969
CRIDDLE, B. *Socialists and European Integration*, London, 1969
CURTIS, M. *Western European Integration*, New York, 1965

DAHL, R. A., ed. *Political Oppositions in Western Democracies*, New Haven, 1966
DAHRENDORF, R. *Society and Democracy in Germany*, N.Y., Garden City, 1967
DALLIN, D. J. *Soviet Foreign Policy After Stalin*, London, 1960
DAVISON, W. P. *The Berlin Blockade*, Princeton, 1958
DELZELL, C. F. *Mussolini's Enemies: The Italian Anti-Fascist Resistance*, Princeton, 1961
DENIAU, J. F. *The Common Market*, London, 1962
DENTON, G., ed. *Economic Integration in Europe*, London, 1969
DEUTSCH, K. and EDINGER, L. J. *Germany Rejoins the Powers*, Stanford, 1959
DEUTSCH, K. et al. *France, Germany and the Western Alliance*, New York, 1967
DEWHURST, J. F. et al. *Europe's Needs and Resources: Trends and Prospects in Eighteen Countries*, New York, 1961
DI PALMA, G. *Apathy and Participation*, New York, 1970
DIEBOLD, W. *The Schuman Plan*, New York, 1959
DIEBOLD, W. *Trade and Payments in Western Europe*, New York, 1952
DONELAN, M. *The Ideas of American Foreign Policy*, London, 1963
DUFFY, J. *Portugal in Africa*, Cambridge, Mass., 1962

EARLE, E. M., ed. *Modern France*, New York, 1964
EDEN, SIR A. *Full Circle*, London, 1960
EDINGER, L. J. *Politics in Germany*, Boston, 1968
EHRMANN, H. W. *Politics in France*, Boston, 1968
EINAUDI, M. et al. *Communism in Western Europe*, Ithaca, 1951

EINAUDI, M. and GOGUEL, F. *Christian Democracy in Italy and France*, South Bend, 1952

EMERSON, R. *From Empire to Nation*, Cambridge, Mass., 1960

EPSTEIN, L. D. *British Politics in the Suez Crisis*, London, 1964

EPSTEIN, L. D. *Britain: Uneasy Ally*, Chicago, 1954

ETZIONI, A. *Political Unification*, New York, 1965

FEIS, H. *Between War and Peace: The Potsdam Conference*, London; 1960

FELD, W. *Reunification and West German–Soviet Relations*, The Hague, 1963

FLORINSKY, M. T. *Integrated Europe?* New York, 1955

FOGARTY, M. P. *Christian Democracy in Western Europe 1820–1953*, London, 1957

FREYMOND, J. *The Saar Conflict, 1945–1955*, London, 1960

FREYMOND, J. *Western Europe Since the War*, New York, 1964

FURNESS, E. S. *France Troubled Ally*, London, 1960

FURNESS, E. S. *France: Keystone of Western Defence*, New York, 1954

GALANTE, P. and MILLER, J. *The Berlin Wall*, London, 1965

GERMINO, D. and PASSIGLI, S. *The Government and Politics of Contemporary Italy*, New York, 1968

GILLESPIE, J. *Algeria: Rebellion and Revolution*, London, 1960

GOLAY, J. F. *The Founding of the Federal Republic of Germany*, Chicago, 1958

GOLDBERG, H. *French Colonialism: Progress or Poverty?* New York, 1959

GOODRICK, H. M. *The United Nations*, London, 1960

GRAHAM, B. D. *The French Socialists and Tripartism 1944–1947*, London, 1965

GRAUBARD, S. R., ed. *A New Europe?* Boston, 1964

GREVE, T. *Norway and NATO*, Oslo, 1959

GRINDROD, M. *The Rebuilding of Italy*, London, 1955

GRINDROD, M. *The New Italy: Transition from War to Peace*, London, 1947

GROSSER, A. *French Foreign Policy under de Gaulle*, Boston, 1967

HAAS, E. B. *The Uniting of Europe*, London, 1958

HAINES, C. G., ed. *European Integration*, Baltimore, 1957

HALLE, L. J. *The Cold War as History*, London, 1967

HALLSTEIN, W. *United Europe: Challenge and Opportunity*, London, 1962

HANKEY, LORD, *Politics, Trials and Errors*, Oxford, 1950

HARRIS, W. R. *Tyranny on Trial: the Evidence at Nuremberg*, Dallas, 1954

HARTMANN, F. H. *Germany Between East and West: The Reunification Problem*, Englewood Cliffs, 1965

HAVILAND, H. F. *The United States and the Western Community*, Haverford, 1957

HEIDENHEIMER, A. J. *Adenauer and the CDU*, Hague, 1960

HEISER, H. J. *British Policy with Regard to the Unification Efforts on the European Continent*, Leiden, 1959

HENRIG, S. and PINDER, J., eds. *European Political Parties*, London, 1969

HEYDECKER, J. J. and LEEB, J. *The Nuremberg Trials*, London, 1962

HISCOCKS, R. *Germany Revived*, London, 1966
HISCOCKS, R. *Democracy in Western Germany*, London, 1957
HISCOCKS, R. *The Rebirth of Austria*, London, 1953
HOFFMAN, S. *et al. France: Change and Tradition*, London, 1963
HOPKINS, H. *The New Look*, London, 1963
HOROWITZ, D. *From Yalta to Vietnam*, London, 1967
HUGHES, H. S. *The United States and Italy*, Cambridge, Mass., 1953
HUNTER, L. *The Road to Brighton Pier*, London, 1959
HURD, V. D. *The Council of Europe*, New York, 1958

INGRAM, K. *History of the Cold War*, London, 1955
ISMAY, LORD. *NATO: The First Five Years 1949–1954*, London, 1955

JACKSON, J. H. *The Postwar Decade*, London, 1961

KENNAN, G. F. *Russia, The Atom and the West*, London, 1958
KENNAN, G. F. *Realities of American Foreign Policy*, London, 1954
KIRCHHEIMER, O. *Political Justice*, Princeton, 1961
KITZINGER, U. W. *Britain, Europe and Beyond*, Leiden, 1964
KITZINGER, U. W. *The Challenge of the Common Market*, Oxford, 1961
KITZINGER, U. W. *German Electoral Politics*, Oxford, 1960
KITZINGER, U. W., ed. *The Second Try: Labour and the EEC*, London, 1968
KLEIMAN, R. *Atlantic Crisis*, London, 1965
KNORR, K., ed. *NATO and American Security*, Princeton, 1959
KOGAN, N. *The Politics of Italian Foreign Policy*, London, 1963
KOGAN, N. *The Government of Italy*, New York, 1962
KOGAN, N. *Italy and the Allies*, Cambridge, Mass., 1956
KRAFT, J. *The Grand Design: from Common Market to Atlantic Partnership*, New York, 1962

LANCASTER, D. *The Emancipation of French Indochina*, New York, 1961
LA PALOMBARA, J. *Interest Groups in Italian Politics*, Princeton, 1964
LAQUEUR, W. *Europe since Hitler*, London, 1970
LAUWERYS, J. A., ed. *Scandinavian Democracy*, Stockholm, 1958
LEITES, N. *On the Game of Politics in France*, Stanford, 1959
LEMARCHAND, R. *Political Awakening in the Belgian Congo*, Berkeley, 1964
LICHTHEIM, G. *Europe and America*, London, 1963
LINDBERG, L. N. *The Political Dynamics of European Economic Integration*, London, 1963
LINDBERG, L. N. and SCHEINGOLD, S. A. *Europe's Would-Be Polity*, Englewood Cliffs, 1970
LINDSAY, K. *European Assemblies: The Experimental Period 1949–1959*, London, 1960
LIPSET, S. M. and ROKKAN, S., eds. *Party Systems and Voter Alignments*, New York, 1967

LISTER, L. *Europe's Coal and Steel Community*, New York, 1960
LITCHFIELD, E. H. *et al. Governing Post-War Germany*, Ithaca, 1953
LORWIN, V. L. *The French Labor Movement*, Cambridge, Mass., 1954
LUARD, E., ed. *The Cold War: A Reappraisal*, London, 1964
LUARD, E. *Britain and Europe*, London, 1961
LUETHY, H. *The State of France*, London, 1955

MCCALLUM, R. B. and READMAN, A. *The British General Election of 1945*, London, 1947
MACKINTOSH, J. M. *Strategy and Tactics of Soviet Foreign Policy*, London, 1962
MACRIDIS, R. C. and BROWN, B. E. *The De Gaulle Republic*, Homewood, 1960
MAMMARELLA, G. *Italy after Fascism*, Montreal, 1964
MARLOWE, J. *Arab Nationalism and British Imperialism*, London, 1961
MASON, H. L. *The ECSC-Experiment in Supranationalism*, The Hague, 1955
MAUGHAM, VISCOUNT. *UNO and War Crimes*, London, 1951
MAYNE, R. *The Recovery of Europe*, London, 1970
MAYNE, R. *The Institutions of the European Community*, London, 1968
MAYNE, R. *The Community of Europe*, London, 1962
MEADE, J. E. *Negotiations for Benelux: An Annotated Chronicle 1943–1956*, Princeton, 1957
MERKL, P. H. *Germany Yesterday and Tomorrow*, New York, 1965
MERKL, P. H. *The Origin of the West German Republic*, New York, 1963
MEYER, F. V. *The Seven*, London, 1960
MICAUD, C. *Communism and the French Left*, London, 1963
MILLER, J. D. B. *The Commonwealth in the World*, London, 1958
MOORE, B. T., ed. *NATO and the Future of Europe*, New York, 1958
MOWAT, R. C. *Ruin and Resurgence*, London, 1966

NEUFELD, M. F. *Italy: School for Awakening Countries*, New York, 1961
NORTHEDGE, F. S. *British Foreign Policy: The Process of Adjustment 1945–1961*, London, 1962
NORTHROP, F. S. C. *European Union and United States Foreign Policy*, New York, 1954
NORVICK, P. *The Resistance versus Vichy*, London, 1968

OEEC. *The OEEC: History and Structure*, Paris, 1956
OSGOOD, R. E. *NATO: The Entangling Alliance*, Chicago, 1962

PALMER, M. *et al. European Unity: A Survey of the European Organizations*, London, 1968
PALMIER, L. H. *Indonesia and the Dutch*, New York, 1962
PFALTZGRAFF, R. L. *Britain Faces Europe*, Philadelphia, 1969
PHILLIPS, C. *The Truman Presidency*, New York, 1966
PICKLES, D. *Algeria and France*, London, 1963
PINDER, J. *Europe Against De Gaulle*, London, 1963

PINDER, J. *Britain and the Common Market*, London, 1961

PINDER, J. and PRYCE, R. *Europe after de Gaulle*, London, 1969

POSTAN, M. M. *An Economic History of Western Europe 1945–1964*, London, 1967

POUNDS, N. J. G. and PARKER, W. N. *Coal and Steel in Western Europe*, Bloomington, 1957

PRICE, H. B. *The Marshall Plan and its Meaning*, Ithaca, 1955

PRYCE, R. *The Political Future of the European Community*, London, 1962

REES, D. *The Age of Containment*, London, 1967

REES, D. *Korea: The Limited War*, London, 1964

RICHARDSON, J. L. *Germany and the Atlantic Alliance*, Cambridge, Mass., 1966

RIEBER, A. J. *Stalin and the French Communist Party, 1940–1947*, New York, 1962

R.I.I.A. *Britain in Western Europe:WEU and the Atlantic Alliance*, London, 1956

ROBERTSON, A. H. *The Council of Europe*, London, 1961

ROBERTSON, A. H. *European Institutions*, London, 1959

ROBERTSON, T. *Crisis: The Inside Story of the Suez Conspiracy*, London, 1964

ROBSON, C. B. *Berlin—Pivot of German Destiny*, Chapel Hill, 1960

RUSSELL, F. M. *The Saar: Battleground and Pawn*, Stanford, 1951

SAMPSON, A. *The New Europeans*, London, 1968

SCHMITT, H. A. *The Path to European Union*, Baton Rouge, 1962

SCHOENBRUN, D. A. *As France Goes*, London, 1957

SEALE, P. and MCCONVILLE, M. *French Revolution 1968*, London, 1968

SHEPHERD, G. *The Austrian Odyssey*, London, 1957

SISSONS, M. and FRENCH, P., eds. *Age of Austerity*, London, 1963

SMITH, B. L. R. *The Governance of Berlin*, New York, 1959

SPANIER, J. W. *American Foreign Policy Since World War II*, London, 1962

SPEIER, H. *Divided Berlin*, London, 1961

SPEIER, H. and DAVISON, W. P., eds. *West German Leadership and Foreign Policy*, Evanston, 1957

SPIRO, H. J. *The Politics of German Codetermination*, Cambridge, Mass., 1958

STOLPER, W. *Germany Between East and West*, Washington, 1960

TABOR, G. M. *John F. Kennedy and a United Europe*, Bruges, 1969

THOMAS, H. *The Suez Affair*, London, 1967

THOMSON, D. *England in the Twentieth Century 1914–1963*, London, 1964

THOMSON, D. *Democracy in France since 1870*, London, 1964

TRUMAN, H. S. *Years of Trial and Hope 1946–1953*, London, 1956

VON SCHMERKING, W. *Outlawing the Communist Party*, New York, 1957

WALLICH, H. C. *Mainsprings of the German Revival*, New Haven, 1955

WARMBRUNN, W. *The Dutch Under German Occupation 1940–1945*, London, 1963

WATT, D. C. *Britain Looks to Germany*, London, 1965

WENDT, F. *The Nordic Council and Cooperation in Scandinavia*, Copenhagen, 1959

BIBLIOGRAPHY

WERTH, A. *The De Gaulle Revolution*, London, 1960
WILLIAMS, P. M. *Crisis and Compromise*, London, 1964
WILLIS, F. R. *Italy Chooses Europe*, New York, 1971
WILLIS, F. R. *France, Germany and the New Europe 1945–1967*, London, 1969
WOLFE, J. H. *Indivisible Germany: Illusion or Reality*, The Hague, 1963
WOLFERS, A., ed. *Alliance Policy in the Cold War*, Baltimore, 1959
WOODHOUSE, C. M. *British Foreign Policy since the Second World War*, London, 1961
WORSWICK, G. D. N., ed. *The Free Trade Area Proposals*, Oxford, 1960
WRIGHT, G. *France in Modern Times*, 1960
WRIGHT, G. *The Reshaping of French Democracy*, London, 1950

ZEMAN, Z. A. B. *Prague Spring: A Report on Czechoslovakia 1968*, London, 1969
ZURCHER, A. J. *The Struggle to Unite Europe 1940–1958*, New York, 1958

Index